SEARCH THEORY AND UNEMPLOYMENT

RECENT ECONOMIC THOUGHT SERIES

Editors:

William Darity, Jr.
University of North Carolina
Chapel Hill, North Carolina, USA

James K. Galbraith
University of Texas at Austin
Austin, Texas, USA

Other books in the series:

SEARCH THEORY
AND UNEMPLOYMENT

edited by

Stephen A. Woodbury
Michigan State University

and

Carl Davidson
Michigan State University

Kluwer Academic Publishers
Boston/Dordrecht/London

Distributors for North, Central and South America:
Kluwer Academic Publishers
101 Philip Drive
Assinippi Park
Norwell, Massachusetts 02061 USA
Telephone (781) 871-6600
Fax (781) 681-9045
E-Mail: kluwer@wkap.com

Distributors for all other countries:
Kluwer Academic Publishers Group
Post Office Box 322
3300 AH Dordrecht, THE NETHERLANDS
Telephone 31 786 576 000
Fax 31 786 576 474
E-Mail: services@wkap.nl

 Electronic Services <http://www.wkap.nl>

Library of Congress Cataloging-in-Publication Data

SEARCH THEORY AND UNEMPLOYMENT
Stephen A. Woodbury and Carl Davidson
ISBN 1-4020-7333-X

A C.I.P. Catalogue record for this book is available
from the Library of Congress.

Table of Contents

Preface

The past twenty-five years have seen a remarkable growth of research on unemployment that takes as its starting point the economic theory of job search. This volume contains eight papers (following an introduction) that trace the development of job search theory and its implications for empirical work and public policy. Following the introductory chapter, chapters 2, 3, and 4 focus on job search theory itself, chapters 5, 6, and 7 treat econometric issues and the estimation of job search models, and chapters 8 and 9 discuss the application of job search theory to public policy.

Drafts of the chapters were first presented at sessions organized by the editors at various regional economic association meetings. We are grateful to the authors and other participants in those sessions—particularly William Alpert, Louis Jacobson, Derek Neal, and Wayne Vroman—for their insightful comments on the drafts.

1

Search Theory and Unemployment: An Introduction

Carl Davidson
Michigan State University

Stephen A. Woodbury
Michigan State University and
W. E. Upjohn Institute

Abstract

The first part of this introductory chapter offers a brief historical survey of job search theory. The goals are to give the reader a sense of how search theory arrived at its current state, to point out some of the roadblocks that search theory has encountered, and to suggest how search theoretic models have evolved so as to overcome those roadblocks. The second part of the chapter offers a brief description of each chapter in the book. Eight chapters follow the introduction, with three devoted to job search theory itself, three to estimating job search models, and two to applying job search theory to public policy.

Unemployment is a persistent and pervasive problem in developed economies. In the last 20 years, every industrialized nation has seen an unemployment rate of 10 percent at least briefly—and in many cases (in Europe and Japan) over a period of years. Industrialized nations spend substantial resources to provide a social safety net for workers who find themselves without a job. Many governments also design and implement programs aimed at either increasing job security (e.g., firing taxes imposed on firms in some European countries) or reducing the time it takes to become reemployed (e.g., government-assisted job search or training programs).

It is remarkable, then, that forty years ago economists had no rigorous explanation of how unemployment could arise and persist in equilibrium. Ad hoc theories existed about "money illusion" and downwardly rigid wages, but it was understood that money illusion could only cause changes in unemployment (it could not explain its existence), and no satisfactory explanation existed of why wages would not fall in the presence of excess supply in the labor market. Economists could not explain unemployment because of the profession's continued reliance on the pristine model of supply and demand as its workhorse. This model rules out (by assumption) all types of transaction costs that might keep markets from operating efficiently. Uncertainty is ruled out, informational problems are assumed away, and economic agents on opposite sides of the market have no difficulty finding each other. Without the presence of such transaction costs, it is hard to imagine unemployment arising as an equilibrium phenomenon.

In the late 1960s, a revolution began in microeconomics as the supply and demand models of Marshall and Walras began to be replaced by models that took transaction costs seriously and used them to explain a wide variety of economic phenomena. For example, the economics of uncertainty provided an explanation of how insurance markets function while the economics of information explained how identical products could sell for different prices in equilibrium.

Among the most important developments offered by "transaction cost economics" were the new models of equilibrium unemployment. These models began to emerge following publication of George Stigler's classic 1961 article on "The Economics of Information." This paper, which many cite as the article that inspired much of the subsequent work on transaction costs, examined the problem faced by a consumer searching for a good that was offered by many firms at different prices. Stigler (1962), J.J. McCall (1965), Dale Mortensen (1970), and others quickly extended the analysis to include the problem faced by an unemployed worker searching for a job across firms that pay different wages. Unemployment would arise if the worker could not find a firm with a vacancy or if it was in the worker's interest to turn down a wage offer that he or she considered too low.

Other theories of unemployment quickly followed. For example, contract theory explained how optimal contracts between risk-neutral firms and their risk-averse employees in the presence of uncertainty and/or asymmetric information might lead to underemployment; that is, a lower level of employment than what would have occurred in a world of certainty and complete information. Efficiency wage models demonstrated that unemployment could arise in equilibrium if firms faced difficulty in monitoring and observing the level of effort exerted by workers on the job. These theories differed from the previous ad hoc explanations of unemployment in that they offered models in which the transaction costs that generated unemployment were completely and carefully specified. Moreover, these theories were internally consistent in that they all provided explanations of unemployment that could persist in equilibrium even though all economic agents were rational and behaving optimally.

Forty years after publication of Stigler's classic article seems an appropriate time to take stock of the new theories of unemployment. Have they really increased our understanding of unemployment? Have they generated insights that could be used to design policies that aid the poor or jobless in better or more efficient ways? What are the weaknesses of these theories that still need to be addressed? This book offers a series of chapters that address these questions for the theory of unemployment that many believe to be most compelling and that has arguably generated the most research to date—search theory. The main message is twofold. First, search theory has been enormously successful in a number of important ways. It has increased understanding of unemployment, provided explanations for a wide variety of observed labor market phenomena, and provided a useful framework for policy analysis. Second, although search theory has taken us in the right direction, it still has far to go. Serious questions about the importance of the theory and methods used for policy analysis remain unanswered. Thus, our hope is that the collection of papers offered here provides a critical, well-balanced view of search theory as it stands today.

The remainder of this introduction is in two parts. The first is a brief survey of how search theory has arrived where it is today. This survey is in not meant to be exhaustive—surveys of the early work in search theory available elsewhere (for example, Mortensen 1986, Davidson 1990, and Mortensen and Pissarides 1999). Further, Monica Merz provides an excellent and up-to-date survey of search theory and the role that it has played in macroeconomics in Chapter 2, and Jose Canals and Steven Stern survey the empirical methods in the field in Chapter 5. Rather, the goal here is to point out some of the roadblocks that search theory has had to overcome and to give the reader a sense of how the basic models of search theory have had to change over time in response. By taking this historical perspective, we hope to emphasize how far search theory and the models of unemployment it offers have come in so short a time.

The second part of this introduction offers a very brief description of each of the chapters in the book. Eight chapters follow the introduction, with three devoted to theory, three to empirical work, and two to policy issues. For any school of economics to survive and thrive, it must be successful in all three. With respect to theory, the models offered must describe some observable phenomena, show internal consistency, and be based on optimizing behavior of rational economic agents. With respect to empirical work, the theories offered must be consistent with the data and explain the data at least as well as competing theories. Finally, the models used must be tractable enough to provide insights into issues of policy analysis and design. Each section of the book includes at least one paper arguing that search theory has been successful in achieving these goals and at least one that raises serious concerns about search theory's performance.

1. Historical Perspective

When Stigler's article appeared, there was optimism that search theory could provide the ideal framework to investigate a host of labor-related issues that had been difficult to analyze in the past. Stigler himself provided such a framework in his 1962 follow-up article "Information in the Labor Market," in which he analyzed how an unemployed worker might go about finding a job in a labor market in which firms offered a variety of employment opportunities. The basic idea was quite simple. Stigler assumed that unemployed workers knew that jobs were available at a variety of wages but that they could only know which firm was offering which wage by contacting the firms. Contacting each firm was costly, so it made no sense to contact them all. Stigler's main concern was to find the best way of searching for a job. He conjectured that the optimal strategy would be to contact a predetermined number of firms (N) and then accept the highest wage offered. Because additional search generates diminishing returns (in terms of the expected wage), the optimal number of firms to contact would be uniquely defined by equating the expected marginal gain from search with the marginal cost of contacting a firm.

Throughout the 1960s a number of authors built on Stigler's insight by first examining the worker's search decision more carefully and then using the basic structure to examine the impact of public policy on unemployment. McCall (1965) argued that Stigler's search rule was not optimal. He showed that, under the assumptions of Stigler's model (in particular, under he assumption that the worker knows the distribution of wage offers), the best strategy is to search *sequentially*. That is, the worker should visit one firm at a time and stop searching as soon as he or she found a wage offer at or above a prespecified "reservation wage." When receiving an offer, the worker could calculate the expected benefit from continuing to search and compare it with the cost of contacting another firm. If the wage offer is low, then the expected benefit would exceed the cost and search should continue. The reservation wage is the wage offer that makes the worker indifferent between stopping (and taking the job) and continuing to search for a higher-wage job. McCall showed that this strategy is better than Stigler's *non-sequential* search rule, which would require the worker to contact $N-1$ more firms even if the first wage offer was exceedingly high.

Once the optimal search rule had been determined, many felt that they had all the tools necessary to start applying the model to practical issues. A typical example of the issues tackled can be found in Mortensen (1970), where a search model is used to show how a "natural rate of unemployment" could be tied to labor market turnover rates and then to show how unemployment would vary with the inflation rate. One of the underlying goals was to provide some theoretical underpinnings for the Phillips curve, which was still in vogue at that time. Mortensen showed that the relationship between unemployment and inflation depended on how the distribution of wages shifted as prices increased.

While some were hurrying to apply the new approach, others were examining the early developments and pointing out flaws. Two related criticisms were viewed as particularly damning. Michael Rothschild (1973) pointed out that search theory was incomplete in that it only provided an analysis of optimizing behavior on one side of the market. While authors were taking pains to make certain that workers were behaving optimally, no one had provided an explanation for why firms would offer different wages in equilibrium. In other words, there had been no serious attempt to model the source of the underlying wage distribution. Rothschild coined the term "partial-partial equilibrium" to refer to this approach of focusing on just one side of one market.

A second criticism, due to Peter Diamond (1971), focused on what would happen if one did try to close such models by carefully modeling the behavior of profit maximizing firms. He argued that if all unemployed workers were to search optimally, then all firms would ultimately offer the same wage. Moreover, this wage would equal the monopsony wage. This result, which became known as the "Diamond paradox," was startling because it implied that optimal search by unemployed workers would eliminate the need to search. Also, the argument behind the result was so compelling it could not be dismissed as a theoretical curiosity. Intuitively, the fact that search is costly means that each firm has a small amount of monopsony power—if the worker rejects an offer, it takes time and effort to generate a new offer from another firm. For this reason, a firm has no incentive to offer the highest wage rate because if it did, it could lower the wage by a small amount (say, the cost of search) without losing any employees. It follows that, in equilibrium, all firms must offer the same wage, and the common wage must equal the monopsony wage. The existence of search costs, no matter how small, gives each firm leeway to vary its wage by a small amount. Diamond's insight was that firms' wage-setting power, combined with optimal search by job seekers, would eliminate any incentive that the firms have to offer different wages.

Much research in the 1970s and early 1980s focused on ways to circumvent the Diamond paradox. Bo Axell (1977) showed that the existence of a significantly large class of consumers with zero search costs could lead to equilibrium wage dispersion. The equilibrium wage distribution would arise because firms would have an incentive to increase their wage offer to attract the zero search-cost workers (provided that there are enough of them). Jennifer Reinganum (1979) demonstrated that if there were heterogeneity on *both* sides of the market (consumers differing in their cost of search, firms differing in labor productivity) the equilibrium wage distribution would be non-degenerate. In this case, the firms offer different wages because they differ on what the monopsony wage is.

Kenneth Burdett and Kenneth Judd (1983) also showed how equilibrium wage dispersion could arise by altering two of the other underlying assumptions of the basic search model. First, they showed that if consumers search *non-sequentially* (as in Stigler's original article) then firms would offer different equilibrium wages. They pointed out that sequential search makes sense in a world in which firms make immediate offers to workers upon contact. In fact, it often takes time for firms to decide whom to offer a job, so there may be a delay between the initial contact and the eventual offer. In such a setting, it makes sense for workers to contact additional firms while they wait for a response. Knowing this, some firms have an incentive to pay high wages in order to attract workers with more than one offer, while others pay low wages and hire the workers without any other offers.

Burdett and Judd (1983) also offered a second model that presented the nature of the search process in a slightly different way. In the standard search model, each time the worker pays the cost of search, he or she contacts one firm and receives one offer. Burdett and Judd altered this by assuming instead that the worker receives a random number of offers. This assumption makes sense if, for example, workers use employment agencies or newspaper want ads to find jobs. They showed that, under certain conditions, equilibrium wage dispersion would arise in this setting for much the same reason that it arose in their first model—some firms pay high wages to attract workers with more than one offer while others pay low wages and hope to attract workers with no other offers.

By the early 1980s it seemed clear that the roadblock created by the Diamond paradox had been overcome. It was clear that models could be built with rational, maximizing agents on both sides of the market that would support a non-trivial distribution of wages. It was now reasonable to return to practical matters and start using the new models to investigate policy-related issues. James Albrecht and Axell (1984) showed that this could be done by extending Reinganum's model in a way that allowed them to investigate the link between unemployment insurance and unemployment. In the old partial-partial equilibrium models it had been argued that a more generous unemployment insurance program would lower the opportunity cost of unemployment, increase reservation wages, and drive up unemployment. Albrecht and Axell correctly pointed out that this argument depended upon an underlying assumption that the equilibrium wage distribution would not change with the program. If workers began to hold out for higher wages, firms would be forced to increase their offers, and it was unclear whether unemployment would rise or fall as the wage-offer distribution changed.

Albrecht and Axel's article clearly illustrated the importance of carefully modeling both sides of the market. Unfortunately, it also revealed a problem with the new search models. In the Albrecht and Axell model, whether unemployment increases or decreases depends on the characteristics of the density function that describes how labor productivity varies across firms. This makes it very hard to know what to expect, because little if anything is known empirically about this distribution. The problem clearly generalizes to other models of this kind. To get equilibrium wage dispersion requires a model that allow for heterogeneity among workers (e.g., in their search costs) or heterogeneity among firms (e.g., in some productivity parameter) or both. The result is not likely to be a model that generates sharp, unambiguous predictions. In addition, the manner in which heterogeneity is introduced plays a crucial role in determining the policy implications of the model. Unfortunately, it is unlikely to be the case that enough is known about the underlying heterogeneity to draw useful conclusions. Little is known about search costs, and it is unlikely that much can be inferred about them from available data.[1] Thus, although the models developed in the 1970s and early 1980s were rigorous and could explain the existence and persistence of equilibrium wage dispersion (along with unemployment), the policy conclusions of those models were tied to ad hoc specifications of underlying heterogeneity that is hard to characterize and usually impossible to observe.

As work aimed at solving the Diamond paradox started to wane, a new approach to search theory was being developed independently by Diamond (1981, 1982a, 1982b, 1984) and Mortensen (1982a, 1982b). In previous search models, unemployment would arise when workers rejected wage offers that were below their reservation wages. Hence, these models focused on the problem faced by workers in finding an acceptable wage offer when sampling from a distribution of wages. The new approach of Diamond and Mortensen focused instead on the problem that unemployed workers and firms with vacancies would face in finding each other. Rather than have firms post wages, they assumed that when an unemployed worker contacts a firm with a job opening, the two parties negotiate over the wage until an agreement is reached. If all workers were alike, then there would be a single equilibrium wage. If workers were to differ, then there would be a distribution of wages; however, in this latter case, the distribution of wages would play no real role in the analysis that followed. What is central in this setting is not the underlying heterogeneity among firms or consumers, but the *matching* or *search* technology that determines the number of new jobs created as a function of the number of unemployed workers and vacancies available.

The basic structure of these "trade friction" models is quite simple. Unemployed workers search for a job while firms with vacancies recruit workers. The matching technology, which is like a neo-classical production function, determines the number of new jobs created as a function of the number of idle factors and the efforts those factors put forth to meet each other. Once they meet, they negotiate a wage and production takes place. Over time, jobs break up (exogenously), and when they do, the newly unemployed worker reenters the search process while the firm looks for a replacement. Over time, workers cycle between periods of employment and unemployment, with the model's dynamics largely driven by the properties of the matching technology.

Much research in the 1980s examined the properties of these models. Two features stood out. First, as Diamond emphasized, if the matching technology exhibits increasing returns to scale, then it is possible for such models to have multiple equilibria. Also, because each equilibrium is characterized by a different unemployment rate, a unique natural rate of unemployment may not exist when trading frictions are present. The logic behind this result is fairly straightforward. The incentive to search for a job or post a vacancy is tied to the expected reward from doing so. If economic activity is vigorous, it will be easy to find a job and/or fill vacancies. Thus, in good times new vacancies will be created and there will be much search activity. As a result, the good times will continue with high production levels and low unemployment. In contrast, if workers expect difficulty finding a job and/or firms expect difficulty filling new vacancies, workers will stay out of the labor market, and firms will not create new jobs. As a result, the economy gets stuck in an equilibrium with a low level of economic activity and high unemployment. In either case, expectations about the level of economic activity are self-fulfilling, making it hard to move from one equilibrium to another. Diamond showed that in such a setting there is a natural role for the government either to manage aggregate demand or to boost confidence in the economy so as to steer it away from the high-unemployment outcome.

The second feature of the trade friction models that drew much attention had to do with the efficiency properties of the equilibria. As Diamond and Mortensen both pointed out, in general, the equilibria in these models will not be efficient because search and recruiting activity both generate externalities. If an unemployed worker searches harder for a job, he or she makes it harder for other unemployed workers to find employment and easier for firms to fill their vacancies. These externalities drive a wedge between the social and marginal productivities associated with various labor market activities, giving rise to inefficiency. Much research was devoted to understanding whether these externalities would generate an equilibrium rate of unemployment that was too high or too low. In either case, though, the fact that equilibrium is not expected to be efficient gives another rationale for government intervention in the market place.

One of the most attractive features of the trade-frictions approach to modeling unemployment is that the driving force behind many of the results, the matching technology, can be estimated from existing data. Papers by Robert Chirinko (1982), Christopher Pissarides (1986), Olivier Blanchard and Diamond (1989), and Ronald Warren (1996), among others, used a variety of data to try to pin down the key characteristics of this function. Chirinko found evidence of diminishing returns with respect search activity while Blanchard and Diamond reported weak evidence of increasing returns to scale. In contrast, Pissarides and Warren concluded that the evidence favors constant returns to scale in the matching technology.

More recently, attention has turned to whether these search models can explain a variety of labor market phenomena. This task has been facilitated by the development of a valuable database on job flows by Steven Davis, John Haltiwanger and Scott Schuh (1996). These data, which track job creation and job destruction rates in U.S. manufacturing industries from 1973 to 1992, have been used to calibrate trade friction models of unemployment. The resulting models have subsequently been examined to see if they have characteristics that are consistent with a variety of the stylized facts associated with economic fluctuations and labor market outcomes. Examples of this type of work include Mortensen and Pissarides (1994) and Cole and Rogerson (1999).

The existence of these two empirical strands of literature sets search theory apart from most of the other micro-based explanations of unemployment. Consider, for example, the efficiency-wage approach, in which unemployment arises because firms cannot directly observe the effort put forth by each worker. In such a setting, full employment cannot be supported in equilibrium because if workers knew that immediate reemployment was available, there would be no need for them to work hard—there would be no penalty attached to being terminated for shirking. Unemployment arises as a disciplinary device. Workers do not shirk because if they are caught shirking and are terminated, it will take time and effort to find a new job. The driving force in these models is the monitoring function that indicates how easy it is for the firm to detect shirking. Unfortunately, it has been impossible to observe or estimate this monitoring function. In addition, existing data cannot be used to calibrate a model that includes such a function in order to see how well it can explain recent data. Consequently, although there have been numerous attempts to test the efficiency wage hypothesis, it seems fair to say that the efficiency wage approach has not been held up to the same level of empirical scrutiny as search theory. (See, for example, the critique of the empirical literature on efficiency wages by Topel (1989).)

One of the most appealing aspects of job search theory is its direct applicability to a variety of policy issues, and particularly to unemployment insurance. In the 1970s, during the same time that job search theory was starting to flourish, concern grew in the United States that unemployment benefits were a cause of unemployment rather than an appropriate remedy for unemployment (Feldstein 1974). The job search model offered a clear justification for this concern—providing unemployed workers with benefits increases workers' reservation wage (or, alternatively, reduces the incentive workers have to search for a new job) and hence leads to longer spells of unemployment.

In the United States, the concern that unemployment insurance caused unemployment led the U.S. Department of Labor and several states to consider various innovative policies that could be grafted onto the unemployment insurance system in order to shorten workers' spells of unemployment and get them back to work quickly. Beginning in the early 1980s, the Labor Department and several states sponsored a series of field experiments based on random assignment in order to test the effectiveness of these innovative polices. Intensive job search assistance was offered as a way to enhance the search skills of unemployed workers (and perhaps also to push workers to search harder for work). Reemployment bonuses, which offered recipients of unemployment benefits a cash bonus if they found a job quickly, were an attempt to alter the financial incentives facing unemployment workers. Incentives for self-employment, which included both financial assistance and training, were tried in two demonstrations with selected groups of workers. The early experience with these programs has been reviewed by Meyer (1995). All three of these policy innovations—intensive job search assistance, the reemployment bonus, and self-employment assistance—were clearly related to the rise of job search theory and its emphasis on the role workers play in determining the duration of unemployment spells.

Much macroeconomic policy research has also taken job search theory as a starting point, as Chapter 2 (by Monica Merz) and Chapter 9 (by Bruce Fallick and William Wascher) make clear. Merz points in particular to the use of job search theory in examining the welfare effects of unemployment insurance (Chapter 8 is an example of this) and the dynamic effects of hiring subsidies, layoff penalties, and payroll taxation. Fallick and Wascher point to the search theoretic underpinnings of the natural rate of unemployment and the Phillips curve, among other constructs that have been important in macroeconomic policy discussions.

2.   An Overview of the Chapters

Chapters 2, 3, and 4 address a range of theoretical issues in search theory and unemployment. Chapter 2, by Monica Merz, offers an insightful critical survey of theoretical developments in macroeconomics using the search approach, with an emphasis on developments since 1986. Merz pays close attention to the ability of search models to explain stylized facts of the macroeconomy and the labor market. She points out that, although the questions motivating the new search approach are essentially similar to those that have motivated past analyses, the more recent analyses are more general, and hence, more convincing. As a result, recent analyses are more relevant to policy analyses and are more likely to provide reasonable quantitative estimates of the welfare implications of policy changes. Throughout, Merz discusses the strengths and weaknesses of existing research and points to potentially fruitful avenues for further research.

Chapter 3, by Andrew John, raises new issues concerning the qualitative nature of search-generated externalities. He presents a model that combines two strands of the literature on the new microfoundations of macroeconomics—search theory and imperfect competition. In his model, agents search for each other in order to create new firms, and the resulting firms compete in an imperfectly competitive output market. More search activity creates more firms and leads to greater product market competition. John shows that this new twist greatly alters the nature of the externalities generated by search behavior, with the externalities generated by imperfect competition effectively swamping the traditional externalities the stem from search activity.

In Chapter 4, Dan Black and Mark Loewenstein offer a new dynamic general equilibrium model of wage dispersion in which workers repeatedly search for jobs non-sequentially. The main goal of the paper is to examine the externalities that arise in such a setting. This fills a surprising gap in the literature. Although many have examined the externalities that are inherent in trade frictions models and reservation wage models with sequential search, Black and Lowenstein are among the first to examine the efficiency properties of models with non-sequential search. In the latter part of the paper, they extend their analysis to allow for business cycles and show that the model is characterized by some surprising features. For example, if the fraction of firms that are hiring falls, workers may choose to search more firms.

Chapters 5, 6, and 7 turn to econometric estimation of job search models. Chapter 5, by Jose Canals and Steven Stern, offers a clear survey of econometric methods that have been developed and used to estimate structural models of job search. Canals and Stern begin with an extensive discussion of the reservation wage model, which they refer to as the classical search model. Included are discussions of measurement error, observed and unobserved heterogeneity, and censored data. The authors include a separate section on the estimation of survival models, which have been used extensively in applied work using unemployment spell data, and conclude with a discussion of estimating equilibrium search models. Canals and Stern's discussion of empirical methods closely parallels the theoretical development of search models and illustrates the remarkable extent to which job search theory and estimation have evolved in tandem.

Chapter 6, by John Engberg, presents a careful and well-executed empirical study of how the duration of unemployment is affected by unemployment insurance benefits. Engberg's contribution is twofold. First, he develops the idea of the present value of remaining unemployment benefits (PVRB), which combines the weekly unemployment benefit amount with the remaining potential duration of benefits to yield an attractive and parsimonious econometric specification. Second, Engberg tests the extent to which different workers show systematically different responses to the exhaustion of unemployment benefits. His main finding—that less educated workers do not appear to increase the intensity of their job search as the end of their unemployment benefits nears—is original and has important implications for unemployment insurance. The finding suggest, for example, that a worker's level of education should be one of the main factors used to allocate job search assistance under unemployment insurance "profiling," which has now been implemented throughout the United States.

In Chapter 7, Theresa Devine applies the job search model to study demographic variation in the rate at which workers become reemployed. Using grouped data on jobless spells from the Survey of Income and Program Participation, she estimates transition rates from unemployment to employment. Her findings suggest that the rate at which job offers arrive varies substantially across the major demographic groups in the U.S. labor force. Moreover, her results suggest that workers' transition rates into employment vary mainly due to this variation in the offer rate, rather than due to variation in the rate at which workers accept job offers. Devine's findings, then, emphasize the importance of the demand side of the labor market in explaining unemployment spells.

Chapters 8 and 9 apply the job search model to policy issues. In Chapter 8, we review some of the main contributions to the literature on optimal unemployment insurance (UI). We also extend the existing research by developing an equilibrium search model that takes account of several theoretical and institutional features that have been treated one-by-one (or not at all) in previous work on optimal UI—varying degrees of worker risk aversion, the job destruction effects of UI, and worker heterogeneity, among others. The main conclusion—that the existing replacement rate of 50 percent is close to optimal but that the current potential duration of benefits (26 weeks) is too short—conflicts with most existing work on optimal UI, but is consistent with the literature on insurance contracts in the presence of moral hazard.

In Chapter 9, Bruce Fallick and William Wascher trace the influence of job search theory on the thinking of macroeconomic policymakers. They note that a number of central concepts in macroeconomic policy—the natural-rate hypothesis, the importance of frictional unemployment, and the Phillips curve—have their origins in early formulations of search theory. However, they also strike a skeptical note and suggest that the more recent contributions of search theory have been far less influential to macroeconomic policy. They point to several reasons for this relative lack of influence: a weakening link between theory and empirical work, an overemphasis on market supply and a corresponding underemphasis of market demand, and the difficulty of reducing recent theoretical contributions to rules of thumb. Nevertheless, Fallick and Wascher are optimistic that search theory has the potential to continue as a source of important ideas in macroeconomic policy.

Taken as a whole, the chapters of this volume illustrate the growth and development of an approach to unemployment that has succeeded theoretically, empirically, and from the standpoint of influencing public policy. As the chapters also reveal, however, many questions and problems remain in job search theory and its related econometric and policy-related fields. It seems reasonable to expect a continued flow of fruitful research—theoretical, econometric, and applied—within the job search paradigm.

Notes

1. The reason is that in theory many underlying distributions could describe the incomplete information that would be consistent with a particular set of observations. When it comes to distribution functions, there are so many degrees of freedom that it would be impossible to pin down a unique distribution that generates the observed data. See Davidson (1990, p. 27).

References

Albrecht, James and Bo Axell. "An Equilibrium Model of Search Unemployment." *Journal of Political Economy* 92 (1984): 824–840.

Axell, Bo. "Search Market Equilibrium." *Scandanavian Journal of Economics* 79 (1977): 20–40.

Blanchard, Olivier and Peter Diamond. "The Beveridge Curve." *Brookings Papers on Economic Activity* (1989): 1–60.

Burdett, Kenneth and Kenneth Judd. "Equilibrium Price Dispersion." *Econometrica* 51 (1983): 955–970.

Chirinko, Robert. "An Empirical Investigation of the Returns to Job Search." *American Economic Review* 72 (1982): 498–501.

Cole, Hal and Richard Rogerson. "Can the Mortensen-Pissarides Matching Model Match the Business Cycle Facts?" *International Economic Review* 40 (1999): 933–960.

Davidson, Carl. *Recent Developments in the Theory of Involuntary Unemployment.* Kalamazoo, Michigan: W.E. Upjohn Institute for Employment Research, 1990.

Davis, Steven, John Haltiwanger, and Scott Schuh. *Job Creation and Destruction.* Cambridge, Massachusetts: MIT Press, 1996.

Diamond, Peter. "A Model of Price Adjustment." *Journal of Economic Theory* 3 (1971): 156–168.

_____. "Mobility Costs, Frictional Unemployment, and Efficiency." *Journal of Political Economy* 89 (1981): 798–812.

_____. "Aggregate Demand Management in Search Equilibrium." *Journal of Political Economy* 90 (1982): 881–894. (a)

_____. "Wage Determination and Efficiency in Search Equilibrium." *Review of Economic Studies* 49 (1982): 217–228. (b)

_____. *A Search Equilibrium Approach to the Microfoundations of Macroeconomics.* Cambridge, Massachusetts: MIT Press, 1984.

Feldstein, Martin. "Unemployment Compensation: Adverse Incentives and Distributional Anomalies." *National Tax Journal* 27 (1974): 231–244.

McCall, J.J. "The Economics of Information and Optimal Stopping Rules." *Journal of Business* 38 (1965): 300–317.

Meyer, Bruce D. "Lessons from the U.S. Unemployment Insurance Experiments." *Journal of Economic Literature* 33 (1995): 91–131.

Mortensen, Dale. "Job Search, the Duration of Unemployment, and the Phillips Curve." *American Economic Review* 60 (1970): 505–517.

————. "Property Rights and Efficiency in Mating, Racing and Related Games." *American Economic Review* 72 (1982): 968–979. (a)

————. "The Matching Process as a Noncooperative Bargaining Game." In *The Economics of Information*, edited by J.J. McCall. Chicago: University of Chicago Press, 1982. Pp. 233–254. (b)

————. "Job Search." In *The Handbook of Labor Economics*, Vol. 2, edited by O. Ashenfelter and R. Layard. Amsterdam: North-Holland, 1986. Pp. 849–919.

Mortensen, Dale and Christopher Pissarides. "Job Creation and Job Destruction in the Theory of Unemployment." *Review of Economic Studies* 61 (1994): 397–415.

————. "New Developments in Models of Search in the Labor Market." In *The Handbook of Labor Economics*, Vol. 3B, edited by O. Ashenfelter and D. Card. Amsterdam: North-Holland, 1999. Pp. 2567–2627.

Pissarides, Christopher. "Unemployment and Vacancies in Britain." *Economic Policy* 3 (1986): 499–560.

Reinganum, Jennifer. "A Simple Model of Equilibrium Price Dispersion." *Journal of Political Economy* 87 (1979): 851–58.

Rothschild, Michael. "Models of Market Organization with Imperfect Information: A Survey." *Journal of Political Economy* 81 (1973): 1283–1308.

Stigler, George. "The Economics of Information." *Journal of Political Economy* 69 (1961): 213–25.

————. "Information in the Labor Market." *Journal of Political Economy* 70 (1962): 94–104.

Topel, Robert. "Comment on 'Industry Rents: Evidence and Implications'." *Brookings Papers on Economic Activity: Microeconomics* (1989): 283–288.

Warren, Ronald. "Returns to Scale in a Matching Model of the Labor Market." *Economics Letters* 50 (January 1996): 135–142.

2

Search Theory Rediscovered: Recent Developments in the Macroeconomics of the Labor Market

Monika Merz

University of Bonn

Abstract

This paper surveys recent work in the area of labor market search and dynamic macroeconomics. It links new developments to the theory's origin, thereby illustrating and critically examining the progress that has been made in terms of studying macroeconomic issues. Labor market search has been used increasingly more often to study the welfare implications of unemployment insurance, or the dynamic effects of labor market policies such as factor taxation, or hiring subsidies. The issues dealt with tend to be familiar, but the methodology applied to them is generally new. The development of tractable dynamic general equilibrium models encompassing many markets has allowed researchers to integrate elements of labor market search into a broader model. This allows them to study the dynamic interaction between the labor market and other markets of the economy. Advances made in developing solution procedures that can handle large state spaces, and a remarkable increase in computing power have spurred the recent development.

1. Introduction

In 1986, according to an eyewitness student, a famous labor economist at the University of Chicago proclaimed in one of his lectures that search theory was dead. This statement coincided with Dale Mortensen publishing his survey article on the theory of labor market search in the *Handbook of Labor Economics*. Mortensen's (1986) survey provides an excellent insight into state-of-the-art research in this field. But his article also illustrates a dilemma from which the theory was suffering at that time. One of the original goals of the theory of labor market search had been to explain aggregate phenomena related to the labor market that existing theories could not address. And yet, until the mid-1980s, search theory had mostly been used for tackling microeconomic issues. According to Mortensen (1992a, p. 163), the limited application in the literature was due in part to the partial equilibrium nature of the theory. It was also due to the lack of a consistent view of how the labor market functions when transactions costs and time lags are important in the job-worker matching process.

Since the early 1990s, macroeconomists seem to have rediscovered labor market search. This development is documented by a steadily growing body of literature casting the theory in a dynamic general equilibrium context and applying it to macroeconomic issues of the labor market. Even though the issues dealt with tend to be old, the methodology applied to them is generally new. The change in methodology is primarily due to the existence of tractable dynamic general equilibrium models encompassing many markets that have allowed researchers to integrate elements of labor market search into a broader model. This has made it possible to study the dynamic interaction between labor market search and other markets of the economy. Advances made in developing solution procedures that can handle a large, and possibly noncontinuous, state space, and a remarkable increase in computing power have spurred the recent development. This movement is a decisive step toward fulfilling one of the original goals of the theory to explain aggregate phenomena related to the labor market.

In this paper, I provide a survey of recent work in the area of labor market search and macroeconomics. This survey is not intended to be exhaustive, but, rather, to include selected representative examples of main developments. I link new developments to the theory's origin. Proceeding in this manner allows me to present them in a consistent framework and to focus on the progress that has been made in terms of studying macroeconomic issues. If applicable, I also contrast new developments against each other in order to stress differences and similarities in methodology and results. In what follows, I first present the development of the theory of labor market search in a historical context in order to stress its original contribution to economics. I distinguish between the theory's two main branches: the information-gathering approach and the trade-frictions approach to search. I proceed by presenting recent developments according to their primary link to either of these approaches. The final section concludes this paper.

2.   The Link to the Theory's Origin

In order to better understand the potential impact that the revival of the theory of labor market search may have on macroeconomics and the type of issues it can help address, it seems appropriate to stress the theory's original contribution when it was first developed. The theory's origin dates back to the late 1960s when the neoclassical and the Keynesian view dominated the way scholars addressed labor market issues. The neoclassical school views labor as being traded in a competitive environment. According to Gale (1986, p. 785), such an environment is characterized by a large number of individually insignificant agents, complete information on the part of each buyer and seller about his or her alternatives, and the absence of transactions costs. In this environment, a fictitious Walrasian auctioneer determines the unique equilibrium wage rate from the households' labor supply schedule and the firms' labor demand schedule in a tâtonnement-process. By construction, the labor market is always in equilibrium, and all unemployment is voluntary, because the unemployed choose not to work at the equilibrium wage. The neoclassical approach has often been criticized for not specifying the microeconomic process of wage formation, thereby leaving it as a black box. Similarly, the approach assumes that an unemployed worker's move to employment and a firm's filling of an open position happen instantaneously, thereby ignoring that the process of creating a job-worker relationship consumes time and resources. According to Walrasian theory, a firm can have at an instant as much labor as it likes at the going wage. The auctioneer is blind as to whom he assigns to being employed, or to being unemployed, in successive periods, a feature which does not allow the model to capture the lasting job-worker relationships that characterize labor markets in the real world. The Keynesian school introduces unemployment by assuming sticky money wages. Wages are sticky either because—in a competitive setting—workers and firms have money illusion, or because—in an oligopolistic setting—menu costs keep both sides from changing prices and wages.

Some economists felt that these two static theories provided rather unsatisfactory explanations—or no explanation at all—for many important labor market issues. They developed the theory of labor market search in an attempt to explain the observed wage dispersion across jobs and workers, the coexistence of unemployment and job-vacancies and their respective duration, the positive link between the level of the unemployment rate and the rate of change of nominal wages, as well as worker flows. What may have shaped the way of thinking of those who developed the theory was a highly influential statement by Milton Friedman (1968) on the natural rate of unemployment that he made in his famous presidential address to the American Economic Association. According to Friedman, "[t]he natural rate of unemployment,..., is the level that would be ground out by the Walrasian system of general equilibrium equations, provided there is imbedded in them the actual structural characteristics of the labor and commodity markets, including market imperfections, stochastic variability in demands and supplies, the cost of gathering information about job vacancies and labor availabilities, the cost of mobility, and so on." By invoking the term Walrasian system of general equilibrium equations, there was a clear implication that Friedman viewed the natural rate of unemployment as part of a constrained Pareto efficient outcome.

The pioneers of the theory, McCall (1970) and the contributors to the Phelps (1970) volume, abandoned the Walrasian paradigm by introducing two novel assumptions, incomplete information and the notion that labor market search requires time and resources.[1] They maintained the neoclassical postulate of lifetime expected utility maximization and net worth maximization, respectively. These changes enabled them to introduce wage dispersion and to explicitly model searching workers' and firms' decision problems. The theory's focus on the process of creating a worker-firm connection underlines its inherent dynamic nature. The structure of the early search models implies a positive relationship between the level of the wage range and the tightness of the labor market measured as the ratio of job-vacancies to unemployment. This positive link has become known as a wage curve. It appears for different labor market structures. A wage curve exists in Phelps' (1970) island model economy where agents are price takers and a Walrasian auctioneer clears the labor market. It also exists in Mortensen's (1970) model where monopsonistic firms set wages in an effort to attract new hires.

The issue of efficiency of search equilibria had initially been of secondary importance to researchers. However, when casting Phelps' (1970) sketch of an island economy into a formal dynamic general equilibrium model, Lucas and Prescott (1974) emphasize that the optimal allocation is constrained Pareto efficient. A Walrasian auctioneer optimally allocates a continuum of searching or working households across infinitely many islands taking as given two sources of frictions, incomplete information on relative wages across islands and search costs due to income foregone. When these frictions disappear, a purely competitive Pareto optimal environment emerges. The work by Peter Diamond (1981, 1982a and 1982b), and Dale Mortensen (1982) in the early 1980s introduces a clear break for the previously still Walrasian-style analysis of search. Their work focuses on search externalities caused by trade frictions and the implications for the wage determination process, and the issue of uniqueness and optimality of equilibria.

This break is largely motivated by Diamond (1971) showing that there can be no wage dispersion in the equilibrium of a game where employers post wages with knowledge of workers' search strategies, workers search randomly, sequentially, and without recall among those offers, and their search is costly. His work eliminates the role of search in revealing information about wages under the given scenario. Diamond (1982a) abandons the assumption of competitiveness when studying the exchange of homogenous goods in an environment with trade frictions. He shows that, even if prices are flexible and all agents in an economy are completely informed so that they correctly perceive prices, the relative ease with which the goods are traded varies with the number of traders present on both sides of the market. For any given trader, a positive externality arises whenever the number of traders on the opposite side of the market increases, and vice versa. This situation is referred to as a thin-market externality, since it facilitates trade. Alternatively, an increase in the number of traders on the same side of the market renders trade more difficult. This situation is commonly referred to as congestion.

The theory of search in an environment with trade frictions is inherently connected to the theory of bargaining. A match is created whenever the surplus associated with it is positive. A match surplus corresponds to the sum of the firm's and workers' utility derived from the match, net of both sides' outside options. The parties involved need to determine how to split the match surplus by finding an acceptable trading price. The earlier literature on search issues takes an axiomatic stand. It simply assumes that a meeting is concluded with an instantaneous agreement which divides the associated surplus in an arbitrary predetermined way. It does not explicitly model the process of splitting the surplus of a match.[2] Binmore, Rubinstein and Wolinsky (1986) replace this axiomatic approach by a strategic one. They explicitly formulate the bargaining process between randomly meeting pairs of two different types of agents. The solution is given by the payoffs to the two players. By imbedding the two person bargaining problem in a large market, the authors can study the extent to which the bargaining positions and agreements reached in any particular meeting are affected by the conditions prevailing in the market. The equilibrium outcome depends on the exact specification of this bargaining process.

It is well known that when wages are negotiated after a job-match is created, there are many equilibrium outcomes, but only one yields efficiency in the sense that all search externalities just offset one another. Hosios (1990) shows that a wage rate exists which, if both parties ex ante agreed upon it and also were committed to it, sets incentives for searching workers and firms so that their respective search effort's marginal contribution to creating a new job-match equals their average contribution, thereby yielding a Pareto optimal allocation. In general, there is nothing inherent in the bargaining process which guarantees that the negotiating parties settle on the efficient wage rate. The bargaining outcome is typically inefficient, as illustrated in Diamond (1982b) and Mortensen (1982).

3. Classification Scheme

The previous section suggests classifying the literature on labor market search according to two aspects. First, when information is incomplete, search plays the role of information-gathering. In this context, a reservation-wage can be derived as a searching agent's wage at which she is indifferent between accepting or rejecting an offer. This environment requires specifying the way in which expectations are formed. It also allows one to study search for perfectly or imperfectly competitive markets. The approach that focuses on the information-gathering aspect of search first appeared in the literature. Exogenous shocks are propagated by searching workers accepting jobs whenever their wage offer exceeds the reservation-wage.

Similarly, firms hire workers whenever wage demands lie below the reservation-wage. In what follows, I will refer to this approach as the *Information-Gathering Approach*.[3] Second, labor market search can be described as consuming time and resources due to the presence of trade frictions. Following Pissarides (1988, p. 363), I will refer to this approach as the *Trade-Frictions Approach*. Pissarides (1990) emphasizes that it assumes the costs and time delay associated with the search process to be due to trade frictions only, and not to information-gathering about wages, or costly wage negotiations. An environment with trade frictions also requires a wage determination scheme which is typically derived from bargaining theory. The theory of bargaining determines how to split the rent from a worker-firm match. The worker's and the firm's reservation-wage enters the wage negotiation as their respective threat point.

3.1 The Information-Gathering Approach

The information-gathering approach is a direct application of the reservation price theory to the labor market. In a seminal paper, Stigler (1961) introduced this theory. It departs from the standard model in that markets are characterized by uncertainty and incomplete information about the quality or the price of the good to be traded. It takes time and resources for agents to gather information. The theory links the necessity for search to various forms of heterogeneity. The market for a certain good can be characterized by price dispersion which leads the agents in that market to search over the distribution of prices until they find one that is acceptable to them. Their minimum acceptable price is called the reservation price.

McCall (1970) applies the basic elements of the reservation price approach to the unemployment phenomenon. This application may have been motivated by the Bureau of Labor Statistic's official definition of unemployment. Workers are classified as unemployed if they are actively searching for a job. McCall studies the decision problem of a single worker in an uncertain environment. He represents the ideas of costly information-gathering and price dispersion by letting workers randomly draw wage offers from a known wage distribution. By assumption, draws are costly. He derives the reservation-wage as the worker's optimal search rule. The optimal search rule also applies to a single firm's decision problem when trying to hire a worker and generating costly wage demands from the known distribution of those demands. McCall's study takes a partial equilibrium approach to a single worker's decision problem. His model has been broadly applied to address issues such as the impact of unemployment insurance or the amount of savings available on the level of a worker's reservation-wage and, hence, the expected duration of unemployment.

In an independent line of research, Phelps (1970) develops an informal version of a reservation-wage model. His setting is that of a competitive product and labor market with homogeneous agents. The key elements, heterogeneous wage rates, costly information-gathering and trade frictions in the labor market are represented by the following scenario. Immobile firms are located on many spatially distinct islands, and workers can migrate between those islands in order to take advantage of higher wages. What complicates a worker's migration decision is the fact that communication between islands is difficult, so that he is only incompletely informed about job alternatives. Furthermore, islands are recurrently hit by demand shocks which affect the local labor demand and wage level. Workers have adaptive expectations. When aggregate demand drops, workers can only observe a decline in their local demand for labor and the going wage rate. They cannot tell for sure whether the decline is island specific or common to all islands. The more workers expect the decline to be idiosyncratic and to persist, the less they adjust their expectations of wages elsewhere—and hence their reservation-wage for accepting a job—downward. They have an incentive to search for a job on another island. To do so, they must forgo income for one period. Hence, in reaction to a drop in aggregate demand, search unemployment rises, and labor supply, employment and output decline, creating an upward pressure for the local real wage rate.

Lucas and Prescott (1974) are the first to cast search theory of the labor market into a general equilibrium framework. They do so by formalizing and extending Phelps' island story which allows them to study the interaction between workers' migration decision and the wage distribution across islands. Workers migrate in search of a higher wage, and since wages are competitively determined on each island, they change in reaction to the migration process. Lucas and Prescott assume agents to have rational expectations in the sense that future events which are relevant for the decision making process are expected to occur with probability distributions generated by the model. The steady state is characterized by worker flows into and out of employment that just offset one another, thereby determining the long-run level of employment and unemployment. Given the assumption of a competitive labor market with incomplete information, there is no room for externalities in the search process. All migrating workers find a job, and the fact that many workers might be searching simultaneously does not affect an individual worker's probability of finding a job. When a favorable demand shock hits an island, the number of vacancies on that island, defined as excess labor demand, increases, together with the local wage rate, which attracts searching workers to the island and leads to an increase in the supply of labor. All vacancies are filled quickly and the local wage declines. This process soon discourages searching workers from considering employment on that island. It leads to a cleared labor market, given the informational constraints.

Mortensen (1970) develops a reservation-wage model of the labor market which can be regarded as a more general case of the island story to which it converges once the importance of trade frictions declines. Mortensen's model economy is populated by homogenous firms and workers who are incompletely informed about their own, as well as each other's, opportunities in the labor market. Contrary to Phelps' competitive labor market in which all agents take wages as given, Mortensen assumes that each firm sets its wage strategically in an attempt to attract new hires. This is because, in a seriously uninformed labor market, information about a firm's wage is acquired only gradually. Thus, each firm possesses dynamic monopsony power at a given point in time. Supposedly, a firm's posted wage rate is positively linked to the number of vacancies it wants to fill. Given the information structure, firms differ in the wage they post, and workers differ in their expectations of those posted wages, and therefore in their reservation-wage. The higher the firm's wage, the higher the proportion of unemployed workers sampling that wage who can be expected to accept it. Hence, when interpreting each firm as representing all firms on a given island, Mortensen's model establishes a link between Phelps' island story and McCall's optimal search rule. Furthermore, when assuming that posting and filling vacancies happens instantaneously, Mortensen's model converges toward the Lucas and Prescott setup.

3.2 The Trade-Frictions Approach

The trade-frictions approach to unemployment was introduced in a series of papers by Pissarides (1985, 1986, 1987, 1988). It is largely motivated by Peter Diamond's work. Diamond studies search externalities that are due to trade-frictions. He emphasizes their implications for the wage determination process, and the uniqueness and optimality of equilibria. Trade-frictions and the process of creating a job-match are represented by the artifact of a matching function. This function links matching output (the flow of newly formed job-worker pairs) to matching input (searching workers and job-advertising firms). Blanchard and Diamond (1990) and Pissarides (1986) use U.S. and British data, respectively, to test for the appropriate specification of the matching function. Both studies provide support for a constant returns to scale specification. They report relative weights of 0.6 and 0.4 on vacancies and unemployment. Both empirical studies have often been quoted by theorists to justify the assumption of constant returns and the focus on unique equilibria. Constant returns to scale imply that, for a worker, the probability of moving from unemployment to employment increases with the vacancy-to-unemployment ratio, while the opposite holds true for a firm's probability of filling a given vacancy. Search externalities are the key element in the transmission of exogenous shocks. An explicit wage determination scheme is required since newly-created job-matches generate a surplus that the worker and the firm involved need to split.

4. Recent Developments

Recent work applying labor market search to macroeconomic issues can be attributed, more or less clearly, to one of the two approaches presented above. Some of these are based primarily and explicitly on the information-gathering approach while the vast majority are more closely linked to the trade-frictions approach. There is some overlap particularly with respect to the important role of the reservation-wage. In what follows, I will sort recent developments according to their primary link.

4.1 Applications of the Reservation-Wage Approach

Few attempts have been undertaken to apply the reservation-wage approach to studying labor market issues in a dynamic general equilibrium context. This lack of application is presumably due to the rather complex economic environment that this approach requires. Simultaneously capturing incomplete information, a non-degenerate wage distribution as the main incentive for agents to search, and possibly heterogeneity among workers and firms, requires strongly simplifying assumptions in order to remain tractable.

Ljungqvist and Sargent (1995a) develop a dynamic general equilibrium model of the labor and goods market à la McCall (1970) that allows them to analyze the dynamic interaction between a wage distribution and the laws of motion of aggregate unemployment and employment. Their goal is to study the implications of certain labor market policies on workers' incentives to search for a job, and hence, on the level and duration of unemployment. In particular, they look at publicly provided unemployment insurance (UI), a progressive payroll tax, and a government stipulated wage threshold level which, if offered and rejected, triggers refusal of unemployment compensation to an unemployed worker. The key variable generating the results is the reservation-wage. Labor market policies tend to change a worker's reservation-wage, thereby affecting his decision to substitute between search and work, or between staying at a job or leaving. In Ljungqvist and Sargent (1995b) the authors use their model to interpret the Swedish unemployment experience since the 1960s.

Ljungqvist and Sargent assume the total labor force to be constant, and workers to be either employed or unemployed. They distinguish between involuntary and voluntary unemployment. Workers are considered involuntarily unemployed when they are entitled to UI benefits. Those who quit their job or were laid off and subsequently refused to accept a suitable wage offer are considered voluntarily unemployed. They don't receive UI benefits. All unemployed workers search at a variable intensity. An increasing search effort increases the probability of receiving a wage offer as well as the disutility arising from search.

By assumption, wage offers are generated following a simple Markov process. This feature is meant to capture relative wage changes—another key feature of the reservation-wage approach—and to make a worker's decision to quit a job only dependent on the tenure of the job and not on time. There is no aggregate uncertainty. Labor is the sole input into the production of output. Furthermore, workers are assumed to be risk neutral, implying that any welfare comparisons between different states of the economy can be based on the different levels of per capita output or consumption. This also implies that welfare benefits arising from UI can be based on the same measure, since there are no gains due to consumption smoothing across different states in the labor market. In this sense, the reported welfare benefit of UI represents a lower bound.

When simulating their model, the authors generate the following results. An increase in the level of unemployment compensation raises an unemployed worker's reservation-wage and reduces his search intensity, thereby raising unemployment duration. Alternatively, when labor income taxes become more progressive, the spread in net wage rates declines. This decreases an unemployed worker's reservation-wage, since it reduces the expected future payoff from search. For the same reason, workers have less of an incentive to quit their job and accept another one, or to quit and start searching. They are locked in their current job. Taken together, an increase in the progressiveness of labor income taxes decreases the level and duration of unemployment, as well as the mobility across jobs, which is equivalent to a less efficient labor allocation.

The authors stress a potential dilemma. When UI benefits increase, the unemployment rate increases and the tax base shrinks. As a consequence, the government raises tax rates on labor income, which reduces search. If the increase in the UI benefit is generous enough, the increasing effect on unemployment dominates. They use this observation in order to interpret the Swedish practice of implementing a suitable wage threshold as an attempt to put a cap on unemployment, thereby reacting to existing distortions in the labor market caused by highly progressive wage taxes and a generous UI scheme.

Cho (1996) has made a preliminary attempt to combine search elements of the Lucas and Prescott (1974) model with a modified version of the standard one-sector stochastic growth model as developed by Kydland and Prescott (1982) and Long and Plosser (1983). He develops a stochastic general equilibrium model with one unproductive and two productive sectors. By assumption, workers can only spend a fraction of their total time endowment in one specific sector at a time. Workers are mobile between the productive sectors, but in order to move from one productive sector to the other, they need to spend at least one period in the nonproductive sector. This feature is intended to capture the idea that search is costly in the sense that it takes time and income or consumption foregone to look for a new job. Sector-specific technology shocks that regularly hit the two productive sectors create the main incentive for workers to move. A major motivation for Cho's work is the empirical observation that in the U.S. economy output of the durable goods sector is much more volatile than output of the consumption good sector. He interprets this as the durable goods sector being more productive than the consumption goods sector in a boom, and less productive in a recession. These cyclical differences in productivity explain cyclical labor reallocation across sectors.

Gomes, Greenwood and Rebelo (1996) build upon the Lucas and Prescott model in their attempt to explain the dynamic behavior of the rate and duration of unemployment and of flows into and out of unemployment. They develop a dynamic general equilibrium economy that is populated by a continuum of self-employed households that can either work or search. In each period, households receive an idiosyncratic and an aggregate shock to technology. Based on the realization of these shocks, they decide whether to work or to search. Households are incompletely insured against nonemployment. When employed, their level of consumption and their disutility from work is higher than when not employed. Households own assets that they use to smooth consumption across different employment states.

Gomes, Greenwood and Rebelo implicitly define the reservation-wage as all possible combinations between accumulated assets and idiosyncratic productivity levels at which households are indifferent between searching and working. The idiosyncratic shock required to render a household indifferent increases with the level of assets, and vice versa. That is, the more wealth a household has accumulated, the better a job offer needs to be for the household to accept it. A novelty in the Gomes, Greenwood and Rebelo paper is the interaction between idiosyncratic and aggregate technology shocks. A positive technology shock increases the variance of the distribution from which idiosyncratic shocks are drawn, thereby increasing the likelihood of an acceptable job offer to arrive. Hence, search becomes more attractive.

Simulation results suggest that the model can replicate the countercyclicality of the rate and duration of unemployment as well as of flows into and out of unemployment. However, the variability of those labor market variables is too low compared to the data. The overall variability increases when the model is augmented by home production as an alternative to search. Home production raises the reservation-wage and the amount of search activity in the model's stationary equilibrium.

4.2 Applications of the Trade-Frictions Approach

The trade-frictions approach has generated a consistent dynamic equilibrium theory of unemployment, job-vacancies and wage formation that has implications for the cyclical behavior of these variables. Pissarides (1990) provides an extensive summary and also sketches possible applications of the approach to a range of primarily macroeconomic issues. His work stresses the need for a broader analytical framework that views the labor market in connection with markets for capital, investment, consumption and output goods if one wants to understand the behavior of the labor market in an overall business cycle context. Pissarides' work has become a natural starting point for recent developments based on the trade-frictions approach. They can be distinguished according to whether they study homogeneous or heterogenous job-matches, whether they are set in a complete or incomplete market environment, and whether there is aggregate uncertainty. Pissarides' work has also spurred interest in studying different wage determination schemes. A possible reason for the popularity of the trade-frictions approach may be the justification that empirical studies have provided.

4.2.1 Homogeneous Job-Matches. The first studies that use elements of the trade-frictions approach to create a link between the labor market and other markets of the economy start from the assumption that all job-matches are equally productive, and that markets are complete. Relaxing both assumptions in ensuing work has enabled researchers to address issues that cannot be dealt within the simpler framework.

4.2.1.1 Complete Markets. In independent lines of research, Merz (1995) and Andolfatto (1996) create a synthesis between the trade-frictions approach to unemployment and the stochastic neoclassical growth model. Their work generalizes and vastly extends a first attempt undertaken by Mortensen (1992b) to integrate the trade-frictions approach into a dynamic stochastic general equilibrium setting. The authors are the first to successfully introduce unemployment into this framework. Their work is motivated by the goal to quantitatively test the qualitative implications that the trade-frictions approach has for aggregate economic variables, thereby assessing the theory's contribution to explaining certain phenomena of the business cycle that existing equilibrium models either have resolved in an unsatisfactory manner or have not been able to address at all.

In particular, they take on the shortcomings of the standard neoclassical growth model which is often referred to as the real-business-cycle (RBC) model. The standard model features a purely competitive labor market. Households can allocate their fixed time endowment across market work and leisure, and firms demand labor up to the point where the marginal product of the last hour equals the hourly real wage. Competitiveness and the absence of trade-frictions imply that the market clearing wage corresponds to the marginal product of labor, and that both behave identically over the cycle. This implication contradicts the empirical observations that real wages fluctuate less and that they are less procyclical than labor productivity. Furthermore, there is no unemployment in the simple RBC model, and the assumption of a Cobb-Douglas production function generates the counterfactual prediction of a constant share of labor's income. Technology shocks are the main driving processes that affect labor productivity and cause shifts in labor demand. When a positive shock hits the economy in a given period, labor demand increases, causing a rise in the real wage, which leads to an increase in labor supply. Consequently, employment and output rise during the period which causes a strongly positive contemporaneous correlation between labor productivity and output. In U.S. data, however, labor productivity leads output and employment by about two quarters over the business cycle.

By replacing a purely competitive labor market with one in which trade-frictions matter as well as bilateral bargaining over wages, Merz and Andolfatto each introduce search unemployment and job-vacancies into the standard stochastic growth model. The new analytical environment, in which two-sided search in the labor market constitutes the key economic propagation mechanism, is characterized by prices that are flexible and correctly perceived by all individuals, by clearing markets, and by maximizing agents who have rational expectations. Their results are qualitatively very similar, even though their analyses differ in the exact model specification.

Merz lets homogenous households divide their total time endowment between market work, and search for a job-match at a variable search intensity. Similarly, homogenous firms can post job-vacancies in order to increase their employment level. Both search activities come at a cost, and all job-matches are equally productive. They start producing one period after they are created. Merz shows that, when trade-frictions are present, the equilibrium real wage at which all search externalities just offset each other deviates from labor productivity. In fact, it can be interpreted as the outcome of a bargaining game that is performed between a worker and a firm after a job-match is created. The efficient equilibrium wage equals the average between the worker's and the firm's threat point, respectively. The worker demands the firm's reservation-wage. It corresponds to the marginal product of the match plus a compensation for the tightness in the labor market. This compensation equals the product of the per unit advertising cost and the vacancy-to-unemployment ratio. The firm offers the worker his reservation-wage corresponding to his disutility from work corrected for search costs foregone. The weight that each threat point has in the average outcome depends on each side's bargaining power. Merz provides an alternative interpretation of the efficient equilibrium wage rate. It is the wage that sets incentives for searching workers and firms such that their respective search effort's marginal contribution to creating a new job-match equals their average contribution. Merz shows that Hosios' (1990) sufficient condition for a Pareto optimal outcome when trade-frictions are present also holds in an environment with physical capital.

The equilibrium of the decentralized model economy is Pareto optimal and can be interpreted as the outcome of a social planning problem. The social planner chooses time paths for per capita consumption, job-vacancies and search intensity in order to maximize the representative household's discounted utility, subject to an aggregate resource constraint, and laws of motion for physical capital, total employment, and aggregate technology. In this environment, the representative household can be thought of as consisting of a very large number of members who either work or search. They pool their income, and thus, provide each other with complete insurance against unemployment. Andolfatto derives a similar planning problem by assuming that labor is indivisible, and that workers are either unemployed and searching at a constant search intensity, or working a given shift-length. His framework nests Hansen's (1985) indivisible labor model as a special case. He explicitly introduces an insurance market so that workers can perfectly insure themselves against income variations arising from unemployment.

The analytical environment created by the work of Merz and Andolfatto has important implications for the dynamic behavior of many labor market variables.

Real wages are less volatile than labor productivity which implies that labor's share of income behaves countercyclically. Moreover, vacancies and unemployment are negatively correlated with each other. When a positive technology shock occurs, labor productivity increases, which leads firms to post more vacancies. The increase in vacancies improves the matching probability for each unemployed worker and leads to an increase in job-matches, thereby reducing unemployment. Since newly-created job-matches become productive only one period later, labor productivity leads output and employment over the business cycle. Compared to Hansen's (1985) setup, unemployment becomes more persistent when trade-frictions are present in the labor market. An increase in the persistence of unemployment translates into more persistent employment and output. When trade-frictions are present, a worker's probability of being employed in the following period depends on his status in the labor market in the current period. When they are absent, this probability is the same for an employed and an unemployed worker.

The analytical framework that Merz and Andolfatto created lends itself to addressing a variety of issues. Shi and Wen (1994) use the framework to examine the dynamic effects that factor income taxation and certain labor market subsidies have on the macroeconomy, and also their welfare implications. They maintain the basic structure of the decentralized model economy with trade-frictions—including the equilibrium wage rate—but modify it in various respects. They eliminate aggregate uncertainty arising from technology shocks and translate the discrete-time setup to continuous time in order to compare the model's predictions to those of existing studies on factor income taxation that assume a competitive labor market. Furthermore, Shi and Wen extend a worker's time allocation decision by letting him or her choose between enjoying leisure, working, or searching for a job. In the aggregate, this can be interpreted as a worker being out of the labor force, employed, or unemployed. The authors introduce complete markets by assuming that households consist of a continuum of workers, differing in their labor market status, who pool their income. Thus, they can invoke a social planner who solves a representative household's optimization problem. With structural policy parameters present, the outcome of this planning problem typically is not Pareto optimal.

Shi and Wen study the short-run and long-run implications that permanent, unforeseen changes in a labor income tax, a capital income tax, an unemployment subsidy, and a vacancy subsidy have on the macroeconomy. Structural policies typically affect either labor demand, or labor supply, or both, since they change the marginal product of a job-match and the equilibrium wage rate. Trade-frictions in the labor market alter the implications that factor income taxes have for the dynamic behavior of many macroeconomic variables. This finding relies on the assumed equilibrium wage rate. It equals a weighted average between a firm's reservation-wage—the marginal product of the match—and the worker's reservation-wage—the disutility from leisure foregone measured in terms of the marginal utility of consumption. A firm considers additional hiring profitable as long as the difference between a match's marginal product and the going wage rate is positive. Similarly, workers find additional labor worth supplying as long as the going wage exceeds their reservation-wage. When a tax is imposed on workers' labor income, the after-tax wage rate declines, thereby increasing the workers' reservation-wage. In addition to the employed workers who react by leaving the labor force, some react by substituting into search unemployment, thereby increasing the unemployment rate. Firms reduce their hiring effort by more than in a competitive labor market environment, since the profitability from posting vacancies is negatively affected by the rise in workers' reservation-wage. Hence, compared to a competitive labor market model, the presence of trade-frictions amplifies the negative impact that a labor income tax has on employment. However, when a tax is imposed on workers' capital income, the trade-frictions dampen its negative impact on employment. A capital income tax reduces the net return from capital and leads to a decline of the capital-labor ratio. Consequently, labor productivity declines, which tends to reduce labor demand as well as worker's reservation-wage by increasing their marginal utility of consumption. The decline in the reservation-wage causes labor supply and demand to increase. Hence, the decline in the reservation-wage partly offsets the drop in labor demand, so that the negative impact on total employment is less than in a competitive labor market environment where the offsetting effect is missing. Shi and Wen show that, for a plausible set of model parameters, the drop in the reservation-wage can outweigh the decline of labor productivity, thereby inducing firms to increase their labor demand, which tends to increase employment.

These findings have important welfare implications. They suggest that the welfare loss in terms of employment foregone due to capital income taxation is less, the one due to labor income taxation is larger, when trade-frictions are present than what they are in a competitive labor market. With trade-frictions, employment resembles a capital good that is augmented by firms and workers investing in time and resource consuming search. Employment wears out by job-matches being destroyed. This characteristic changes the rules for efficient factor taxation that are derived for a competitive environment.

Shi (1995) uses the continuous-time intertemporal optimization framework with trade-frictions and extends it to a small open economy in order to study the macroeconomic implications of tariffs. His findings are primarily driven by the observation that the assumed equilibrium wage rate differs from the marginal product of labor which affects labor demand and supply. In conventional models, tariffs reduce the marginal product of labor and lead to less labor demand and employment. When trade-frictions are present, this decline is counteracted by a decline in the reservation-wage. Shi shows that, contrary to conventional wisdom, tariffs can actually lead to an increase in employment, output, and the current account.

4.2.1.2 Incomplete Markets. When studying dynamic general equilibrium models, the fiction of a social planner solving a representative household's problem comes in handy, since it renders an otherwise very complex problem much more tractable. This fiction relies on the assumption that all agents in the economy are *ex ante* identical, because they can perfectly insure themselves against income differences arising from different states in the labor market. Particularly when it comes to studying certain labor market issues, this assumption is commonly regarded as problematic, since it eliminates differences that may be highly relevant for an individual's decision problem. Assuming perfect insurance eliminates from a macroeconomist's potential research agenda many issues that are of interest from a labor or a finance perspective, such as the interaction between a worker's labor market status and his consumption and savings behavior. The work by Andolfatto and Gomme (1996), Costain (1995) and Valdivia (1995) has started filling this gap. In what follows, I will present Valdivia's work in more detail, since it most naturally fits into the framework presented so far.

Valdivia (1995) studies the macroeconomic costs and benefits of a simple publicly provided unemployment insurance (UI) scheme. He eliminates aggregate uncertainty from the framework developed by Merz and Andolfatto and contrasts their complete markets setting with one of incomplete markets. He does so in order to analyze the dynamic interaction between publicly provided unemployment insurance, a worker's decision about consumption, savings and labor supply, as well as a firm's labor demand decision. His work represents one of the first attempts to extend earlier partial equilibrium settings analyzing the impact of UI on a worker's labor supply decision for a given wage distribution to a general equilibrium framework with risk averse agents.[4] According to these models, unemployed workers search for high wage rates and accept employment whenever a wage offer exceeds their reservation-wage. Providing UI subsidizes search, raises reservation-wages, lengthens the duration of unemployment, and raises the unemployment rate. The effect of UI on savings and on the capital stock typically is not analyzed; nor are the implications for firms' labor demand. Valdivia's general equilibrium framework makes it possible to link all of these issues.

The equilibrium wage rate is assumed to equal the efficient wage derived in Merz (1995). Introducing a publicly provided UI that is financed by a tax on households' labor income raises a worker's reservation-wage and also the equilibrium wage. The rise in both wage rates causes workers to substitute from employment to search unemployment, and firms to post fewer vacancies, since an increased wage reduces their payoff from doing so. Taken together, a UI scheme raises the equilibrium wage, reduces the number of posted vacancies, increases the extent and duration of unemployment, and lowers aggregate consumption and—as a result of more unemployment—lowers savings. Savings decline, since workers need less of a private cushion to protect themselves against unemployment when they have access to a public UI scheme.

Valdivia studies the model with and without UI in a complete market environment and also in an incomplete market setting. He does so in order to assess the implications that a publicly provided UI scheme has for the level of aggregate variables, and also for the distribution of per capita wealth, consumption, and utility.

For the sake of comparison, he maintains the assumed equilibrium wage rate under both scenarios. Interestingly enough, introducing incomplete markets leaves aggregate per capita consumption, savings and output largely unaffected. But it drastically changes individual variables. When markets are complete, all workers consume and save the same amount, regardless of their status in the labor market. In contrast, when markets are incomplete, workers consume and save less when unemployed than when employed. In that case, UI causes the unemployed workers' average consumption level to rise, and the average level and variance of employed workers' consumption to decline. It also reduces the average level and variance of wealth in the economy.

4.2.2 Heterogeneous Job-Matches. In two related papers, Mortensen and Pissarides (1993, 1994) have developed an analytical framework that has become widely known as the Mortensen-Pissarides model, or the MP-model in brief. Their analysis builds upon earlier work by Pissarides (1985) in which he introduces productivity differences across firms. The authors combine this element with a dynamic stochastic version of the trade-frictions approach. They also study various wage determination schemes. Their analytical framework is path-breaking as it enables them to study a firm's endogenous decision to create or destroy a job in a dynamic general equilibrium setting. It has been extended and modified in various directions and has proven to be a valuable workhorse for studying aggregate labor market phenomena.

4.2.2.1 The Mortensen-Pissarides Model. In the original MP-model, there is a continuum of firms that create or destroy jobs at no cost. Matching takes place between a job and a worker. A job can be unfilled or filled. Filling jobs with a suitable worker is costly, however. All jobs are identical *ex ante*, but once they are filled, they are exposed to recurring aggregate productivity shocks, and also to idiosyncratic shocks which may change their idiosyncratic productivity level. *Ex post* heterogeneity exists among jobs, and firms endogenously decide which job to dissolve and which to maintain. When a job is destroyed, the accompanying job-match is destroyed and the worker becomes unemployed. Jobs are destroyed for two separate reasons. A job is destroyed either because an idiosyncratic shock decreases its productivity below the firm's reservation-productivity, or because the reservation-productivity rises beyond the job's given labor productivity. Of course, a job is also destroyed if both events occur simultaneously. By assumption, all newly filled jobs exhibit the highest productivity level before being exposed to aggregate and idiosyncratic shocks. Shocks to idiosyncratic productivity levels are modelled as a jump process characterized by a Poisson arrival frequency and a drawing from a common distribution of labor productivity levels with bounded support. This stochastic process causes the job-specific productivity levels to be positively correlated over time, even though—conditional on change—a job's existing productivity level does not affect its new level.

The optimization problem implicit in the MP-setup can be interpreted as follows.[5] Firms maximize their profit subject to the production technology, and household-workers maximize their utility subject to a budget. Primarily for the sake of numerical tractability, Mortensen and Pissarides assume households to be risk neutral and the production technology to linearly depend on aggregate and match-specific productivity shocks. At the beginning of every period, firms take as given the distribution of their jobs across productivity levels and also the realization of the aggregate shock. They choose the number of vacancies to post and the reservation-productivity level. Then jobs are hit by idiosyncratic shocks, and, based on the outcome, firms decide which jobs to maintain and which to destroy. Together with the newly matched jobs, those that are maintained each produce one unit of output. Workers are either matched with a job and employed, or unmatched and unemployed. By assumption, only the unemployed workers have a chance to be rematched with an unfilled job. Due to trade-frictions, this matching process exhibits externalities.

The wage that workers receive when matched can be determined in various ways. A firm and a worker can negotiate it by agreeing on how to split the resulting match surplus, or the firm can simply decide to pay the worker his reservation-wage and to keep all of the match surplus. Both wage determination schedules are compatible with an equilibrium in the model economy.

When simulating their model, Mortensen and Pissarides find that it generates some of the stylized facts describing the cyclical behavior of job creation and destruction in the U.S. manufacturing sector that have been found by Davis and Haltiwanger (1990, 1992). Due to recurring idiosyncratic shocks, job creation and destruction occur simultaneously. Job destruction is countercyclical and varies more than the procyclical series of job creation. The cyclical behavior of job creation and destruction is governed by an asymmetry in the reaction of job destruction and job creation to recessions compared to booms. Job destruction is a jump process that takes place immediately in response to aggregate shocks while job creation requires a time consuming matching process.

When a negative aggregate shock hits the economy, firms post fewer vacancies and increase their reservation-productivity. The rise in the separation threshold leads to an immediate sharp increase in the incidence of firms destroying jobs whose idiosyncratic productivity lies below the increased reservation value. Furthermore, job destruction increases since more jobs are likely to receive a bad idiosyncratic shock that reduces their idiosyncratic productivity below the reservation value. As a consequence, unemployment increases. The negative aggregate shock also decreases the number of posted vacancies which eventually reduces the number of newly filled jobs. However, the decrease in job creation due to fewer vacancies is mitigated by an increase due to a rise in the unemployment rate. When a positive technology shock occurs, firms post more vacancies and reduce their reservation-productivity level. These actions cause a symmetrical movement in job creation and job destruction. The observed asymmetry in the movement of both series in a recession that is due to the immediate destruction of low productivity jobs, has no counterpart in a boom.

A major shortcoming of the original MP-model lies in its prediction of job creation and job destruction being positively correlated with each other, even though upon the impact of an aggregate shock, they both move in opposite directions. This behavior arises, since job creation depends on the reaction of vacancies and of unemployment. While vacancies react in such a fashion that the implied job creation moves in the opposite direction of job destruction, the unemployment rate counteracts this behavior, ultimately causing job creation and job destruction to move in the same direction. Subsequent research has addressed this issue.

4.2.2.2 Extensions and Applications. The MP-model with heterogeneous jobs and persistent unemployment has quickly become a popular framework for studying aggregate phenomena of the labor market that are inherently linked to heterogeneity. It has been modified and used for tackling a broad set of issues. Garibaldi (1998), Millard (1994) and Millard and Mortensen (1997) extend it to account for various labor market policies that affect firms' hiring and firing decisions and the workers' decision to provide labor. Millard and Mortensen eliminate aggregate uncertainty and include a payroll tax, a publicly provided UI policy, a firing penalty, severance pay, and a hiring subsidy, and different wage formation schemes. The authors pursue two related goals. They use their model to study the quantitative implications that the above listed labor market policies and different wage setting schemes have for the incidence and duration of unemployment, and for economic welfare. The endogenously determined reservation-productivity and the vacancy-to-unemployment ratio are the two main variables generating the results. Unemployment incidence, the probability of an employed worker becoming unemployed, is positively linked with the reservation-productivity. Unemployment duration, the inverse of the probability of an unemployed worker becoming employed, decreases in the vacancy-to-unemployment ratio. With their findings in hand, they proceed to assess the impact that reforming labor market policies have on unemployment and welfare. Since agents are assumed to be risk neutral and not to save, welfare corresponds to net output or consumption per worker.

By assumption, all separations are efficient in that they only occur if it is in both the firm's and the worker's best interest to dissolve the job-match. Both parties agree to dissolve the match whenever its net surplus becomes negative. Labor market policies affect the decision to separate by affecting the net match surplus that is to be shared between a matched firm and worker. This net surplus equals the expected present value of the sum of the future incomes of the firm and worker were they to continue the match corrected for the capital value of separation. The capital value equals the expected present discounted value of future worker and firm incomes were they separate, corrected for the impact of various labor market policies. The capital value increases by the expected present discounted value of UI benefits received by the worker during his subsequent unemployment spells and also by severance or redundancy pay received from the firm. The capital value decreases by any firing cost that the employer has to bear. For a given net match surplus, different wage determination schemes determine how this surplus is split between a worker and a firm.

Labor market policies affect firms' and workers' respective threat points in the wage bargaining process, and therefore the equilibrium wage rate. The key to Millard's and Mortensen's results lies in the link between the equilibrium wage—corresponding to the wage that ensures efficient separation—and labor demand and supply. Labor demand consists of firms' decisions to create new job-matches and to maintain or dissolve existing ones. Labor supply consists of workers' decisions to be employed rather than unemployed and searching. Introducing UI, for example, leads to a rise in the going wage caused by a rise in the workers' reservation-wage. This rise leads to a decline in firms' profitability due to posting vacancies, and therefore in job creation. The authors show that the reservation-productivity level equals the worker's reservation-wage. Hence, UI raises the reservation-productivity, thereby raising the level and incidence of unemployment. Together with the change in job creation, this also causes an increase in the duration of unemployment. When assessing the implied welfare loss due to reduced per capita consumption, the authors stress that their result is an upper bound to the true loss, since they ignore potential welfare gains due to UI smoothing consumption across different states in the labor market.

Alternatively, a hiring subsidy implemented in the form of a fixed payment to a firm for every newly hired worker increases the firm's profitability due to posting vacancies. It also makes new job-matches relatively more profitable than existing low productivity matches and leads to a rise in the reservation-productivity. Taken together, the duration of unemployment declines while its incidence increases, leaving the net impact on the unemployment rate ambiguous. The authors analyze the remaining labor market policies and wage determination schemes analogously.

Cabrales and Hopenhayn (1995) modify the MP-framework as depicted in Millard and Mortensen (1997) by introducing a stochastic process governing idiosyncratic shocks that exhibit persistence conditional on a change in productivity. They do so in order to address two undesirable implications of the original model. In the original MP-setup, conditional on its productivity changing, a job's existing productivity level does not affect its new level. This implies that a job's hazard of being dissolved is the same for all jobs, regardless of their duration. Furthermore, the average wage associated with a job is the same for all jobs. By introducing history-dependence, Cabrales and Hopenhayn explain the empirical observations that the hazard rate of job-termination declines, and that the average wage associated with a job-match increases with the duration of the match. Furthermore, they use their model to study the implications of a payroll tax and severance pay on the unemployment rate and the rate of labor turnover.

Mortensen (1994) departs from the original MP-model to study the cyclical behavior of job and worker flows. His work is largely motivated by the observation that, even though not identical, job and worker flows are closely interrelated. Furthermore, Akerlof, Rose and Yellen (1988) have documented for the U.S. economy that job-to-job movements are an important phenomenon of total labor turnover. These movements account for about 40 percent of all separations and are strongly procyclical. Mortensen modifies the original MP-model by also letting employed workers search for a new job, thereby allowing for the empirically important observation that workers can move from one job to another without first becoming unemployed. In order to provide incentives for an employed worker to search at all, he assumes that when a new match is created, the worker participates in the resulting match surplus. In fact, he assumes the equilibrium wage rate to be efficient. Consequently, all separations in his model economy are efficient, since they only occur when it is in both the firm's and the worker's best interest to dissolve the job-match. With this modified setup, Mortensen (1994) improves on the original model's prediction regarding the correlation between job creation and destruction.

Compared to the original version, job creation and job destruction each include quits as a component. Including quits enhances the procyclicality of job creation and mitigates the countercyclicality of job destruction enough to generate a negative contemporaneous correlation between the two time series. At the same time, this change does not affect the observation that job destruction is more volatile than job creation, even though it reduces the volatility of both series compared to the original model. Eliminating quits from the new measure of job destruction and of job creation yields measures of worker flows from employment to unemployment, and from unemployment to employment, respectively. Both worker flows are countercyclical and positively correlated with each other.

Merz (1999) creates a synthesis between a modified version of the original MP-framework and the standard one-sector stochastic growth model. She introduces physical capital and standard functional forms of utility and production technology into the MP-framework in order to compare its quantitative predictions to those of existing models of the business cycle. In particular, she provides a model framework that is capable of generating some of the dynamic features characterizing worker flows into and out of unemployment. Both flows simultaneously occur over the business cycle, and it is striking how closely they move together. They are countercyclical with inflows leading outflows by one quarter. Moreover, the hazard of an unemployed worker becoming employed is procyclical, while the unemployment rate is countercyclical. Her model's predictions are consistent with the dynamic behavior of more commonly studied variables such as per capita consumption, capital, investment, employment, unemployment, and output. Merz deviates from the original model by assuming that all endogenous separations are temporary. This change allows her to introduce temporary layoffs and recalls, in addition to new hires and permanent layoffs, as the main propagation mechanism of aggregate shocks. By assumption, only permanently laid off workers can be rematched. She also assumes the productivity of new job-matches to be drawn from the same distribution as idiosyncratic shocks. This formulation captures Jovanovic's (1979) idea that the quality of a job-match is a random variable, and that the true quality is revealed only after its creation.

Simulation results suggest that the model performs well in generating the observed dynamics of flows into and out of unemployment, the unemployment rate, the hazard to move from unemployment to employment, and also of more standard variables of the business cycle. When a positive technology shock hits the economy, the reservation-productivity level drops immediately and the number of vacancies posted increases. Both movements increase employment and reduce the stock of temporarily laid off workers. Flows into unemployment decline, since fewer employed job-matches receive an idiosyncratic shock that reduces their productivity level below the decreased reservation-productivity. Also, fewer of the newly-created matches are immediately dissolved. Flows out of unemployment decline, since recalls decline. The stock of temporarily laid off matches has been sufficiently reduced, so that fewer are exposed to idiosyncratic shocks that might change their productivity above the reservation level. This effect dominates a slight increase in outflows due to an increase in new hires. The decline in inflows outweighs the decline in outflows upon impact of the shock, leading to an immediate decline in the unemployment rate, which reduces outflows even further. Together with a rise in new hires, this causes an increase in the matching probability for all permanently unemployed workers and, ultimately, a rise in flows out of unemployment. It also explains why inflows lead outflows over the cycle.

Merz (1996) uses an extended version of her model to mimic the composition bias that is present in many aggregate statistics on labor market variables. The bias is due to the fact that when time series of aggregate variables are constructed, the composition of individuals underlying these series systematically varies over time. The author generalizes the distribution from which idiosyncratic shocks are drawn. This setup enables her to assess the quantitative impact that advertising costs, or the shape of the distribution of workers across different productivity levels, have on the size of the composition bias in the aggregate statistics on hours, average wages, and labor productivity. The setup also allows her to distinguish between efficient equilibrium wages and labor productivity, since trade-frictions in the labor market keep these two variables from being identical.

When simulating the model, the author finds that it performs well in mimicking the presence of a composition bias and also in generating the dynamic behavior of more commonly studied variables. Its key feature, an endogenously determined countercyclical reservation-productivity level, generates such a bias when she distinguishes between hours worked, that are weighted by their respective productivity level, and those that are unweighted. In an economic upswing, employment is increased by new job-matches and by recalling existing matches. Since, on average, recalls are less productive than new matches, productivity-adjusted hours increase by less than unadjusted hours which translates into the adjusted average wage and labor productivity increasing by more than their unadjusted counterparts. In a downswing, low-productivity matches are the first to be temporarily laid off, which leads to the quality-adjusted average wage and labor productivity declining by more than their unadjusted equivalents. This composition bias is enhanced by the presence of advertising costs for creating new job-matches which makes recalling existing matches more attractive, and also by a distribution from which idiosyncratic shocks to labor productivity are drawn that are skewed to the right.

Cole and Rogerson (1996) investigate in great detail the capability of the MP-model to generate not only the cyclical characteristics of job creation and destruction but also their degree of persistence and the dynamic behavior of employment. They show that the model suffers from a built-in tension between volatility and persistence when used for studying the dynamic behavior of job flows.

4.3 Wage Determination Schemes

It is well known in the search literature stressing externalities that even though an efficient wage rate exists, which splits the rent associated with a match, there is nothing inherent in the model which guarantees that this wage will be the one that the negotiating parties settle on. Mortensen (1982) emphasized this incentive incompatibility of an efficient wage when bargaining takes place. Moen (1997) and Shimer (1995) address the issue of implementing the efficient equilibrium wage rate. They suggest *ex ante* wage announcements by firms as alternative to *ex post* bargaining. They assume that firms can communicate wage offers to potential workers before they are matched by also announcing the accompanying offered wage when posting a vacancy. The economy consists of many submarkets that differ in their degree of labor market tightness, expressed by the respective vacancy-to-unemployment ratios. When applying Mortensen's (1970) ideas to this setup, a firm can be viewed as a monopsonist operating in a given submarket. With an increase in the relative number of vacancies in this market, the firm needs to signal a higher wage to applicants if it wants to fill all its open slots. In equilibrium, the wage rate offered in each submarket is positively linked to the prevailing vacancy-to-unemployment ratio in this market, and the resulting allocation of resources is efficient. Hence, Moen and Shimer provide a competitive setup that can circumvent the incentive compatibility problem associated with *ex post* wage bargaining if one views *ex ante* wage announcements as credible and as the ones that are actually implemented.

5. Conclusions

In this paper, I have surveyed representative examples of recent developments in the field of labor market search and macroeconomics. I have linked these developments to the origins of search theory of the labor market in order to assess the progress that has been made toward explaining aggregate phenomena related to this market. The survey indicates that many of the topics addressed are by no means new. They are to a large extent the same topics that the founding fathers of the theory were interested in. But the fact that they are now studied in a new and often broader analytical environment renders the results more general, and more relevant, for economic policy. Take as an example publicly provided UI and its impact on the level and duration of unemployment. Early search theory studied the issue by mainly focusing on the increase in a searching worker's reservation-wage that UI causes. By casting search in a dynamic general equilibrium model encompassing many possibly incomplete markets, economists can more accurately assess the quantitative implications of UI. They can study the effect that UI has on a workers' and firms' labor supply and demand decision, respectively, and also on a worker's saving decision. Thus, they can more precisely determine welfare costs and benefits and provide better guidelines for policymakers.

This survey also indicates that the recent developments in labor market search and macroeconomics have opened many avenues for future research. Much more work can be done in exploring topics related to open economy macroeconomics, to multisectoral analyses, or to the interaction between the labor market and financial issues, for example. There is a lot of potential for improving the assessment of the quantitative implications that search theory of the labor market has for economics.

Notes

I thank David Andolfatto, Carl Davidson, and Shouyung Shi for valuable comments. All remaining errors are mine.

1. Phelps (1970, p. 4) introduced his volume as an attempt to develop the microeconomic underpinning for the natural rate of unemployment, and for the Phillips curve—the negative link between the unemployment rate and the rate of change of nominal wages.

2. See Diamond (1981, 1982b) and Mortensen (1982), for example.

3. Pissarides (1988, p. 363) labels this approach the reservation wage approach. He explains his choice of words by the fact that the reservation wage plays a key role in propagating exogenous shocks in this part of the search literature. Pissarides' choice of words is misleading, since the reservation wage can be shown to play a similarly important role in the trade frictions approach.

4. This early work is based on McCall's (1970) paper. It thus belongs to the reservation wage approach to search unemployment. Mortensen (1986) provides an extensive survey.

5. Merz (1997) provides a microeconomic structure that can be used to reformulate the social planner's problem of a generalized version of the MP-model as a decentralized market economy. While this microeconomic structure lends itself to an interpretation that establishes its relationship to the existing literature on trade frictions in the labor market, it is not unique. The model presented deviates from the MP-framework in several respects. It is more general, as it allows for risk aversion among workers, a more broadly defined production function, and

physical capital. It is more restrictive, as it focuses on the special case of a Pareto optimal environment.

References

Akerlof, George, Andrew Rose, and Janet Yellen. "Job Switching and Job Satisfaction in the U.S. Labor Market." *Brookings Papers on Economic Activity* (1988): 495–582.

Andolfatto, David. "Business Cycles and Labor Market Search." *American Economic Review* 86 (1996): 112–132.

Andolfatto, David and Paul Gomme. "Unemployment Insurance and Labor-Market Activity in Canada." *Carnegie-Rochester Conference Series on Public Policy* 44 (1996): 47–82.

Blanchard, Olivier Jean and Peter Diamond. "The Aggregate Matching Function." In *Growth/Productivity/Unemployment*, edited by Peter Diamond. Cambridge, Massachusetts: MIT Press, 1990. Pp. 159–201.

Binmore, Ken, Ariel Rubinstein, and Asher Wolinsky. "The Nash Bargaining Solution in Economic Modelling." *Rand Journal of Economics* 17 (1986): 176–188.

Cabrales, Antonio and Hugo A. Hopenhayn. "Job Dynamics, Correlated Shocks and Wage Profiles." Unpublished manuscript. Universitat Pompeu-Fabra, 1995.

Cho, Gyeong L. "Search, Unemployment, and the Business Cycle: A Multisectoral Dynamic General Equilibrium Model." Unpublished manuscript. University of Texas at Austin, 1996.

Cole, Harold and Richard Rogerson. "Can the Mortensen-Pissarides Matching Model Match the Business Cycle Facts?" Unpublished manuscript. Federal Reserve Bank of Minneapolis, 1996.

Costain, James S. "Unemployment Insurance in a General Equilibrium Model of Job Search and Precautionary Savings." Unpublished manuscript. University of Chicago, 1995.

Davis, Steven and John Haltiwanger. "Gross Job Creation and Destruction: Microeconomic Evidence and Macroeconomic Implications." *NBER Macroeconomic Annual* 5 (1990): 123–168.

_____. "Gross Job Creation, Gross Job Destruction, and Employment Reallocation." *Quarterly Journal of Economics* 107 (1992): 819–863.

Diamond, Peter A. "A Model of Price Adjustment." *Journal of Economic Theory* 3 (1971): 156–168.

_____. "Mobility Costs, Frictional Unemployment, and Efficiency." *Journal of Political Economy* 89 (1981): 789–812.

_____. "Wage Determination and Efficiency in Search Equilibrium." *Review of Economic Studies* 49 (1982): 217–227 (a).

_____. "Aggregate Demand Management in Search Equilibrium." *Journal of Political Economy* 90 (1982): 881–894 (b).

Friedman, Milton. "The Role of Monetary Policy." *American Economic Review* 58 (1968): 1–17.

Gale, Douglas. "Bargaining and Competition Part I: Characterization." *Econometrica* 54 (1986): 725–745.

Garibaldi, Pietro. "Job Flow Dynamics and Firing Restrictions." *European Economic Review* 42 (1998): 245–275.

Gomes, Joao, Jeremy Greenwood, and Sergio Rebelo. "Equilibrium Unemployment." Unpublished manuscript. University of Rochester, 1996.

Hansen, Gary D. "Indivisible Labor and the Business Cycle." *Journal of Monetary Economics* 16 (1985): 309–327.

Hosios, Arthur J. "On the Efficiency of Matching and Related Models of Search and Unemployment." *Review of Economic Studies* 57 (1990): 279–298.

Jovanovic, Boyan. "Job Matching and the Theory of Turnover." *Journal of Political Economy* 87 (1979): 972–990.

Kydland, Finn E. and Edward C. Prescott. "Time to Build and Aggregate Fluctuations." *Econometrica* 50 (1982): 1345–1370.

Ljungqvist, Lars and Thomas J. Sargent. "Welfare States and Unemployment." *Economic Theory* 6 (1995): 143–160 (a).

_____. "The Swedish Unemployment Experience." *European Economic Review* 39 (1995): 1043–1070 (b).

Long, John B. and Charles Plosser. "Real Business Cycles." *Journal of Political Economy* 91 (1983): 39–69.

Lucas, Robert E., Jr. and Edward Prescott. "Equilibrium Search and Unemployment." *Journal of Economic Theory* 7 (1974): 188–209.

McCall, John J. "Economics of Information and Job Search." *Quarterly Journal of Economics* 84 (1970): 113–126.

Merz, Monika. "Search in the Labor Market and the Real Business Cycle." *Journal of Monetary Economics* 36 (1995): 269–300.

_____. "Heterogenous Job-Matches and Real Wages: The Composition Bias Revisited." Unpublished manuscript. Rice University, 1996.

_____. "A Market Structure for an Environment with Heterogeneous Job-Matches, Indivisible Labor, and Persistent Unemployment." *Journal of Economic Dynamics and Control* 21 (1997): 853–872.

_____. "Heterogenous Job-Matches and the Cyclical Behavior of Labor Turnover." *Journal of Monetary Economics* 43 (1999): 91–124.

Millard, Stephen P. "The Effect of Employment Protection Legislation on Labour Market Activity: A Search Approach." Unpublished manuscript. Bank of England, 1994.

Millard, Stephen P. and Dale T. Mortensen. "The Unemployment and Welfare Effects of Labour Market Policies: A Comparison of the USA and the UK." In *Unemployment Policy: Government Options for the Labour Market*, edited by Guillermo de la Dehesa and Dennis J. Snower. Cambridge, England: Cambridge University Press, 1997. Pp. 545–572.

Moen, Espen R. "Competitive Search Equilibrium." *Journal of Political Economy* 105 (1997): 385–411.

Mortensen, Dale T. "A Theory of Wage and Employment Dynamics." In *Microeconomic Foundations of Employment and Inflation Theory*, edited by Edmund S. Phelps. New York: W. W. Norton, 1970. Pp. 167–211.

_____. "Property Rights and Efficiency in Mating, Racing, and Related Games." *American Economic Review* 72 (1982): 968–980.

_____. "Job Search and Labor Market Analysis." In *Handbook of Labor Economics*, Volume II, edited by O. Ashenfelter and R. Layard. Amsterdam: Elsevier Science Publishers, 1986. Pp. 849–919.

_____. "Search Theory and Macroeconomics." *Journal of Monetary Economics* 29 (1992): 163–167 (a).

_____. "Equilibrio de Busqueda y Ciclos Economicos Reales (Search Equilibrium and Real Business Cycles)." *Cuadernos Economicos* 51 (1992): 151–172 (b).

_____. "The Cyclical Behavior of Job and Worker Flows." *Journal of Economic Dynamics and Control* 18 (1994): 1121–1142.

Mortensen, Dale T. and Christopher A. Pissarides. "The Cyclical Behavior of Job Creation and Destruction." In *Labour Demand and Equilibrium Wage Formation*, edited by J.C. van Ours, G.A. Pfann, and G. Ridder. Amsterdam: North-Holland, 1993. Pp. 201–222.

_____. "Job Creation and Destruction in the Theory of Unemployment." *Review of Economic Studies* 61 (1994): 397–415.

Phelps, Edmund S., ed. *Microeconomic Foundations of Employment and Inflation Theory.* New York: Norton, 1970.

Pissarides, Christopher A. "Short-Run Equilibrium Dynamics of Unemployment, Vacancies, and Real Wages." *American Economic Review* 75 (1985): 676–690.

_____. "Unemployment and Vacancies in Britain." *Economic Policy* 3 (1986): 499–559.

_____. "Search, Wage Bargains and Cycles." *Review of Economic Studies* 54 (1987): 474–483.

_____. "The Search Equilibrium Approach to Fluctuations in Employment." *American Economic Review Papers and Proceedings* 78 (1988): 363–368.

_____. *Equilibrium Unemployment Theory.* Oxford: Basil Blackwell, 1990.

Shi, Shouyong. "Tariff, Unemployment, and the Current Account: An Intertemporal Equilibrium Model." Unpublished manuscript. Queen's University, 1995.

Shi, Shouyong and Quan Wen. "Labor Market Search and the Dynamic Effects of Factor Taxation." Unpublished manuscript. Queen's University, 1994.

Shimer, Robert. "Contracts in a Frictional Labor Market." Unpublished manuscript. Massachusetts Institute of Technology, 1995.

Stigler, George J. "The Economics of Information." *Journal of Political Economy* 69 (1961): 213–225.

Valdivia, Victor H. "Evaluating the Welfare Benefits of Unemployment Insurance." Unpublished manuscript. Northwestern University, 1995.

3

Search, Bargaining, and the Business Cycle

Dan A. Black
Syracuse University

Mark A. Loewenstein
Boston University

Abstract

In this paper we construct a model where workers engaging in repeated nonsequential search auction their labor services to the highest bidder. The auction mechanism results in a nondegenerate equilibrium wage distribution. Under the assumption that the cumulative distribution function of match specific productivity is log concave, workers search more than the socially efficient number of firms. If workers can repeatedly engage in nonsequential search, the workers' reservation wage is too low for the efficient matching of workers and employers when firms make take-it-or-leave-it employment offers. When workers make take-it-or-leave-it employment offers, however, the workers' reservation wage is set too high for the efficient matching of workers and employers. Finally, we allow for business cycle effects by assuming that only a portion of firms are hiring at any given time. Contrary to the standard sequential search model, we show that the marginal gains to additional search may increase as the portion of firms hiring declines.

1. Introduction

After the publication of John McCall's (1965) seminal paper, "The Economics of Information and Optimal Stopping Rules," most economists abandoned Stigler's (1961) fixed-sample size search in favor of sequential search as a way of modeling the search behavior of workers.[1] Yet, we conjecture that few, if any, of these economists followed a sequential search rule when finding their own jobs. Casual observation suggests that workers in other markets also do not follow a sequential search rule. Morgan and Manning (1985) provide one explanation of this apparent paradox: Because it takes time for employers to evaluate job candidates and make job offers, workers will not wait for a reply to one job application before making another application, but rather will apply to several employers at once. In this paper, we provide another reason why workers may choose nonsequential search: to improve their bargaining position with prospective employers.

We know from Diamond (1971) that when the wage offer distribution is endogenous, there will not generally exist an equilibrium with participation if workers adopt a sequential search strategy. The existence problem stems from the fact that sequential search by workers gives employers monopsony power that they cannot credibly commit to refrain from using. Because this difficulty does not arise when workers adopt a fixed sample size search strategy, Lang (1991) is able to obtain an equilibrium under very general conditions.

The model we present in Section 2 is like Lang's in that workers choose a fixed sample size search strategy, but as in Jovanovic (1979) we assume that workers are not all equally productive at a given employer. Our wage offer game thus reduces to a private-value auction in which firms bid against one another for workers' services, with each worker selecting the employer who offers the highest wage. If employers' wage offers are verifiable, the offer game has a very simple and appealing equilibrium. As we demonstrate, workers' equilibrium search intensity does not generally maximize social welfare. There are two conflicting forces at work: The fact that workers must share the returns to favorable matches with employers causes workers to search too little, while the fact that workers can increase their share of match returns by increasing the number of firms bidding for their services provides an incentive for workers to search too much. If the distribution of match-specific productivity has a decreasing inverse hazard function (as is the case for many common distributions, including the normal and the uniform), the latter effect dominates and there is too much search.

In Section 3, we extend the analysis by allowing workers to engage in repeated, nonsequential search, which requires the worker to choose both an optimal number of firms to search and a reservation wage. Unlike the standard sequential search model with endogenous wage offers, our non-sequential repeated search model readily admits a nondegenerate equilibrium. A reservation wage above the worker's value of leisure is made credible in our model by the fact that if the worker stays unemployed and continues to search there will eventually be two (or more) employers bidding for his services in some future period. The equilibrium wage distribution that results is therefore nondegenerate, although it has a mass point at the reservation wage. Because workers must share the returns to favorable matches with employers, a worker's value of search and reservation wage is too low for efficient matching when firms make take-it-or-leave-it wage offers to workers. When workers are given the right to make take-it-or-leave-it offers to firms, however, we show that the worker sets a reservation wage that is too high for socially efficient matching. Because these two cases represent the polar extremes in the distribution of bargaining power, these results indicate that the efficiency of the matching of worker and firm depend crucially on the distribution of bargaining power.

In Section 4, we allow for business cycle effects by assuming that only a portion of firms are hiring at any given time. We then examine how the number of firms that the worker searches changes as the portion of firms hiring changes. Surprisingly, we find that when the fraction of firms hiring declines, workers may choose to search more firms. Finally, in Section V, we offer a brief summary.

2.   A Model with Multiple Job Applications

Consider a labor market populated with N employers and M workers. To obtain employment, a worker must search for a job. If it takes time for employers to evaluate job candidates and make job offers, workers will not wait for a reply to one job application before making another application, but will search nonsequentially, applying to several employers at once. For simplicity, we assume that workers adopt a fixed sample size search strategy. Our search-wage offer game thus starts with workers choosing the number of firms, n, to search. After a worker applies to all n firms, firms evaluate him and tender wage offers. The worker then selects the employer who offers the highest wage.

As workers are not all equally productive at a given employer, let the ith worker's expected productivity at the jth employer he visits be given by the random variable ε_{ij}. An employer can ascertain a worker's match-specific productivity only after the worker applies for the position. Assuming a linear production technology, the employer receives an expected profit of $\varepsilon_{ij} - w_{ij}$ if the worker accepts his wage offer of w_{ij}. We may suppose that the random variable ε_{ij} is distributed on the interval $[\underline{\varepsilon}, \bar{\varepsilon}]$ with density function $f(\cdot)$ and cumulative distribution function $F(\cdot)$. We will also make the standard assumption that the inverse hazard function $m(\varepsilon) \equiv [1 - F(\varepsilon)]/f(\varepsilon)$ is decreasing.[2]

The worker auctions his labor services to the highest bidder, with each of the competing employers formulating his bid on the basis of the realized value of the worker's match-specific productivity ε. As employers are risk-neutral, the Revenue-Equivalence Theorem of auction theory (see, for example, McAfee and McMillan,

1987 or Milgrom, 1989) tells us that the English, Dutch, Vickery, and sealed-bid, first-price auctions all yield the same expected wage. Given risk-neutral workers, it makes no difference for our analysis which mechanism we choose, although the English auction would seem to bear the most resemblance to the real world where we observe employers making offers and counteroffers as they bid for a worker's services. Employer j will continue to bid for worker i until some other employer offers a wage above ε_{ij}. This process continues until only one firm remains, and this firm pays a wage equal to the second highest value of ε. That is, worker i receives a wage equal to the $(n-1)^{\text{th}}$ order statistic for the sample $\{\varepsilon_{i1}, \varepsilon_{i2}, ..., \varepsilon_{in}\}$.

One might expect that the worker can increase his expected wage by searching a larger number of employers. This conjecture is correct, as one can prove

Lemma 1: Let $E(\varepsilon_{[k],n})$ denote the expected value of the kth order statistic from a random sample of productivity draws at n different employers. Then $E(\varepsilon_{[n-1],n})$ is increasing in n.

Proof: See Appendix.

Although a worker can increase his expected wage by searching a larger number of employers, the marginal gains to search fall as n increases. The following lemma, adapted from McAfee and McMillan, is helpful in showing this.

Lemma 2: Let $J(\varepsilon) \equiv \varepsilon - m(\varepsilon)$. Then the expected value of the $(n-1)^{\text{th}}$-order statistic is equal to the expected value of the function $J(\varepsilon)$ evaluated at the nth-order statistic, or

$$E\left(\varepsilon_{[n-1],n}\right) = n \int_{\underline{\varepsilon}}^{\overline{\varepsilon}} J(\varepsilon)[F(\varepsilon)]^{n-1} f(\varepsilon)d\varepsilon = E\left[J\left(\varepsilon_{[n],n}\right)\right].$$

Proof: See Appendix.

Using Lemma 2, it is straightforward to prove

Lemma 3: $E(\varepsilon_{[n-1],n}) - E(\varepsilon_{[n-2],n-1})$ is decreasing in n.

Proof: From Lemma 2, we have

$$E\left(\varepsilon_{[n-1],n}\right) - E\left(\varepsilon_{[n-2],n-1}\right) = n \int_{\underline{\varepsilon}}^{\overline{\varepsilon}} J(\varepsilon)\{nF(\varepsilon)^{n-1} - (n-1)F(\varepsilon)^{n-2}\} f(\varepsilon)d\varepsilon$$

$$= \int_{\underline{\varepsilon}}^{\bar{\varepsilon}} J(\varepsilon) F(\varepsilon)^{n-2} \{ nF(\varepsilon) - (n-1) \} f(\varepsilon) d\varepsilon \, .$$

As $J(\varepsilon)$ is independent of n and $F(\varepsilon)^{n-2}$ is decreasing in n, we need only show that $nF(\varepsilon) - (n-1)$ is nonincreasing in n. Differentiating this expression with respect to n yields $F(\varepsilon)-1$, which is less than zero.

Presumably a worker who searches more firms increases not only his expected wage but also his search costs. The worker selects n, the number of firms to visit, so as to maximize his expected wage net of search costs. Let $c(n)$ denote the worker's total search cost and let n^* denote the worker's optimal value of n. Because it pays the worker to keep increasing the size of his sample as long as the increase in the expected wage from an additional search exceeds the increase in search cost, n^* is the largest integer less than or equal to N such that

(1) $E(\varepsilon_{[n-1],n}) - E(\varepsilon_{[n-2],n-1}) \geq c(n) - c(n-1).$

As Lemma 3 ensures that the marginal return to search falls with n, nondecreasing marginal search costs are sufficient to ensure that there exists a unique global maximum to the worker's search problem.

Given n, it is straightforward to determine employers' expected profits. An employer who succeeds in hiring a worker receives output $\varepsilon_{[n],n}$ and pays the wage $\varepsilon_{[n-1],n}$. Because an employer hires a job applicant with probability $(1/n)$, the expected profit per applicant is given by

(2) $\rho(n) \equiv [E(\varepsilon_{[n],n}) - E(\varepsilon_{[n-1],n})]/n.$

As each employer can expect to be searched by (nM/N) workers, total expected profit is simply $(nM/N)\rho(n)$.[3]

Several characteristics of the labor market equilibrium warrant mention. First, as Lang (1991) emphasizes, workers' ability to apply for several positions simultaneously is sufficient to induce a dispersed wage equilibrium. Job matching considerations are absent from Lang's model; the equilibrium dispersion in wages occurs because firms have differing costs of vacancies. In contrast, the equilibrium variation in wages occurs in our model because of variations in match-specific productivity. As firms compete directly for workers, they must give workers a portion of the returns to favorable matches in the form of higher wages. In contrast, if we had adopted the standard assumption of sequential search, firms' resultant monopsony power would preclude the existence of an equilibrium with labor force participation (as first pointed out by Diamond, 1971).

Second, a worker's expected wage depends on the number of firms that he searches, not on the number of firms in the market. If $N > n$, an increase in the number of firms in the market has no effect on a worker's expected wage, but a fall in the marginal cost of search increases the number of firms that workers will search, thereby increasing competition among employers for workers' services. Thus, holding the distribution of ε constant, workers are able to capture a greater share of match-specific rents in markets where search is relatively inexpensive.

Third, the equilibrium level of search will generally differ from the level that maximizes expected output net of search cost. The social planner selecting search to maximize expected output net of search costs would have the worker keep increasing the size of his sample as long as the expected increase in output exceeds the additional cost of searching an extra firm, or

(3) $E(\varepsilon_{[n],n}) - E(\varepsilon_{[n-1],n-1}) \geq c(n) - c(n-1).$

A comparison of equations (1) and (3) reveals that the private benefit to a worker from searching an additional employer generally differs from the social benefit. While the social planner cares about the expected increase in the nth order statistic, the worker is interested in the $(n-1)^{th}$ order statistic. Because workers must share the returns to favorable matches with employers, one's intuition might suggest that workers will generally search too little. As the following example illustrates, however, this need not be the case. Suppose that $F(\cdot)$ is normal with a mean of 30 and a standard deviation of 10. In addition, suppose that $c(n) = n$. Making use of the fact that

$$E\left(\varepsilon_{[n],n}\right) = \int_{\underline{\varepsilon}}^{\overline{\varepsilon}} \varepsilon n F\left(\varepsilon\right)^{n-1} f\left(\varepsilon\right) d\varepsilon ,$$

one can calculate that the efficient number of searches is 5. Making use of equation (1) and Lemma 2, however, one finds that the worker will choose to search 7 employers.

In our example, the worker's search intensity thus exceeds the Pareto optimal search intensity by 40 percent. Increasing the number of searches from 5 to 7 raises the worker's expected wage by 2.5 (from to 34.5 to 37), but only increases his expected productivity by 1.7 (from 41.2 to 42.9). To understand this result, note that a worker's private gain from searching an additional employer differs from the social gain for *two* distinct reasons. First, as noted above, if searching the additional employer results in a better match, the worker captures only part of the return, the remaining part accruing to the employer. While this effect alone would cause the private return to search to be less than the social return, there is another offsetting consideration: Even if additional search does not lead to a better match, the increased competition among potential employers may nevertheless enable the worker to increase his share of match-specific rents. In our example, this second effect dominates the first and there is too much search. The question that naturally arises is how sensitive this result is to the choice of the distribution function $F(\varepsilon)$ and cost function $c(n)$.

Interestingly, the tendency toward too much search holds generally. To show this, we first use Lemma 2 to rewrite the worker's marginal gain to search as

(4) $$E(\varepsilon_{[n-1],n}) - E(\varepsilon_{[n-2],n-1}) = E(\varepsilon_{[n],n}) - E(\varepsilon_{[n-1],n-1}) + \Delta$$

where

(5) $$\Delta \equiv (n-1)\int_{\underline{\varepsilon}}^{\bar{\varepsilon}} m(\varepsilon)[F(\varepsilon)]^{n-2} f(\varepsilon)d\varepsilon - n\int_{\underline{\varepsilon}}^{\bar{\varepsilon}} m(\varepsilon)[F(\varepsilon)]^{n-1} f(\varepsilon)d\varepsilon .$$

According to equation (4), the worker's private gain to search is greater (less) than the social gain as $\Delta > (<) \, 0$. Using this result, it is straightforward to prove

Proposition 1: A worker's marginal gain to search is greater than the social gain.

Proof: Let $\hat{\varepsilon} \equiv F^{-1}((n-1)/n)$ and note that $(n-1)F(\varepsilon)^{n-2} < nF(\varepsilon)^{n-1}$ as $\varepsilon > (<)\hat{\varepsilon}$. As $m(\varepsilon)$ is decreasing, it follows from equation (5) that

$$\Delta = \int_{\underline{\varepsilon}}^{\hat{\varepsilon}} m(\varepsilon)\{(n-1)F(\varepsilon)^{n-2} - nF(\varepsilon)^{n-1}\}f(\varepsilon)d\varepsilon + \int_{\hat{\varepsilon}}^{\bar{\varepsilon}} m(\varepsilon)\{(n-1)F(\varepsilon)^{n-2} - nF(\varepsilon)^{n-1}\}f(\varepsilon)d\varepsilon$$

$$> \int_{\underline{\varepsilon}}^{\hat{\varepsilon}} m(\hat{\varepsilon})\{(n-1)F(\varepsilon)^{n-2} - nF(\varepsilon)^{n-1}\}f(\varepsilon)d\varepsilon + \int_{\hat{\varepsilon}}^{\bar{\varepsilon}} m(\hat{\varepsilon})\{(n-1)F(\varepsilon)^{n-2} - nF(\varepsilon)^{n-1}\}f(\varepsilon)d\varepsilon$$

$$= m(\hat{\varepsilon})\{\int_{\underline{\varepsilon}}^{\bar{\varepsilon}} (n-1)F(\varepsilon)^{n-2} f(\varepsilon)d\varepsilon - n\int_{\underline{\varepsilon}}^{\bar{\varepsilon}} F(\varepsilon)^{n-1} f(\varepsilon)d\varepsilon\} .$$

As a density function must integrate to 1, $n\int_{\underline{\varepsilon}}^{\bar{\varepsilon}} F(\varepsilon)^{n-1} f(\varepsilon)d\varepsilon = 1$ for all $n \geq 2$. We thus have

$$\Delta > m(\hat{\varepsilon})\{\int_{\underline{\varepsilon}}^{\bar{\varepsilon}} (n-1)F(\varepsilon)^{n-2} f(\varepsilon)d\varepsilon - n\int_{\underline{\varepsilon}}^{\bar{\varepsilon}} F(\varepsilon)^{n-1} f(\varepsilon)d\varepsilon\} = 0 .$$

It follows immediately from Proposition 1 that the worker searches more than the socially optimal number of employers. Interestingly, it follows immediately from the proof of Proposition 1 that the worker will search too few firms if the inverse hazard function is increasing. (To see this, note that if $m(\varepsilon)$ is increasing, the inequality in the second line of the proof is reversed.) Similarly, search is socially efficient if the inverse hazard function is a constant. Thus, we have

Corollary 1: If ε is distributed exponentially, then search is socially efficient.

The intuition behind these results is simple. The social planner cares about the increase in the expected value of the nth-order statistic as the number of firms searched increases, but the worker cares about the distribution of the $(n-1)^{th}$-order statistic. When the distribution of match-specific productivity is exponential, the impact of increasing the number of firms searched is the same for both statistics. When the inverse hazard rate is declining, then the increase in the expectation of the $(n-1)^{th}$-order statistic is larger than the increase for the nth-order statistic, and the worker searches too much for social efficiency.

3.   Repeated Nonsequential Search

We now extend the model by allowing workers to engage in repeated, nonsequential search. A worker engaging in repeated, nonsequential search selects not only a number of firms to search, but also a reservation wage, w_r, which functions as a reserve price in an auction. If the worker does not receive an offer at least as high as the reservation wage, he chooses to forego employment and search again next period.

The mechanics of repeated, nonsequential search are relatively straightforward. Operationally, the worker chooses that employer who offers him the highest wage, provided that this wage offer is at least as high as w_r. If the worker's wage offers are all below w_r, then he continues to search in the subsequent period. An employer will obviously never offer a worker a wage above his match-specific productivity, and the employer also knows that there is no point in extending a wage offer below w_r, which may help explain Barron, Black, and Loewenstein's (1989) observation that on average only one out of 3.7 job applicants receives an offer.

Before proceeding with the formal analysis, one subtlety requires attention: The wage offers that a worker receives depends on the bargaining positions of the worker and firm. To see why, let V denote an unemployed worker's "value of search"; that is, V is the difference between the worker's expected discounted wage income and expected discounted search cost. Suppose that among the employers searched in the current period, worker i's discounted value of marginal product is less than V at all employers other than j and exceeds V at employer j. Then, worker i can become employed at employer j at any wage between V and w_r. The actual solution to this general bargaining problem will depend on the relative bargaining strengths of the employer and worker. We will consider the two polar cases. In the first, the employer has the right to make a take-it-or-leave-it wage offer if the worker has no other currently viable employment alternatives. In the second, the worker has the right to make a take-it-or-leave-it wage demand. In the first case, all bargaining power effectively rests with the employer, while in the second, it lies with the worker. Search models in which the wage distribution is endogenous usually assign the employer the right to make a take-it-or-leave-it offer, thereby giving him all the bargaining power.

3.1 Employers Make Take-it-or-Leave-it Offers

In this section, we will assume that employers have the right to make take-it-or-leave-it wage offers. The standard sequential search model with endogenous take-it-or-leave wage offers by employers cannot support a (subgame perfect) equilibrium with participation because a worker cannot credibly insist on a reservation wage sufficiently high to ensure that he recoups his search costs. When search is non-sequential, this is not a problem. Even if a worker's productivity exceeds his reservation wage at only one of the employers searched in the preceding period, a reservation wage above the worker's value of leisure is made credible by the fact that if the worker continues to search there will eventually be two (or more) employers bidding for his services in some future period, provided that $n \geq 2$. The equilibrium wage distribution that results is nondegenerate but has a mass point at the reservation wage.

In order to characterize equilibrium search behavior, note that if worker i's match-specific productivity exceeds w_r at two or more firms in the current period, then the reserve price is not binding and the worker receives a wage equal to the $(n-1)^{th}$ order statistic for the sample $\{\varepsilon_{i1}, \varepsilon_{i2}, ..., \varepsilon_{in}\}$. If the worker's match-specific productivity is less than w_r at each of the n firms that he visits in the current period, then no employer will be willing to offer the worker his reservation wage, and the worker will continue to search next period. Finally, if the worker's match-specific productivity exceeds w_r at firm j and is less than w_r at all other firms, firm j will offer the worker a wage of w_r. When the worker searches $n \geq 2$ firms, the value of search is thus given by

$$V = -c(n) + \beta F(w_r)^n V + n[1-F(w_r)]F(w_r)^{n-1}w_r$$

$$+\{1-F(w_r) - n[1-F(w_r)]F(w_r)^{n-1}\}E(\varepsilon_{[n-1],n} \mid \varepsilon_{[n-1],n} \geq w_r),$$

where $0 < \beta < 1$ is the worker's discount factor and where we assume, for simplicity of notation, that wage and productivity are denoted in terms of their discounted present values. When rearranged, this yields

(6) $$V = \frac{n[1 - F(w_r)]\{F(w_r)\}^{n-1} w_r + \int_{w_r}^{\bar{\varepsilon}} \varepsilon n(n-1)[1 - F(\varepsilon)]F(\varepsilon)^{n-2} f(\varepsilon)d\varepsilon - c(n)}{1 - \beta F(w_r)^n}.$$

Using an argument similar to that in Lemma 2, equation (6) can be rewritten as

(7) $$V = \frac{\int_{w_r}^{\bar{\varepsilon}} J(\varepsilon) n F(\varepsilon)^{n-1} f(\varepsilon)d\varepsilon - c(n)}{1 - \beta F(w_r)^n}.$$

The derivative of V with respect to w_r is given by $\frac{\partial V}{\partial w_r} = [\beta V - J(w_r)]\frac{n(F(w_r))^{n-1} f(w_r)}{1 - \beta(F(w_r))^n}$. Setting this equal to zero yields

(8) $\beta V - J(w_r) = 0.$

From equation (8), it immediately follows that the reservation wage $w_r = J^{-1}(\beta V)$ maximizes V. As $J^{-1}(\beta V) > \beta V$, the worker would like to threaten to refuse some offers that exceed the value of continued search. While such a strategy would represent a Nash Equilibrium, however, it would not satisfy a requirement of subgame perfection because it would allow the worker to commit to behavior that is not optimal *ex post*. *Ex post* the worker will find it optimal to accept any take-it-or-leave-it wage offer that is at least as high as the expected payoff he would receive from remaining unemployed and searching another period. Subgame perfection thus requires that the reservation wage equal the discounted value of search, or $w_r = \beta V$.

Substituting βV for w_r in equation (7) and rearranging terms, one obtains

(9) $$\int_{\beta V}^{\bar{\varepsilon}} [J(\varepsilon) - \beta V] n F(\varepsilon)^{n-1} f(\varepsilon)d\varepsilon - (1 - \beta)V = c(n).$$

By the implicit function theorem, we can use equation (9) to solve for the value of search as a function of n, or $V = V(n)$. The worker chooses the number of searches, n^*, so as to maximize $V(n)$. Of course, the equilibrium reservation wage is simply $\beta V(n^*)$.

To illustrate the effects of repeated search, suppose that, as above, $F(\cdot)$ is normal with a mean of 30 and a standard deviation of 10 and $c(n) = n$. In addition, suppose that the discount factor β is equal to 0.98. Then using equation (9), one can show that the worker's optimal reservation wage is 29.5 and his optimal number of searches each period is 7. Note that the probability of the worker receiving an acceptable offer in a given period is equal to $1-(F(29.5))^6 = 0.988$, so that the expected number of search periods is 1.02. As the worker searches 6 firms each period, he can expect to search 6.072 employers in all. Recall that the worker's optimal number of searches was seven in the one period model. When search cannot be repeated beyond one period, a firm's ability to appropriate the rents from a match is limited only by the presence of other firms also bidding for the worker's services. When search is repeated, the positive reservation wage also serves to limit the rents that an employer can extract. In effect, the firm seeking to hire a worker must compete not only against the firms that the worker has searched in the current period, but also against those that he will search in the future if he remains unemployed. Because searching an additional employer has a smaller effect on the worker's share of match returns, the worker's optimal number of searches is lower when search can be repeated beyond one period.

A social planner would select the reservation value of ε, ε_r, and the number of searches k so as to maximize

(10)
$$v = \frac{\int_{\varepsilon_r}^{\bar{\varepsilon}} \varepsilon k F(\varepsilon)^{k-1} f(\varepsilon) d\varepsilon - c(k)}{1 - \beta F(\varepsilon_r)^k}.$$

Differentiating equation (10) yields the necessary condition

(11) $\partial v / \partial \varepsilon_r = (\beta v - \varepsilon_r) = 0.$

Substituting equation (11) into equation (10) and simplifying gives us

(12) $\int_{\beta v(k)}^{\bar{\varepsilon}} [\varepsilon - \beta v(k)] k F(\varepsilon)^{k-1} f(\varepsilon) d\varepsilon - (1-\beta) v(k) = c(k).$

Equation (12) implicitly defines the social planner's value of search as a function of k, or $v = v(k)$. The socially optimal number of searches, k^*, maximizes $v(k)$ and the socially optimal reservation wage is $\beta v(k^*)$. In our example, it can be shown that the socially efficient reservation wage is 36.1 and the socially efficient number of searches each period is 6. Thus, the worker's reservation wage is below the socially efficient reservation wage and the number of employers that he searches exceeds the socially efficient number. Do these results hold in general?

Others have shown that a worker's reservation wage is generally too low when search is sequential.[4] This inefficiency arises from the fact that workers must share the returns to favorable matches with employers. The following proposition shows that the same inefficiency arises when search is nonsequential:

Proposition 2: When employers make take-it-or-leave it offers, the worker's equilibrium reservation wage, w_r, is too low for efficient matching.

Proof: Let

$$\phi(x,y,n) = \int_{\beta x}^{\bar{\varepsilon}} \left[J(\varepsilon) - \beta x \right] nF(\varepsilon)^{n-1} f(\varepsilon) d\varepsilon - (1-\beta)x - \int_{\beta y}^{\bar{\varepsilon}} \left[\varepsilon - \beta y \right] nF(\varepsilon)^{n-1} f(\varepsilon) d\varepsilon - (1-\beta)y$$

and note that $\phi(x,x,n) = \int_{\beta x}^{\bar{\varepsilon}} -m(\varepsilon)nF(\varepsilon)^{n-1} f(\varepsilon) d\varepsilon < 0$. Differentiation of $\phi(\cdot)$ yields

$$\frac{\partial \phi(x,y,n)}{\partial x} = \beta m(\beta x)nF(\beta x)^{n-1} f(\beta x) - \int_{\beta x}^{\bar{\varepsilon}} \beta nF(\varepsilon)^{n-1} f(\varepsilon) d\varepsilon - (1-\beta)$$

$$= \beta(1 - F(\beta x))nF(\beta x)^{n-1} - \int_{\beta x}^{\bar{\varepsilon}} \beta nF(\varepsilon)^{n-1} f(\varepsilon) d\varepsilon - (1-\beta)$$

$$= \beta \int_{\beta x}^{\bar{\varepsilon}} n\left(F(\beta x)^{n-1} - nF(\varepsilon)^{n-1} \right) f(\varepsilon) de - (1-\beta)$$

$$< 0 .$$

As equations (9) and (12) imply that $\varphi(V(n), v(n), n) = 0$, it follows immediately that $V(n) < v(n)$ for all n. As the worker's value of search is given by $w_r^* = \max_n \{\beta V(n)\}$ and as the socially optimal reservation wage is given by $\varepsilon_r^* = \max_n \{\beta v(n)\}$, it must be the case that $w_r^* < \varepsilon_r^*$.

Workers not only have a socially inefficient reservation wage, but they also do not search the efficient number of firms. As discussed in the previous section, there are two conflicting forces at work: The fact that workers must share the returns to favorable matches with employers causes workers to search too little, while the fact that workers can increase their share of match returns by increasing the number of firms bidding for their services provides an incentive for workers to search too much. When search is not repeated, the latter effect dominates, and the worker searches too many firms. Our example above indicates that the worker may also search too many employers when search is repeated. While it is easy to find other examples where this is true, it cannot be proved in general. As noted above, when search is not repeated, a firm's ability to appropriate the rents from a match is limited only by the presence of other firms also bidding for the worker's services. When search is repeated, however, the positive reservation wage also serves to limit the rents that an employer can extract. As searching additional firms has a smaller effect on the worker's share of match returns, the worker is less likely to search an inefficiently large number of firms.

3.2 Workers Make Take-it-or-Leave-it Wage Demands

Instead of allowing employers to make take-it-or-leave-it offers, let us now consider the case where workers make take-it-or-leave-it wage demands. As before, if worker i's match-specific productivity exceeds w_r at two or more firms in the current period, the worker's reservation price is not binding and the worker receives a wage equal to the $(n-1)^{\text{th}}$ order statistic for the sample $\{\varepsilon_{i1}, \varepsilon_{i2}, ..., \varepsilon_{in}\}$. If the worker has no other currently viable employment alternatives, employer j's optimal strategy is simply to offer the worker a wage equal to his reservation wage demand provided that the worker's productivity ε_{ij} is at least as high as w_r. Thus, the value of search is still given by equation (7). As the worker has the right to make a take-it-or-leave-it demand, however, he can now insist on a wage above V. The reservation wage that the worker ends up choosing will be the one that maximizes the value of search.

Differentiating equation (7) with respect to w_r yields the first-order condition

$$\frac{\partial V}{\partial w_r} = [\beta V - J(w_r)] = 0$$

from which it follows that

(13) $\beta V + m(w_r) = w_r.$

According to equation (13), a worker's optimal take-it-or-leave-it reservation wage demand exceeds the value of continued search. This result reflects the fact that the distribution of wage offers is not exogenous but depends on the worker's reservation wage demand. Specifically, an increase in the reservation wage w_r increases the wage offer a worker receives from firm j if the worker's match-specific productivity is less than w_r at all firms other than firm j but greater than w_r at firm j. Of course, if the worker's match-specific productivity at firm j were initially just equal to w_r, then an increase in w_r would preclude the worker from obtaining employment at firm j, resulting in a loss of $w_r - \beta V$. Optimality requires that the worker choose the reservation wage to balance the expected gain from a further increase against the expected loss.

Substituting $J^{-1}(\beta V)$ for w_r in equation (7) and rearranging terms yields

(14) $\displaystyle\int_{J^{-1}(\beta V)}^{\bar{\varepsilon}} [J(\varepsilon) - \beta V]nF(\varepsilon)^{n-1} f(\varepsilon)d\varepsilon - (1-\beta)V = c(n) .$

By the implicit function theorem, we can solve equation (14) for the value of search as a function of n, or $V = V(n)$. The worker chooses the number of searches, n^*, so as to maximize $V(n)$. The equilibrium reservation wage is $J^{-1}(\beta V(n^*))$.

To illustrate the effects of giving bargaining power to the worker instead of the employer, let us return to the case where $F(\cdot)$ is normal with a mean of 30 and a standard deviation of 10, the cost of search is given by $c(n) = n$, and the discount factor β is equal to 0.98. In this case, calculations reveal that when the worker has the right to make a take-it-or-leave-it wage offer, his optimal reservation wage demand is 38.5 and his optimal number of searches is 3. Recall that when employers had the right to make take-it-or-leave-it offers, the equilibrium reservation wage was 29.5 and the number of searches was 6. Thus, at least in our example, the equilibrium reservation wage is higher and the equilibrium number of searches is lower when the worker rather than the employer has the ability to make a take-it-or-leave-it offer. This result makes intuitive sense. When the worker has the power to make a take-it-or-leave-it offer, he sets a higher reservation price and extracts a greater share of match rents. As noted above, the worker searches not only to find more efficient matches, but also to limit the employer's share of rents. But when the worker can make a take-it-or-leave wage demand, his higher reservation price also limits the employer's rent extraction. As a result, the worker's marginal gain to search is lower, and he searches fewer firms in equilibrium.

The result that the worker's reservation wage is higher when he has the right to make a take-it-or-leave-it-offer is not unique to our example but can be shown to hold in general. In fact, as the following proposition indicates, one can prove a stronger result.

Proposition 3: When the worker makes a take-it-or-leave-it wage demand, the reservation wage w_r is too high for efficient matching.

Proof: See the Appendix.

Proposition 3 indicates that when workers make take-it-or-leave-it wage demands, a worker's reservation wage exceeds the level that is socially optimal. This reflects the fact that in attempting to maximize his share of match-specific returns, the worker sets a reservation wage demand that is sufficiently high to preclude some mutually beneficial matches.[5]

Thus, depending on who has the power to make take-it-or-leave-it offers, the reservation wage is set either too high or too low for efficient job matching. When an employer is able to make a take-it-or-leave-it offer to a worker who does not have an acceptable alternative, the employer acts as a monopsonist and sets a wage giving him all the gains accruing to the match. Because workers bear the full cost of search but do not realize all of the returns, their reservation wage is too low for efficient matching. On the other hand, when the worker is allowed to make a take-it-or-leave-it offer, the worker acts as price setter and sets a price that is too high for efficient matching.

4. Search and the Business Cycle

Our analysis thus far has assumed that every employer searched by the worker actually has a vacancy. We now relax this assumption. Among other things, this will allow us to examine search behavior over the business cycle.

To simplify the discussion, let us return to the one period model where workers adopt a fixed sample size search strategy. Now suppose that an employer searched by a worker has a vacancy with probability p. Thus, if a worker searches n firms, the probability that exactly i employers will have vacancies is

$$(15) \qquad P(n,i) = \frac{n!}{i!(n-i)!} p^i (1-p)^{n-i}$$

and the expected number of offers is $p \times n$. As before, our search-wage offer game starts with workers choosing the number of firms, n, to search. After a worker applies at all n firms, those firms with vacancies evaluate him and tender wage offers. The worker then selects the employer who offers the highest wage.

As before, it pays for the worker to choose the number of searches such that the expected marginal gain from an additional search equals the marginal cost. Ascertaining the marginal gain to additional search, however, is somewhat more complicated when employers may not have vacancies. To determine the marginal gain to search, suppose that the worker's first $(n-1)$ searches yield i offers from firms with vacancies. Now suppose that the worker searches an nth firm. If this firm does not have a vacancy, then the marginal gain to search is zero. If the firm has a vacancy, then the worker's expected wage increases from $E(\varepsilon_{[i-1],i})$ to $E(\varepsilon_{[i],i+1})$. Thus, if the worker's first $n-1$ searches yield ($i \geq 2$) offers from firms with vacancies, the expected marginal gain to searching an nth employer is

$$(16a) \qquad p(E(\varepsilon_{[i],i+1}) - E(\varepsilon_{[i-1],i})) = p \int_{\underline{\varepsilon}}^{\bar{\varepsilon}} J(\varepsilon) F(\varepsilon)^{i-1} \{(i+1)F(\varepsilon) - (i)\} f(\varepsilon) d\varepsilon \ .$$

Note also that if only one of the employers searched by the worker has a vacancy, then that employer can hire the worker for essentially nothing. Thus, if $i = 1$, the expected marginal gain to searching an nth employer is

$$(16b) \qquad p(E(\varepsilon_{[1],2}) - E(\varepsilon_{[0],1})) = p \int_{\underline{\varepsilon}}^{\bar{\varepsilon}} J(\varepsilon) F(\varepsilon) \{2F(\varepsilon)\} f(\varepsilon) d\varepsilon$$

and if $i = 0$, there is no gain to searching an additional employer.

Naturally, the worker does not know how many of the first $(n-1)$ employers will have vacancies. He does know, however, the probability that there will be exactly i vacancies. In fact, from equations (15) and (16), it follows immediately that the expected gain to searching the nth firm is given by

$$(17) \quad MG(n) = \sum_{i=1}^{n-1} P(n-1,i) p\left(E\left(\varepsilon_{[i],i+1}\right) - E\left(\varepsilon_{[i-1],i}\right)\right)$$

$$= \sum_{i=2}^{n-1} \frac{(n-1)!}{i!(n-1-i)!} p^{i+1} (1-p)^{n-1-i} \int_{\underline{\varepsilon}}^{\bar{\varepsilon}} J(\varepsilon) F(\varepsilon)^{i-1} \{(i+1)F(\varepsilon) - i\} f(\varepsilon) d\varepsilon$$

$$+ \frac{(n-1)!}{(n-2)!} p^2 (1-p)^{n-2} \int_{\underline{\varepsilon}}^{\bar{\varepsilon}} J(\varepsilon) F(\varepsilon) \{2F(\varepsilon)\} f(\varepsilon) d\varepsilon .$$

We are now ready to analyze search behavior over the business cycle. Presumably, p will fall during a recession and rise during an expansion. A change in p affects search behavior through its impact on the marginal gain to search. If the marginal gain to search rises (falls), then the worker will search more (fewer) employers. For example, consider our previous example, where $F(\cdot)$ is normal with a mean of 30 and a standard deviation of 10 and where $c(n) = n$. As discussed above, if each firm searched has a vacancy, then the worker's optimal number of searches is 7. If p is 0.7, then the optimal number of searches is 8. If p falls to 0.4, then the optimal number of searches increases to 12.

In our example, a reduction in p thus increases the worker's search intensity. This is in contrast to the standard sequential search model, where a reduction in the proportion of employers who have vacancies unambiguously lowers the marginal gain to search. To gain further insight into the effect of a change in p on the marginal gain to search, let us differentiate equation (17) with respect to p:

$$(18) \qquad \frac{dMG(n)}{dp} = \sum_{i=1}^{n-1} P(n-1,i)\left(E\left(\varepsilon_{[i],i+1}\right) - E\left(\varepsilon_{[i-1],i}\right)\right)$$

$$+ \sum_{i=1}^{n-1} \frac{dP(n-1,i)}{dp} p\left(E\left(\varepsilon_{[i],i+1}\right) - E\left(\varepsilon_{[i-1],i}\right)\right).$$

From equation (18), we see that when search is nonsequential, a reduction in p has two conflicting effects on the marginal gain to search. First, there is a direct effect that is analogous to the effect occurring in the sequential search model. Specifically, a fall in p means that the nth employer is less likely to have a vacancy, which by itself reduces the marginal gain to search. This effect is represented by the term

$$\sum_{i=1}^{n-1} P(n-1,i)(E(\varepsilon_{[i],i+1}) - E(\varepsilon_{[i-1],i}))$$ in equation (18). Note that this term is unambiguously positive.

When search is nonsequential, a change in p has an additional indirect effect that needs to be taken into account. This second effect is represented by the term

$$\sum_{i=1}^{n-1} \frac{dP(n-1,i)}{dp} p(E(\varepsilon_{[i],i+1}) - E(\varepsilon_{[i-1],i})),$$

which can be shown to be negative. If p falls, then the worker's first $(n-1)$ searches can be expected to yield fewer vacancies. Recall from Lemma 3 that $E(\varepsilon_{[i],i+1}) - E(\varepsilon_{[i-1],i})$ is decreasing in i. Thus, if the first $(n-1)$ searches yield fewer vacancies, an additional employer bidding for the worker's services will have greater value in raising the worker's wage. This indirect effect works in the opposite direction of the direct effect and reflects the fact that the marginal gain to search is a nonlinear function of p. In contrast, when search is sequential, the marginal gain to search is linear in p.

In our example, the indirect effect of a reduction in p exceeds the direct effect so that search intensity moves counter-cyclically. One can easily find other examples where this is true, although we doubt that it can be proved in general. Note too that although a reduction in p may cause the marginal gain to search to increase, it is straightforward to show that an unemployed worker's total gain from search unambiguously falls. Thus, there is a critical value p^* with the property that an unemployed worker participates if and only if $p > p^*$. In our example p^* is approximately 0.12.

Contrary to the prediction of the neoclassical model, empirical research has generally found that productivity and wages move cyclically. One important feature missing from the neoclassical model is the process by which workers are matched to firms. Other things the same, a reduction in p means that there will be fewer employers bidding for a worker's services. As average match quality would fall, this could help explain cyclical movement in both productivity and wages.

Of course, as discussed above, if search is nonsequential, workers may compensate for a smaller probability of a vacancy by searching more firms. Note, however, that in our example the increase in n only partially compensates for the reduction in p, so that the expected number of bidders for a worker's services still falls. Thus, while the number of firms searched by the worker moves counter cyclically, the expected number of bidders moves cyclically. Specifically, when the probability of a vacancy is 0.7, the worker searches 8 firms, which means that the expected number of bidders is 5.6. If p falls to 0.4, n increases to 12 so that the expected number of bidders falls to 0.48. We suspect that this result may hold under fairly general conditions.[6] To see why, recall that a fall in p has two effects on the marginal gain to search: a direct negative effect and an indirect effect caused by the fact that the marginal gain to search tends to fall as the expected number of bidders increases. If n were to rise sufficiently to cause an increase in the expected number of bidders, then the indirect effect would tend to be negative. But this would in turn mean that the marginal gain to search was lower, so that n could not increase.[7]

5. Conclusion

As we mentioned in the introduction, nonsequential search appears to be a standard feature of the labor market for Ph.D. economists in the United States. Similarly, every year graduating college seniors and M.B.A. students engage in nonsequential search for employment. Morgan and Manning (1985) argue that search becomes nonsequential when it takes time for potential employers to tender offers. Price offers are exogenous in Morgan and Manning's model. When one makes offers endogenous, however, there is another reason why workers may choose nonsequential search. When there are match-specific returns, the wages that employers offer and workers demand will depend on bargaining considerations. By engaging in nonsequential search, workers can improve their bargaining position with prospective employers and thus obtain higher wage offers. We have shown that workers who search nonsequentially may choose to search too many firms for efficient job matching.

We have extended the basic analysis by allowing workers to engage in repeated, nonsequential search, which requires the worker to choose both an optimal number of firms to search and a reservation wage. Our nonsequential repeated search model easily admits a nondegenerate equilibrium: The equilibrium wage distribution has a mass point at the reservation wage but differs from the reservation wage when multiple firms bid for the worker's services. We have shown that when firms make take-it-or-leave-it wage offers to workers, the reservation wage is too low for socially efficient matching, but when workers make take-it-or-leave-it offers to firms, the reservation wage is too high for socially efficient matching. Thus, the efficiency of the matching of worker and firm depends crucially on the distribution of bargaining power. Finally, we have allowed for business cycle effects by assuming that only a portion of firms are hiring at any given time. We show that when the fraction of firms hiring declines, workers may choose to search more firms. The fact that this tends to only partially compensate for the reduced probability of a vacancy may help explain cyclical movement in both productivity and wages.

Notes

We thank Paul Anglin, Mike Baye, Kevin Lang, Rich Jensen, Keith Crocker, and Tom Gresik for helpful discussions, and seminar participants at the University of Kentucky, Pennsylvania State University, and Purdue University for useful comments on previous versions of the paper. Any remaining errors are our responsibility. The views expressed here are those of the authors and do not necessarily reflect the views of the U.S. Bureau of Labor Statistics.

1. Exceptions include Benhabib and Bull (1983), Burdett and Judd (1983), Lang (1991), and Black and Loewenstein (1995).

2. Many standard distributions, including the normal and the uniform, have an inverse hazard function $m(\varepsilon)$ that is strictly decreasing. Dagsvik, Jovanovic, and Shepard (1985) present evidence that the distribution of ε may be approximated by the normal distribution.

3. For convenience, we are assuming that employers' search costs are zero.

4. This effect is analyzed by Mortensen (1982a, 1982b), Diamond (1981, 1982), Pissarides (1984, 1985), and Davidson, Martin, and Matusz (1987). See Mortensen (1986) and Davidson (1990) for good reviews of the literature.

5. This is consistent with Bulow and Roberts (1989) who show that a seller's problem of devising an optimal auction is identical to the problem facing a monopolist engaging in third degree price discrimination.

6. One complication that should be noted is that the number of firms searched is a discrete variable. Thus if the number of firms increases from n_1 to n_1+1 when p falls to p_1, then a reduction in p from $p_1+\delta$ to p_1 will clearly cause the expected number of bidders to rise if δ is sufficiently small. On the other hand, away from a switch point, a small fall in p will not affect n and thus will unambiguously lead to a reduction in expected number of bidders. Of course, what we are really interested in is the change in the expected number of firms when p itself falls by a discrete amount. It seems that the appropriate way to analyze this would be to examine the change in the expected number of bidders as p moves from one switch point to the next.

7. To simplify the discussion in the text, we have glossed over the fact that pn is not sufficient statistic for the multinomial distribution $P(n,i)$. If a fall in p is partially offset by an increase in n, then the tails of the multinomial distribution $P(n,i)$ will become fatter. As the marginal gain to search falls as the number of bidders increases, the spreading out of the distribution to the right would also tend to lower the marginal gain to search. One might at first think that the spreading out of the distribution to the left would work in the opposite direction. However, this is not necessarily the case since the marginal gain to an extra bidder is 0 when the number of bidders is 0.

References

Barron, John M., Dan A. Black, and Mark A. Loewenstein. "Job Matching and On-the-Job Training." *Journal of Labor Economics* 7 (1989):1–19.

Benhabib, Jess and Clive Bull. "Job Search: The Choice of Intensity." *Journal of Political Economy* 91 (October 1983): 747–764.

Black, Dan A. and Mark A. Loewenstein. "Bidding for Workers." Unpublished manuscript, University of Kentucky, 1995.

Bulow, Jeremy and John Roberts. "The Simple Economics of Optimal Auctions." *Journal of Political Economy* 97 (October 1989): 1060–1090.

Burdett, Kenneth and Kenneth L. Judd. "Equilibrium Price Dispersion." *Econometrica* 51 (July 1983): 955–965.

Davidson, Carl. *Recent Developments in the Theory of Involuntary Unemployment.* Kalamazoo, MI: W.E. Upjohn Institute, 1990.

Davidson, Carl, Lawrence Martin, and Steven Matusz. "Search, Unemployment, and the Production of Jobs." *Economic Journal* 97 (1987): 857–876.

Dagsvik, John, Boyan Jovanovic, and Andrea Shepard. "A Foundation for Three Popular Assumptions in Job Matching." *Journal of Labor Economics* 3 (October 1985): 403–420.

Diamond, Peter A. "A Model of Price Adjustment." *Journal of Economic Theory* 3 (1971): 156–168.

_____. "Mobility Costs, Frictional Unemployment, and Efficiency." *Journal of Political Economy* 89 (August 1981): 798–812.

_____. "Wage Determination and Efficiency in Search Equilibrium." *Review of Economic Studies* 49 (April 1982): 217–227.

Jovanovic, Boyan. "Job Matching and the Theory of Turnover." *Journal of Political Economy* 87 (October 1979): 972–990.

Lang, Kevin. "Persistent Wage Dispersion and Involuntary Unemployment." *Quarterly Journal of Economics* 106 (February 1991): 181–202.

McAfee, R. Preston and John McMillan. "Auctions and Bidding." *Journal of Economic Literature* 27 (June 1987): 699–738.

McCall, John J. "The Economics of Information and Optimal Stopping Rules." *Journal of Business* 38 (1965): 300–317.

Milgrom, Paul R. "Auctions and Bidding: A Primer." *Journal of Economic Perspectives* 3 (Summer 1989): 3–22.

Morgan, Peter and Richard Manning. "Optimal Search." *Econometrica* 53 (July 1985): 923–944.

Mortensen, Dale T. "The Matching Process as a Noncooperative Bargaining Game." In *The Economics of Information and Uncertainty*, edited by John J. McCall. Chicago: University of Chicago Press, 1982. Pp. 233–258. (a).

_____. "Property Rights and Efficiency in Mating, Racing, and Other Games." *American Economic Review* 72 (December 1982): 968–979 (b).

_____. "Job Search and Labor Market Analysis." In *Handbook of Labor Economics*, Volume II, edited by O. Ashenfelter and R. Layard. Amsterdam: Elsevier Science Publishers, 1986. Pp. 849–919.

Pissarides, Christopher A. "Search Intensity, Job Advertising, and Efficiency." *Journal of Labor Economics* 2 (January 1984): 128–143.

_____. "Taxes, Subsidies and Equilibrium Unemployment." *Review of Economic Studies* 52 (January 1985): 121–133.

Stigler, George J. "The Economics of Information." *Journal of Political Economy* 69 (June 1961): 213–225.

Appendix

Lemma 1: Let $E(\varepsilon_{[k],n})$ denote the expected value of the kth order statistic from a random sample of productivity draws at n different employers. Then $E(\varepsilon_{[n-1],n})$ is increasing in n.

Proof: As the expected value of the $(n-1)^{\text{th}}$ order statistic is given by

$$E\left(\varepsilon_{[n-1],n}\right)=\int_{\underline{\varepsilon}}^{\bar{\varepsilon}}\varepsilon n(n-1)F\left(\varepsilon\right)^{n-2}\left(1-F\left(\varepsilon\right)\right)d\varepsilon\,,$$

we have

$$E\left(\varepsilon_{n-1,n}\right)-E\left(\varepsilon_{n-2,n-1}\right)$$

$$=\ \int_{\underline{\varepsilon}}^{\bar{\varepsilon}}\varepsilon(n-1)(n-2)F\left(\varepsilon\right)^{n-2}\left(1-F\left(\varepsilon\right)\right)d\varepsilon-\int_{\underline{\varepsilon}}^{\bar{\varepsilon}}\varepsilon(n-2)(n-3)F\left(\varepsilon\right)^{n-3}\left(1-F\left(\varepsilon\right)\right)d\varepsilon$$

$$=\ (n-2)\int_{\underline{\varepsilon}}^{\bar{\varepsilon}}\varepsilon(1-F\left(\varepsilon\right))F\left(\varepsilon\right)^{n-3}\left\{(n-1)F\left(\varepsilon\right)-(n-3)\right\}d\varepsilon\,.$$

Letting $\hat{\varepsilon}=F^{-1}\left(\dfrac{n-1}{n-3}\right)$ and noting that $(n-1)F(\varepsilon)>n-3$ as $\varepsilon>(<)\ \hat{\varepsilon}$, we have

$$E(\varepsilon_{[n-1],n}) - E(\varepsilon_{[n-2],n-1}) = \int_{\underline{\varepsilon}}^{\hat{\varepsilon}} \varepsilon(n-2)(1-F(\varepsilon))F(\varepsilon)^{n-3}\{(n-1)F(\varepsilon)-(n-3)\}d\varepsilon$$

$$+ \int_{\hat{\varepsilon}}^{\bar{\varepsilon}} \varepsilon(n-2)(1-F(\varepsilon))F(\varepsilon)^{n-3}\{(n-1)F(\varepsilon)-(n-3)\}d\varepsilon$$

$$> \int_{\underline{\varepsilon}}^{\hat{\varepsilon}} \hat{\varepsilon}(n-2)(1-F(\varepsilon))F(\varepsilon)^{n-3}\{(n-1)F(\varepsilon)-(n-3)\}d\varepsilon$$

$$+ \int_{\hat{\varepsilon}}^{\bar{\varepsilon}} \hat{\varepsilon}(n-2)(1-F(\varepsilon))F(\varepsilon)^{n-3}\{(n-1)F(\varepsilon)-(n-3)\}d\varepsilon$$

$$= 0,$$

where the last line stems from the fact that an order statistic's density function must integrate to zero.

Lemma 2: Let $J(\varepsilon) \equiv \varepsilon - m(\varepsilon)$. Then the expected value of the $(n-1)^{th}$-order statistic is equal to the expected value of the function $J(\varepsilon)$ evaluated at the nth-order statistic, or

$$E\left(\varepsilon_{[n-1],n}\right) = n\int_{\underline{\varepsilon}}^{\bar{\varepsilon}} J(\varepsilon)[F(\varepsilon)]^{n-1} f(\varepsilon)d\varepsilon = E\left[J\left(\varepsilon_{[n],n}\right)\right].$$

Proof:
$$E\left(\varepsilon_{[n-1],n}\right) = \int_{\underline{\varepsilon}}^{\bar{\varepsilon}} \varepsilon n(n-1)[F(\varepsilon)]^{n-2}[1-F(\varepsilon)]f(\varepsilon)d\varepsilon$$

$$= \int_{\underline{\varepsilon}}^{\bar{\varepsilon}} \varepsilon n[1-F(\varepsilon)]\frac{d[F(\varepsilon)]^{n-1}}{d\varepsilon}d\varepsilon.$$

Integration by parts yields

$$E\left(\varepsilon_{[n-1],n}\right) = n\varepsilon[F(\varepsilon)]^{n-1}[1-F(\varepsilon)]\Big|_{\underline{\varepsilon}}^{\bar{\varepsilon}} + n\int_{\underline{\varepsilon}}^{\bar{\varepsilon}} \{\varepsilon f(\varepsilon)-[1-F(\varepsilon)]\}[F(\varepsilon)]^{n-1}d\varepsilon$$

$$= n\int_{\underline{\varepsilon}}^{\bar{\varepsilon}} [\varepsilon - m(\varepsilon)][F(\varepsilon)]^{n-1} f(\varepsilon)d\varepsilon = n\int_{\underline{\varepsilon}}^{\bar{\varepsilon}} J(\varepsilon)[F(\varepsilon)]^{n-1} f(\varepsilon)d\varepsilon = E\left[J\left(\varepsilon_{[n],n}\right)\right].$$

Proposition 3: When the worker makes a take-it-or-leave-it wage demand, the reservation wage w_r is too high for efficient matching.

Proof: Let $w_r(n)$ denote the worker's optimal reservation wage when he searches n employers and let $\varepsilon_r(n)$ denote the socially optimal reservation wage when the worker searches n employers. Differentiating equations (7) and (10) yields

$$(A1)\ \frac{\partial V(n)}{\partial w_r}\Big|_{w_r=\varepsilon_r(n)} = \left\{ \beta \frac{\int_{\varepsilon_r}^{\varepsilon} J(\varepsilon)nF(\varepsilon)^{n-1}f(\varepsilon)d\varepsilon - c(n)}{1-\beta F(\varepsilon)^n} - J(\varepsilon_r(n)) \right\} nF(\varepsilon_r)^{n-1}f(\varepsilon_r)$$

$$(A2)\ \frac{\partial v(n)}{\partial \varepsilon_r}\Big|_{\varepsilon_r=\varepsilon_r(n)} = \left\{ \beta \frac{\int_{\varepsilon_r}^{\varepsilon} \varepsilon nF(\varepsilon)^{n-1}f(\varepsilon)d\varepsilon - c(n)}{1-\beta F(\varepsilon_r(n))^n} - \varepsilon_r(n) \right\} nF(\varepsilon_r(n))^{n-1}f(\varepsilon_r(n)) = 0.$$

Subtracting (A2) from (A1) yields

$$\frac{\partial V(n)}{\partial w_r}\Big|_{w_r=\varepsilon_r(n)} = \left\{ \beta \frac{-\int_{\varepsilon_r}^{\varepsilon} m(\varepsilon)nF(\varepsilon_r)^{n-1}f(\varepsilon)d\varepsilon}{1-\beta F(\varepsilon_r)^n} + m(\varepsilon_r) \right\} nF(\varepsilon_r(n))^{n-1}f(\varepsilon_r(n))$$

$$> \left\{ \beta \frac{-m(\varepsilon_r)\int_{\varepsilon_r}^{\varepsilon} nF(\varepsilon_r)^{n-1}f(\varepsilon)d\varepsilon}{1-\beta F(\varepsilon_r)^n} + m(\varepsilon_r) \right\} nF(\varepsilon_r(n))^{n-1}f(\varepsilon_r(n))$$

$$= m(\varepsilon_r)\left(-\frac{\beta[1-F(\varepsilon_r)^n]}{1-\beta F(\varepsilon_r)^n} + 1 \right) nF(\varepsilon_r(n))^{n-1}f(\varepsilon_r(n))$$

$$> 0,$$

where the first inequality arises because $m(\cdot)$ is monotonically decreasing. Because $\partial V/\partial w_r$ is positive when evaluated at $w_r = \varepsilon_r(n)$, it must be the case that $w_r(n) > \varepsilon_r(n)$.

Since the worker chooses n to maximize $V(n) = \left(\dfrac{1}{\beta}\right) J(w_r(n))$ and since $J(\cdot)$ is increasing, it must be the case that $w_r^* > \varepsilon_r^*$.

4

Search Externalities in an Imperfectly Competitive Economy

Andrew John

INSEAD and AJK Executive Consulting

Abstract

The paper brings together two strands of the New Keynesian literature: search externalities and imperfect competition. In the model of the paper, agents engage in costly search in order to form firms, which then compete in an imperfectly competitive environment. Search thus plays the role of an endogenous entry cost, and the degree of imperfect competition is likewise endogenous. The main result of the paper is that, since the externalities from search include its effects on the degree of market power, increased search by one agent imposes net negative externalities on potential partners. The increased probability of being matched is outweighed by lower expected profits. The endogeneity of the degree of market power also magnifies the multiplier effects associated with demand shocks in the product market.

1. Introduction

It is well known that if agents cannot carry out transactions costlessly, but must instead engage in costly search, externalities emerge. Such externalities can result in inefficiencies and coordination failures (multiple, Pareto-ranked equilibria). Search externalities in partial and general equilibrium have been analyzed by Diamond (1982), Mortensen (1986), Davidson, Martin and Matusz (1987, 1988, 1994), Howitt (1990), Howitt and MacAfee (1988), and Hosios (1990), among others.

Search models focus on how the matching of agents creates surplus in a setting where such matching carries a cost. A successful match brings a surplus that in general will be divided between the matched parties. Externalities arise in search models because increased effort by one side increases the likelihood that potential partners will gain some surplus. For example, a job-seeker who puts extra effort into finding a job bestows a positive externality on all the firms who might hire her. Another, possibly offsetting, externality arises if different agents are competing for the same match. The worker who puts forth extra effort is more likely to be matched with a given job—which means that other workers are less likely to be matched with that job.

The focus of this paper is on a different externality that arises in a particular class of search models, where search plays the role of an entry cost in an imperfectly competitive economy. In the model presented here, agents engage in costly search in order to form firms; these firms then compete in imperfectly competitive markets. When more agents are successfully matched, there is greater competition, and so the gain from being matched falls. Under fairly general conditions, this radically alters search externalities: increased search effort imposes negative externalities on potential partners. The increased probability of a match is more than offset by the decreased expected value of matches.

The paper brings together two strands of the New Keynesian literature. Some authors in this literature have utilized search models, while others have developed models with imperfect competition.[1] Both approaches have appeal. There is direct and indirect evidence that there is significant market power in some sectors of the U.S. economy.[2] Imperfect competition thus seems a natural microeconomic distortion to incorporate in macroeconomic models. For analysis of labor markets, meanwhile, explicit consideration of search activity by workers and firms also has appeal.[3]

While researchers have actively pursued both search models and imperfect competition models in isolation, there has been very little work that incorporates both distortions. Drazen (1986) is an exception. He focuses upon spillovers from the labor market to aggregate demand, and vice versa. In his model, increased search activity by workers directly encourages greater search intensity on the part of firms (and conversely). In addition, increased search intensity increases employment, leading to increased aggregate demand, and hence increased demand for labor by firms. This indirect linkage also results in greater search intensity on the part of firms. As in

Diamond (1982), Drazen finds that multiple Pareto-ranked equilibria may result, with involuntary unemployment present at low-level equilibria.

The model of this paper also emphasizes linkages between search activity and product market activity. One feature of this paper is that the distortion in the product market is endogenous. The analysis therefore has something in common with Chatterjee and Cooper (1989) and Chatterjee, Cooper and Ravikumar (1993), who also endogenize entry in imperfectly competitive models. As is the case in this paper, that research shows that entry and exit can lead to increased multiplier effects and countercyclical markups. Chatterjee-Cooper and Chatterjee-Cooper- Ravikumar treat entry costs as exogenous, however, and focus on multiplicity of equilibria and the possibility of sunspot equilibria. In the current model, the cost of entry and the benefit from entry are both endogenous. The endogenous distortion in the product market affects the benefit of entry and so feeds back into the entry (that is, search) decision. Search decisions by all agents in turn determine the effective cost of entry. These feedbacks are the focus of the current work.

Section 2 sets out the model and Section 3 characterizes equilibrium. Section 4 contains discussion of the main results, and Section 5 concludes.

2. The Model

2.1 Overview

Before presenting the detailed specification of the structure, technology and preferences of the model, this section briefly sets out the workings of the model and informally describes equilibrium.

The model is populated by a continuum of identical agents. There is a total of N agents distributed evenly across a unit continuum of sectors, so there are N agents in each sector. Each sector has associated with it a single distinct good. All produced goods enter symmetrically into utility. There is also a nonproduced numeraire good, endowed in equal quantities to all agents and consumed by all agents.

Agents play a three stage game. In the first stage of the game, agents in each sector expend effort in an attempt to form production teams. Production teams are formed through a random matching process, where the probability of forming a team depends upon the effort of all agents in the sector. A team consists of two agents, and is called a firm. Effort is a source of disutility. In this first stage, there is no connection between the different sectors of the economy.

In the second stage of the game, the two agents who make up the firm behave cooperatively, and expend effort in order to produce output. Firms in each sector decide upon their level of production. Firms behave as Cournot-Nash competitors, taking as given the output produced by other firms in their sector and the demand curve faced by the sector. In the final stage of the game, markets clear and agents consume.

The equilibrium concept adopted is that of symmetric Nash equilibrium. A symmetric equilibrium is described by a symmetric choice of effort (e) by all agents in all sectors. As a consequence of this effort choice and the matching process, firms are formed in each sector. Symmetric Nash equilibrium within each sector determines the aggregate level of output in the sector.

Since there is randomness in the matching process, the number of firms in a sector (F) is a random variable. The law of large numbers implies that, for given effort choices, the distribution of firms is fixed, however. The aggregate output produced in the second-stage production game will vary across sectors, because the number of firms varies. Given preferences and given the vector of outputs produced in the second stage, market clearing in the third stage gives rise to a fixed distribution of equilibrium prices.

Firms in the second stage of the game take as given the output of other firms in their sector. They also take as given the demand curve facing their sector, which depends in general on the output chosen by all other firms in all other sectors. All firms correctly perceive the demand curve that they face. All firms maximize profits, which is equivalent to maximizing utility. The value of profits in terms of utility depends upon the marginal utility of income, which depends in turn on the prices agents face as consumers in the third stage of the game.

The monopoly profits that firms can earn provide the incentive for agents to expend effort in the first stage of the game. The gain from being matched is given by these monopoly profits, and depends in general upon the number of firms in the sector and on the prices in all other sectors. Agents choose their search effort to equate the marginal expected gain from search to the marginal disutility of searching. Agents take as given the search efforts of all other agents in all sectors; hence they take as given the distribution of firms and prices. The effort chosen by all agents thus induces distributions on prices, quantities, and the number of firms; in equilibrium, agents correctly perceive these distributions when choosing their level of effort.

2.2 Preferences and Technology

There is a unit continuum of sectors with N agents per sector. Each sector has associated with it a distinct good, indexed by $s \in [0, 1]$. There is also a non-produced good, which is taken to be the numeraire. Agents have utility defined over all produced goods, the non-produced good, and effort:[4]

$$(1) \qquad U(c_s, m, e, x) = \left| \int (c_s)^\rho ds \right|^{\alpha/\rho} m^{(1-\alpha)} - k(e + x); \ \rho \in (-\infty, 1);$$

where c_s denotes consumption of good s, m is consumption of a non-produced good, and $(e + x)$ is total effort expended in both searching for a production partner (e) and producing output (x). One interpretation of effort is that it represents time input. Assume that $e \in [0, \bar{e}]$ and $x \in [0, \bar{x}]$. Each agent is endowed with $\bar{m}$ units of the non-produced good, so the total endowment of the numeraire good equals $N\bar{m}$.

The production technology utilized in the second stage characterizes the output of the produced good as a function of the input of the efforts expended by the two agents who make up a firm. This technology is of the following CES form:

(2)
$$q = 2^{(\xi-1)/\xi}\left((x_i)^\xi + (x_j)^\xi\right)^{1/\xi}.$$

When agents choose the same level of output ($x_i = x_j$), the technology implies that total output $q = 2x_i = 2x_j$, and that the marginal product of either agent equals one. It is assumed that the profits earned by a firm are divided evenly between the two agents.

The matching technology requires more elaboration. Recall that each sector contains N agents. To characterize the matching technology in a given sector, first define $\bar{F}$ to be the largest integer $\leq N/2$ and $\underline{F}$ to be the smallest integer $>1-\rho$. Here, $\bar{F}$ is the maximum feasible number of firms, and $\underline{F}$ is the minimum number of firms; the restriction imposed on $\underline{F}$ ensures that all firms face elastic demand and so will produce positive output. Note that, by assumption, the matching process guarantees that each sector contains a positive number of firms. It is assumed that $\bar{F} > \underline{F}$; a necessary condition for this is obviously $\rho > 1-N/2$. Define $\hat{F}$ to be the set of integers $\{\underline{F}, \underline{F}+1, ...\bar{F}\}$, The matching function is assumed always to deliver a number of firms $F \in \hat{F}$.

Now define N^F to be the set of all subsets of N that contain exactly $2F$ members, where $F \in \hat{F}$, and define $\hat{N} = \cup N^F$. Thus N^F represents all possible combinations of agents who could be matched to give rise to F firms, and $\hat{N}$ is all possible combinations of agents who could be matched to give rise to some number of firms between $\underline{F}$ and $\bar{F}$. Let $M(N_k)$ be the event that the agents in the set $N_k \subseteq \hat{N}$ are successfully matched, and let π_k be the probability that the event $M(N_k)$ occurs. These probabilities depend in general upon the efforts expended by all agents in the sector. The matching process is thus described in general by a collection of functions:

(3)
$$\pi_k = \pi_k(e_j), \ j = 1, ... \ N$$

one for each event $M(N_k)$, where e_j is the vector of efforts chosen by all agents. It is assumed that these functions are continuous and differentiable. Because the matching process always generates some $F \in \hat{F}$, the probabilities in (3) must satisfy

$$\sum_{N_k} \pi_k = 1.$$

The probability that the matching process results in the formation of exactly F firms is given by

(4)
$$\sum_{N_k \in N^F} \pi_k(e_j) \equiv \psi^F(e_j).$$

Obviously,

$$\sum_{F \in \hat{F}} \psi^F(e_j) \equiv 1 .$$

Thus $\psi^F(e_j)$ describes the distribution of firms in the sector.

Now define M_i^F to be the probability that agent $i \in N$ is matched, conditional on there being exactly F firms:

(5)
$$M_i^F(e_i, e_j) \equiv \frac{\sum_{N_k \in N_i^F} \pi_k(e_i, e_j)}{\sum_{N_k \in N^F} \pi_k(e_i, e_j)} , j \neq i$$

where $N_i^F \subset N^F$ is the set of all subsets of N^F that include agent i as a member. Note that

(6)
$$\sum_i M_i^F \equiv 2F,$$

which implies

(7)
$$\sum_i \partial\left(M_i^F(e_i, e_j)\right)/\partial e_j = 0, \forall j.$$

It is convenient to place some restrictions directly on $\psi^F(e_j)$ and $M_i^F(e_j)$:

(A1) $\psi^F(e_j)$ is symmetric in all its arguments;

(A2) $M_i^F(e_j)$ is symmetric in all arguments $e_j, j \neq i$;

(A3) $\dfrac{\partial}{\partial e_j}\left[\sum_{n=E}^{r} \psi^F(e_j)\right] \leq 0, \forall r \in \hat{F}, \forall j.$

Assumptions (A1) and (A2) are natural symmetry assumptions to impose.[5,6] Assumption (A3) is first-order stochastic dominance: increases in the effort of any agent result in a new distribution of firms with the property that its cumulative distribution function lies everywhere below the cumulative distribution of the original function.

Individual i's probability of being matched is given by

(8) $$\pi_i(e_i, e_j) = \sum_{F \in \hat{F}} \psi^F(e_i, e_j) M_i^F.$$

That is, it is equal to the probability that there are exactly F firms, multiplied by agent i's conditional probability of being matched given that there are F firms, summed over all admissible F.

2.3 Equilibrium

A symmetric subgame perfect Nash equilibrium for this model is a symmetric level of effort chosen by all agents in all sectors, and associated distributions of firms, prices, and quantities $\{e, \tilde{F}, \tilde{P}, \tilde{Q}\}$ such that the following hold.

(i) Taking as given the efforts of others in the sector and the outcome of the subgames associated with the realization of a given number of firms in the sector, each agent chooses effort to maximize expected utility;

(ii) Taking as given the output chosen by all other firms in all sectors, and taking as given the demand curve faced by the sector, each firm chooses output to maximize utility, and all firms within a sector choose the same level of output;

(iii) Markets clear.

3. Equilibrium

The model is solved backwards.

3.1 Third Stage

In the third stage, there is a given quantity of output in each sector (Q_s). Agents' demands for the goods produced in each sector are derived from utility maximization. Consider the problem of an agent with income I. She solves

$$\max_{\{c_s, m\}} \left[\int (c_s)^\rho ds \right]^{\alpha/\rho} m^{(1-\alpha)} + \lambda \left[I - \int P_s c_s ds - m \right],$$

where λ is a Lagrange multiplier and P_s is the price of good s. Note that e and q are sunk costs at this point. Standard analysis yields

(9) $$m = (1 - \alpha)I$$

(10)
$$c_s = \left(\frac{P_s}{P}\right)^{\frac{1}{(\rho-1)}} \alpha\left(\frac{I}{P}\right)$$

where P is a price index given by

(11)
$$P = \left[\int (P_r)^{\rho/(\rho-1)} dr\right]^{\frac{\rho-1}{\rho}}$$

Hence the total demand for good s is

(12)
$$Q_s^d = \left(\frac{P_s}{P}\right)^{\frac{1}{(\rho-1)}} \alpha\left(\frac{Y}{P}\right)$$

where Y is the total income in the economy:

(13)
$$Y = N\overline{m} + \int P_r Q_r dr.$$

Market clearing for good s implies that

(14)
$$P_s Q_s = P_s Q_s^d = \left(\frac{P_s}{P}\right)^{\frac{\rho}{(\rho-1)}} \alpha Y.$$

Summing the market clearing conditions (14) over all goods yields

(15)
$$\int P_r Q_r dr = \alpha Y.$$

From (13) and (15), it follows that

(16)
$$Y = N\overline{m}/(1-\alpha).$$

Hence the equilibrium demand curve for good s is

(17)
$$Q_s^d = \left(\frac{\alpha}{1-\alpha}\right)\left(\frac{P_s}{P}\right)^{\frac{1}{(\rho-1)}}\left(\frac{N\overline{m}}{P}\right).$$

Firms in sector s take this demand curve as given in the second stage of the game.

Equation (17) implies that

(18)
$$\left(P_s\right)^{\frac{\rho}{(\rho-1)}} = \left(Q_s\right)^\rho (P)^{\frac{\rho^2}{(\rho-1)}} \left(\alpha Y\right)^{-\rho}$$

(19)
$$P = \left(\int (Q_s)^\rho\right)^{-1/\rho} \alpha Y.$$

Equation (19) gives the solution for the price index for an arbitrary vector of quantities. As expected, higher quantities imply a lower value of the price index.

The indirect utility of an agent with income I can be written as

$$v(P)I,$$

where

(20)
$$v(P) = \alpha^\alpha (1-\alpha)^{1-\alpha} P^{-\alpha}.$$

The multiplicative form of indirect utility is a consequence of the homotheticity of preferences. Higher prices reduce the utility from a given level of income: $v'(P)$.

3.2 Second Stage

Now consider the decision problem facing a firm in the second stage of the game. The assumption that there is a continuum of sectors means that individual agents rationally perceive that their actions have no effect on the equilibrium distribution of prices. Thus agents take P as given. Because all agents possess the same utility functions, behave cooperatively, and divide profits evenly, the agents who make up the firm choose x_i, x_j to maximize[7]

$$v(P)\left(P_s(Q_s, P) q(x_i, x_j)\right) - k(x_i + x_j),$$

where $P_s(Q_s, P)$ is obtained by inverting the demand curve (17). The firm takes as given the output of other firms in the sector. The agents choose identical levels of effort, which implies from the production technology (4) that the marginal product of effort is unity. Hence, the two first-order conditions from this problem are identical:

(21)
$$P_s'()q + P_s() - \frac{k}{v(P)} = 0.$$

Each agent receives half of the profit, so the profit of an individual agent is given by

(22)
$$\pi(x) = v(P)\left(P_s(Q_s, P)x\right) - kx,$$

since $q = 2x$.

In symmetric equilibrium within the sector, $q = Q_s / F$, so

(23)
$$P_s = \left(\frac{F_s}{F_s - (1-\rho)}\right)\left(\frac{k}{v(P)}\right) = \mu_s\left(\frac{k}{v(P)}\right).$$

This is the standard solution for Cournot-Nash competition: price is set as a markup, μ_s, over marginal cost, where the markup depends upon the elasticity of the residual demand curve. The markup in sector s is a decreasing function of F_s. It is also decreasing in ρ: higher values of ρ imply that goods are closer substitutes, which means that firms face relatively elastic demand curves and so have less ability to exploit their market power.

For each sector, there is an equation like (23) defining the price in that sector as a function of the number of firms in the sector and the general price level, P. From (23), and from the definition of the price index (11), it is therefore possible to solve for the price level in terms of the distribution of firms in the different sectors. From (11) and (18),

$$P = \left[\int (\mu_s)^{\rho/(\rho-1)} ds\right]^{\frac{\rho-1}{\rho}}\left(\frac{k}{v(P)}\right)$$

(24)
$$P^{1-\alpha} = \left[\int (\mu_s)^{\rho/\rho-1} ds\right]^{\frac{\rho-1}{\rho}}\left(\frac{k}{\alpha^\alpha(1-\alpha)^{1-\alpha}}\right)$$

$$P = \left(\frac{\mu k}{\alpha^\alpha(1-\alpha)^{1-\alpha}}\right)^{\frac{1}{1-\alpha}}$$

where

(25)
$$\mu = \left[\int (\mu_s)^{\rho/(\rho-1)} ds\right]^{\frac{\rho-1}{\rho}}.$$

(Alternatively, equation (24) can be derived by taking the first-order condition (23), substituting into the demand curve (17) to obtain the equilibrium quantities produced in each sector, and then using (19).)

From (23) and (24), the equilibrium solution for P_s is given by

$$P_s = \left(\frac{\mu_s k}{\alpha^\alpha (1-\alpha)^{1-\alpha}} \right) P^\alpha$$

$$(26) \qquad = \left(\frac{\mu_s k}{\alpha^\alpha (1-\alpha)^{1-\alpha}} \right) \left(\frac{\mu k}{\alpha^\alpha (1-\alpha)^{1-\alpha}} \right)^{\frac{\alpha}{1-\alpha}}$$

$$= \left(\frac{k}{\alpha^\alpha (1-\alpha)^{1-\alpha}} \right)^{\frac{1}{1-\alpha}} (\mu)^{\frac{\alpha}{1-\alpha}} \mu_s$$

From (24) and (20) the indirect utility from income I is given by:

$$v(P)I = vI;$$

$$v = \alpha^\alpha (1-\alpha)^{1-\alpha} \left(\frac{\mu k}{\alpha^\alpha (1-\alpha)^{1-\alpha}} \right)^{\frac{-\alpha}{1-\alpha}} = \left(\alpha^\alpha (1-\alpha)^{1-\alpha} \right)^{\frac{1-2\alpha}{1-\alpha}} (\mu k)^{\frac{-\alpha}{1-\alpha}}.$$

3.3 First Stage

Finally, consider the choice problem of an agent who has to decide how much effort to expend in searching for a partner. The gain from being matched naturally depends upon how many other firms were formed in the same sector: the smaller the number of firms, the greater the monopoly power. Using (21) and (23), the gain from being matched in sector s, given that there are F_s firms in the sector, is simply the profit that can be earned:

$$\pi(F_s) = vP_s x - kx$$

$$= (\mu_s - 1)kx$$

$$(27)$$

$$= (\mu_s - 1)k \left(\frac{Q_s}{2F_s} \right).$$

Recall from (17) that

$$Q_s = \left(\frac{\alpha}{1-\alpha} \right) \left(\frac{P_s}{P} \right)^{\frac{1}{(\rho-1)}} \left(\frac{N\overline{m}}{P} \right).$$

Substituting into (27), and using (20) and (23)

$$\pi(F_s) = (\mu_s - 1) k \left(\frac{\alpha}{2(1-\alpha)} \right) \left(\frac{P_s}{P} \right)^{\frac{1}{(\rho-1)}} \left(\frac{N\bar{m}}{P} \right) F_s^{-1}$$

(28)
$$= (\mu_s - 1) k \left(\frac{\alpha}{2(1-\alpha)} \right) \left(\frac{\mu_s k}{v(P)} \right)^{\frac{1}{(\rho-1)}} \left(\frac{N\bar{m}}{P} \right) F_s^{-1} (P)^{\frac{-1}{(\rho-1)}}$$

$$= \left(\frac{\alpha(1-\rho)}{2(1-\alpha)} \right) \left(\alpha^{\alpha}(1-\alpha)^{1-\alpha} \right)^{\frac{-1}{(\rho-1)}} (\mu_s k)^{\frac{\rho}{(\rho-1)}} (F_s)^{-2} (P)^{\frac{\alpha-\rho}{(\rho-1)}} N\bar{m}.$$

Substituting out for P yields

(29)
$$\pi(F_s) = \alpha^{1/(1-\alpha)} \left(\frac{1-\rho}{2} \right) (\mu_s k)^{\frac{\rho}{(\rho-1)}} (F_s)^{-2} N\bar{m}.$$

Equation (29) gives the gain to being matched for an agent in sector s, given that there are F_s firms in the sector. Agent i's expected gain from being matched is

(30)
$$E\pi_i = \sum_F \psi^F M_i^F \pi(F).$$

Taking others' efforts as given, agent i chooses e_i in the first stage to maximize $E\pi - ke_i$:

$$\sum_F \psi^F(e_i, e_j) M_i^F(e_i, e_j) \pi(F) - ke_i, \ j \neq i.$$

The first-order condition from this problem is

(31)
$$\sum_F \left(\psi^F \left[\frac{\partial M^F(e_i, e_j)}{\partial e_i} \right] + M_i^F() \left[\frac{\partial \psi^F(e_i, e_j)}{\partial e_i} \right] \right) \pi(F) = k.$$

In symmetric equilibrium, $e_i = e_j = e$, all j. In this case the condition is:

(32)
$$\sum_F \left(\psi^F(e, e) \left[\frac{\partial M^F(e, e)}{\partial e_i} \right] + \left(\frac{2F}{N} \right) \left[\frac{\partial \psi^F(e, e)}{\partial e_i} \right] \right) \pi(F) = k.$$

Now consider the following mapping from $[0, \bar{e}]$ to $[0, \bar{e}]$. Given a value of e, $\psi(e)$ defines a distribution of firms, $\tilde{F}$. Equation (26) yields a distribution of prices, $\tilde{P}$ and (24) yields a value for P. From equation (28), P and $\tilde{F}$ together yield a distribution of gains from matching, $\tilde{\pi}$. Finally, given $\tilde{\pi}$, equation (32) gives a solution (or solutions) for e.[8] A symmetric Nash equilibrium for the model is a fixed point of this mapping.

4. Discussion

The focus throughout is on symmetric equilibria.

4.1 Externalities

The main results of this paper concern the externalities from the matching technology. The literature on search emphasizes that matching technologies are a source of externalities: the efforts of a given agent impose externalities on the other agents in the sector. Typically, it is assumed that increased search effort bestows an external benefit on potential partners. (It is sometimes also assumed that there are two types of agent, and that increased search imposes negative externalities on agents of the same type—that is, there are positive external effects on those on the other side of the matching market, and negative external effects on those on the same side of the market. The main results of this paper still go through in such a setting.)

Increased effort of agent j, by first-order stochastic dominance, increases the expected number of firms in the sector. Other things equal, this increases the likelihood that agent $i \neq j$ would be matched. But increased effort by agent j also affects the probability, conditional on a given number of firms, that agent j will be matched. For a given number of firms, however, if it is more likely that agent j will be matched, then it is less likely that agent $i \neq j$ will be matched. The net effect of agent j's action on agent i's probability of matching is therefore ambiguous in general:

$$\frac{\partial \pi_i(e_i, e_j)}{\partial e_j} = \sum_F \psi^F(e_i, e_j) \left[\frac{\partial M_i^F(e_i, e_j)}{\partial e_j} \right] + \sum_F M_i^F(e_i, e_j) \left[\frac{\partial \psi^F(e_i, e_j)}{\partial e_j} \right] \gtrless 0.$$

In the current setting, there is an additional externality that does not typically arise in search models. Suppose that agent j increases her search effort. Other agents in the sector may benefit from being more likely to be matched. But the increase in agent j's effort also affects the distribution of firms in the sector—specifically, the expected number of firms increases. This means that, if an agent's chance of being matched increases, she is also likely to be in a more competitive sector, and so should expect to make lower monopoly profits. As the following analysis shows, the nature of the search externalities is radically altered as a consequence.

Lemma 1: $F\pi(F)$ is decreasing in F.

Proof: Recall that

$$\pi(F_s) = \left(\frac{\alpha}{1-\alpha}\right)\left(\alpha^{\alpha}(1-\alpha)^{1-\alpha}\right)^{\frac{-1}{(\rho-1)}}(\mu_s k)^{\frac{\rho}{(\rho-1)}}(F_s)^{-2}(P)^{\frac{\alpha-\rho}{(\rho-1)}}N\overline{m}$$

(33)

$$F_s\pi(F_s) = \left(\frac{\alpha}{1-\alpha}\right)\left(\alpha^{\alpha}(1-\alpha)^{1-\alpha}\right)^{\frac{-1}{(\rho-1)}}(\mu_s k)^{\frac{\rho}{(\rho-1)}}(F_s)^{-1}(P)^{\frac{\alpha-\rho}{(\rho-1)}}N\overline{m},$$

where $\mu_s = \left(\dfrac{F_s}{F_s-(1-\rho)}\right)$.

Although this expression is only economically relevant for integer values of F_s, it is a well-defined continuous and differentiable function.

Differentiation yields

(34)
$$\frac{\partial}{\partial F_s}\left(F_s\pi(F_s)\right) = -\left(\frac{F_s-1}{F_s}\right)\pi(F_s)\mu_s .$$

For $F_s > 1$, this expression is negative.

Lemma 1 is intuitive. It states that as the number of agents in a sector increases, total profits in the sector fall (and the profits of an individual firm fall a fortiori).[9]

Proposition 1: In symmetric equilibrium, an increase in search effort by one agent imposes negative externalities on other agents in the same sector.

Proof: Recall that

$$E\pi_i = \sum_F \psi^F(e_i, e_j) M_i^F(e_i, e_j) \pi(F) .$$

Suppose that agent $j, j \neq i$, increases her search effort. The effect on agent i is given by

(35)
$$\frac{\partial E\pi_i}{\partial e_j} = \sum_F \pi(F)\left[\psi^F(e_i, e_j)\left(\frac{\partial M_i^F(e_i, e_j)}{\partial e_j}\right) + M_i^F(e_i, e_j)\left(\frac{\partial \psi^F(e_i, e_j)}{\partial e_j}\right)\right].$$

Summing over all i yields

$$\sum_i \frac{\partial E\,\pi_i}{\partial e_j} = \sum_i \sum_F \pi(F) \left[\psi^F(e_i, e_j) \left(\frac{\partial M_i^F(e_i, e_j)}{\partial e_j} \right) + M_i^F(e_i, e_j) \left(\frac{\partial \psi^F(e_i, e_j)}{\partial e_j} \right) \right]$$

$$= \sum_F \pi(F) \left[\sum_i \psi^F(e_i, e_j) \left(\frac{\partial M_i^F(e_i, e_j)}{\partial e_j} \right) + \sum_i M_i^F(e_i, e_j) \left(\frac{\partial \psi^F(e_i, e_j)}{\partial e_j} \right) \right]$$

$$= \sum_F \pi(F) \left[\sum_i M_i^F(e_i, e_j) \left(\frac{\partial \psi^F(e_i, e_j)}{\partial e_j} \right) \right]$$

$$= 2 \sum_F F \pi(F) \left(\frac{\partial \psi^F(e_i, e_j)}{\partial e_j} \right)$$

since

$$\sum_i \partial \left(M_i^F(e_j) \right) / \partial e_j = 0$$

and

$$\sum_i M_i^F(e_i, e_j) = \sum_i 2F/N = 2F.$$

By Lemma 1, $F\pi(F)$ is decreasing in F. By (A3), it follows that

$$\sum_i \frac{\partial E\,\pi_i}{\partial e_j} < 0.$$

Using the first-order condition, the aggregate external effect is therefore

$$\sum_i \frac{\partial E\,\pi_i}{\partial e_j} - \frac{\partial e\,\pi_j}{\partial e_j} = \sum_i \frac{\partial E\,\pi_i}{\partial e_j} - k < 0,$$

By symmetry, an increase in agent j's effort imposes a negative externality on other agents in the sector.

Proposition 1 reveals that the within-sector externalities are unambiguously negative in symmetric equilibrium, even though increases in effort may increase others' probability of matching. The reason is simple. Any change in effort that increases a typical agent's likelihood of being matched must also increase the expected number of firms. Greater competition lowers expected profits from being matched, and this effect outweighs the increased probability of being matched.[10]

The result does depend on the assumption that the matching function always generates some positive number of firms. In terms of Lemma 1, total profits in a sector are zero if a sector contains no firms, and are positive if the sector contains one firm. So total profits *increase* as the number of firms goes from zero to one, and decrease thereafter. So, if increased effort increases the probability that there will be a non-zero number of firms, the result in Proposition 1 would not necessarily go through. (Note that for the CES preferences specified here, the model is not well defined when $\rho < 0$ unless there is a strictly positive number of firms in all sectors.)

The negative within-sector externalities are replaced by positive across-sector externalities.

Proposition 2: In symmetric equilibrium, an increase in search effort by agents in other sectors benefits agents in sector s if $\alpha > \rho$.

Proof: Suppose that all agents in some positive measure of sectors increase their search effort. From (A3), this increase in effort will increase the expected number of firms in those sectors. The new distribution of firms will lie to the right of the old distribution. From (23), markups—and hence prices—will fall on average in those sectors. Hence the general price level will fall. Equation (28) reveals that, if $\alpha > \rho$, the fall in P will increase the gain from matching for an agent in sector s, for all F_s. Hence the expected gain from matching rises. Finally, the reduction in the price level increases the utility from the endowment of the non-produced good.

Note that agents who are unmatched unambiguously benefit ex post from increased search effort elsewhere. Note also that, even if $\alpha < \rho$, agents benefit from the fact that their endowment of numeraire is more valuable. Hence, even if $\alpha < \rho$, there may be positive externalities across sectors.

Proposition 3: The total of the within-sector and cross sector externalities can be either positive or negative.

Proof: The proof is by example. Suppose $\alpha = \rho = \frac{1}{2}$ and $\overline{m} = 64$. Suppose also that $F \in \{1, 2\}$. Let $\psi = \text{prob } (F = 2)$ and $1 - \psi = \text{prob } (F = 1)$. It is easily shown that

$$\mu_1 = 2, \mu_2 = 4/3, \mu = 4/(2 + \psi), P_1 = 32k^2/(2 + \psi), P_2 = 64k^2/(2 + \psi), P = 64k^2/(2 + \psi)^2,$$

$$v = (2 + \psi)/16k, Q_1 = 4N/k^2, Q_2 = 9N/k^2, \pi(1) = 2N/k \text{ and } \pi(2) = 3N/4k.$$

To calculate the external effect, suppose that all agents in all sectors increase their search effort. First note that

$$E\pi_i = (1 - \psi) M_i^1 (2N/k) + \psi M_i^2 (3N/4k).$$

The aggregate within-sector externality is equal to

$$N\left(\sum_i \frac{\partial E\pi_i}{\partial e_i} - k\right) = N\left(\left((4/N)(3N/4k) - (2/N)(2N/k)\right)\psi' - k\right),$$

where $\psi' = N\partial\psi(\ )/\partial e_j$; that is, ψ' gives the effect on ψ of a simultaneous increase in effort by all agents. Thus the aggregate within-sector effect is

$$-N\psi'/k - Nk < 0.$$

Calculation of the aggregate cross-sector effect is simplified by the assumption that $\alpha = \rho$, since this means that increased effort in one sector has no effect on the value of profits in other sectors (see equation (28)). The cross sector effect is given by

$$N\left(64\,(\partial v/\partial\psi)\,\psi'\right) = 4N\psi'/k.$$

The total within- and cross-sector effect is therefore

$$3N\psi'/k - Nk \gtrless 0.$$

Agents may expend too much or too little search effort, from a social perspective.[11] Note also that the effect of increased search on others' probability of matching can also be positive or negative, and that the sign of these effects can be different from the sign of the overall externality.[12]

4.2 Complementarities

There are four strategic interactions in the model: within sectors in the second stage, across sectors on the second stage, within sectors in the first stage, and across sectors in the first stage. In general, all four can exhibit either strategic complementarity of strategic substitutability. If there are sufficiently strong strategic complementarities, multiple equilibria are possible.[13]

Proposition 4: There is strategic complementarity within a sector when the number of firms equals $\underline{F}$. There is strategic substitutability within a sector when the number of firms exceeds $\underline{F}$.

Proof: Recall from (21) that the first-order condition for an individual firm is

$$P'_s(\overline{Q} + q) q + P_s(\overline{Q} + q) - \frac{k}{v(P)} = 0 ,$$

where $\overline{Q}$ is the output of other firms in the sector. It follows that

(36)
$$\frac{\partial q}{\partial Q} = \frac{P''(\ ) q + P'(\ )}{P''(\ ) q + 2P'(\ )} .$$

The denominator is negative by the second order condition.[14] The numerator equals $(P'/F)(F+\rho-2)$ in symmetric equilibrium. By assumption, $\underline{F}$ is the smallest integer greater than $1-\rho$. It follows that $\partial q/\partial Q > 0$ when $F = \underline{F}$, and $\partial q/\partial Q < 0$ otherwise.

There is strategic complementarity within a sector in the second stage only with the minimum permissible number of firms. Of course, it need not be the case that the matching function delivers $\underline{F}$ firms with positive probability. Note that even when $F = \underline{F}$, the slope of the reaction function is less than one, so there is insufficient complementarity to generate multiple equilibria.

Proposition 5: If $\alpha > \rho$, there is strategic complementarity across sectors in the second stage. If $\alpha < \rho$, there is strategic substitutability across sectors in the second stage.

Proof: Fix the distribution of firms, and suppose that all the firms in some positive measure of sectors increase their output. From (19), this results in a decrease in the general price level. From equation (26), the equilibrium price in other sectors will also fall. It falls less than proportionately, however: the elasticity of P_s with respect to P is equal to $\alpha < 1$. As a consequence, the price of good s rises relative to other produced goods. Since the price of good s falls relative to the numeraire, but rises relative to other produced goods, the direction of change in the output of good s is in general ambiguous. From (17),

$$Q_s = \left(\frac{\alpha}{1-\alpha} \right) \left(\frac{P_s}{P} \right)^{\frac{1}{(\rho-1)}} \left(\frac{N\overline{m}}{P} \right) .$$

Substituting for P_s from equation (26) yields

(37)
$$Q_s = \left(\frac{\alpha N\overline{m}}{1-\alpha} \right) \left(\frac{\mu_s k}{\alpha^\alpha (1-\alpha)^{1-\alpha}} \right)^{\frac{1}{(\rho-1)}} (P)^{\frac{\alpha-\rho}{(\rho-1)}}$$

If $\alpha > \rho$, the decrease in P leads to an increase in Q_s. In this case there is strategic complementarity across sectors; if $\alpha < \rho$, there is strategic substitutability across sectors.

A low value of α implies that the price of good s relative to other produced goods increases substantially. A high value of ρ means that goods are close substitutes, so the higher relative price causes consumers to switch to other produced goods. When α is low and ρ is high, therefore, an increase in the output of other sectors leads to a decrease in production in sector s.

Proposition 6: There is strategic complementarity within a sector in the first stage if

$$(38) \quad \sum_F \left\{ \psi^F() \left[\frac{\partial^2 M_i^F()}{\partial e_i \partial e_j} \right] + \left(\frac{2F}{N} \right) \left[\frac{\partial^2 \psi^F()}{\partial e_i \partial e_j} \right] + \left(\frac{N-2}{N-1} \right) \left[\frac{\partial \psi^F()}{\partial e_i} \right] \left[\frac{\partial M_i^F()}{\partial e_i} \right] \right\} \pi(F) > 0 \,.$$

Proof: The condition for complementarity within a sector is:

$$\partial^2 E\pi_i / \partial e_i \partial e_j > 0, \ j \neq i.$$

That is, there is complementarity if

$$\sum_F \left\{ \psi^F() \left[\frac{\partial^2 M_i^F()}{\partial e_i \partial e_j} \right] + \left(M_i^F \right) \left[\frac{\partial^2 \psi^F()}{\partial e_i \partial e_j} \right] + \left[\frac{\partial \psi^F()}{\partial e_i} \right] \left[\frac{\partial M_i^F()}{\partial e_j} \right] + \left[\frac{\partial \psi^F()}{\partial e_j} \right] \left[\frac{\partial M_i^F()}{\partial e_j} \right] \right\} \pi(F) > 0 \,.$$

In symmetric equilibrium, $M_i^F = 2F/N$. Also, in symmetric equilibrium, for all F, $\partial M_i^F / \partial e_j = \partial M_j^F / \partial e_i$ and $\partial \psi^F / \partial e_i = \partial \psi^F / \partial e_j$. Finally, from (9), $\sum_i \partial M_i^F() / \partial e_j = 0$. The result follows.

The terms in (38) cannot be signed without specifying more details of the matching process.

Proposition 7: In stable symmetric equilibrium, there is strategic complementarity across sectors in the first stage if $\alpha > \rho$.

Proof: Suppose that all agents in some positive measure of sectors increase their search effort. Recall from (A3) that this increase in effort will increase the expected number of firms in those sectors. The new distribution of firms will lie to the right of the old distribution. From (23), markups—and hence prices—will fall on average in those sectors. Hence the general price level will fall. Equation (28) reveals that, if $\alpha > \rho$, the fall in P will increase the gain from matching for an agent in sector s, for all F_s. Hence the expected gain from matching rises. From equation (32), this will lead to a rise in the equilibrium effort in sector s (given that the original equilibrium is stable).[15] It therefore turns out that the condition for complementarity across sectors in the first stage is again $\alpha > \rho$.

4.3 Comparative Statics and Multipliers

In common with Chatterjee and Cooper (1989), the multiplier effects of demand shocks in this model are increased by the first-stage search. Consider the effect of a change in $\overline{m}$, the endowment of the non-produced good. Recall equations (17), (24) and (26):

$$Q_s = \left(\frac{\alpha}{1-\alpha} \right) \left(\frac{P_s}{P} \right)^{\frac{1}{\rho-1}} \left(\frac{N\overline{m}}{P} \right);$$

$$P = \left(\frac{\mu k}{\alpha^\alpha (1-\alpha)^{1-\alpha}} \right)^{\frac{1}{1-\alpha}};$$

$$P_s = \left(\frac{\mu_s k}{\alpha^\alpha (1-\alpha)^{1-\alpha}} \right) P^\alpha.$$

From these equations it follows that the elasticity of Qs with respect to $\overline{m}$ equals 1, holding fixed the number of firms (since P_s and P are independent of $\overline{m}$). An increase in $\overline{m}$ shifts out the demand curves faced by all sectors: equilibrium prices are unchanged and quantities increase proportionately.

The partial equilibrium effect of a change in the endowment of the non-produced good is smaller. Specifically, suppose that $\overline{m}$ is increased but that quantities in sectors other than *s* are held fixed. From (19), this change will lead to a proportionate increase in P. This shifts in the demand curve facing sector *s*, and leads to an increase in P_s. It is easily shown from (17) and (26) that the elasticity of Q_s with respect to $\overline{m}$, holding other quantities fixed, is equal to $(1-\alpha)/(1-\rho)$, which is less than 1 for $\alpha > \rho$. Thus, provided that $\alpha > \rho$, the general equilibrium consequence of an increase in the non-produced good exceeds the partial equilibrium change. This is the multiplier effect noted in Cooper and John (1988).

There is an additional effect in this model arising from the entry decision. An increase in $\overline{m}$, from equation (29), also increases the gain from matching. In equilibrium, therefore, agents will incur extra search effort, and so the expected number of firms will increase. The average markup, μ, will fall, and so the price index, P, will fall also. Output will rise.

The other comparative statics in the model are straightforward. An increase in *k* (the marginal cost of production) leads to an increase in P and a decrease in output. The profit from being matched falls. Search effort falls because of this effect, and also because k also represents the marginal cost of search effort. An increase in ρ (which means that goods become closer substitutes) results in a decrease in the markup.

5. Conclusion

The analysis here brings together two strands of the recent New Keynesian literature: models with search externalities and models with imperfect competition. While most macroeconomic models with imperfectly competitive markets exogenously impose the degree of competitiveness, the degree of imperfect competition is endogenous is this model. Costly search in the labor market plays the role of an endogenous entry cost.

The paper has two main conclusions. First, the externalities from search now include the effect of search activity on the degree of competition in the economy. Under fairly general conditions, this means that increased search by one agent imposes net negative externalities on potential partners. In contrast to the model of Drazen (1986), the externalities from search and from market power do not reinforce each other. A corollary is that positive search externalities generally emerge across sectors. Second, the model has implications for the multiplier effects associated with demand shocks in the product market. Increased demand increases the gain from being matched, and thus encourages greater search activity. This leads to the formation of more firms and hence to increased competition; this in turn implies increased output.

The analysis of this paper can be extended in a number of ways. Since firms take such a particular symmetric form in this paper, it would be instructive to investigate how the results obtained here are altered in a model where there is a hiring decision that is distinct from the formation of the firm. A model with richer dynamics, where firms existed for a number of periods, is also worthy of investigation. Finally, it would be interesting to conduct a more complete analysis of government policy in the model.

Notes

1. See for example Hart (1982), Heller (1986), Kiyotaki (1988), Blanchard and Kiyotaki (1987), and many others.

2. See, for example, Bils (1987), Shapiro (1987), Hall (1988), Domowitz, Hubbard, and Petersen (1988), and Basu (1995) for discussions of the degree of market power and the cyclical behavior of markups in the U.S. economy. Rotemberg and Woodford (1992), meanwhile, argue that a calibrated dynamic general equilibrium model, where firms have market power, outperforms a standard real business cycle model.

3. There is by now a large literature on the search approach to labor markets. See Mortensen (1986), Davidson (1990), and Merz (1998) for surveys.

4. Such a specification of preferences has become quite common in the literature on macroeconomic models with imperfect competition, since the homotheticity of the utility function makes it relatively easy to characterize equilibrium. (For example, this is similar to the utility

function utilized by Blanchard and Kiyotaki (1987), although an important difference is that they include real money balances rather than a non-produced good.) As will be clear, the assumption that utility is linear in effort also simplifies they analysis.

5. (A1) and (A2) should be viewed as being derived from an underlying assumption of symmetry in the $\pi_k(\ )$ functions as follows. For a given N_k, partition the arguments of $\pi_k(\ )$ into two subsets: the effort supplied by agents who are members of N_k, and the effort put forth by agents who are in N/N_k. Symmetry implies that the $\pi_k(\ )$ function is symmetric with respect to the arguments in each subset. Moreover, symmetry implies that there will be identical probability functions (up to the relabeling of the arguments) for all subsets, N_k, of a given size F.

6. Obviously, other specifications of the matching process are possible. For example, there might be two types of agents in each sector, each endowed with a different type of capital, and a successful match would require one of each type. The main results of the paper are unaltered in such a specification.

7. The utility of an agent equals this expression plus $v(P)\overline{m}-ke$, which is constant from the perspective of an individual agent—P is exogenous to the agent, and e is a sunk cost.

8. This description assumes interior solutions. Nothing in this argument is altered if agents choose corner values for e or q.

9. Lemma 1 is used in Proposition 1 below. The condition in Lemma 1—that aggregate profits are declining in F—is sufficient but not necessary for the result of the proposition. Since Lemma 1 derives in part from the assumptions made about preferences and technology, it is natural to ask if it holds more generally.

It is obviously not the case that aggregate profit, $F\pi(F)$, is declining in F for any demand curve and any specification of costs. But Lemma 1 does hold in a fairly general set of circumstances. In particular, the following results can be shown. First, if there is constant marginal cost, then a sufficient (not necessary) condition for Lemma 1 is that the elasticity of demand in the sector is non-increasing in aggregate output. This condition holds for both constant-elasticity demand curves and linear demand curves. Second, with increasing marginal cost and constant-elasticity demand curves, a sufficient (not necessary) condition for Lemma 1 is that demand be inelastic. (If marginal cost is increasing, then the decrease in output per firm from increased competition acts in the direction of increased aggregate profits, because individual firms produce more efficiently.) Third, with an elastic (constant-elasticity) demand curve and increasing marginal cost, Lemma 1 holds for small F.

10. The externality here is distinct from the class of external effect labeled "income externalities" by Davidson (1990, p. 33). Those externalities arise because individuals do not take account of the act that their effort raises the income of those with whom they are matched. The actions of one agent affect the welfare of all matched agents in the sector ex post, not just that agent's partner. Moreover, the effect discussed here is a negative rather than a positive externality.

11. Mankiw and Whinston (1986) analyzed the entry decisions of firms into an imperfectly competitive market and showed that there is a tendency towards too many firms if the second-stage game is characterized by strategic complementarity.

12. Strategic decisions are of course made in stages 1 and 2 of this game, and external effects arise in both cases. A planner who could internalize all externalities would choose zero effort in the first stage, and then instruct firms in the second stage to produce the competitive level of output.

Because firms have constant marginal cost, one firm can produce a given level of output at the same cost as many firms could. Moreover, the matching technology guarantees at least $\underline{F}$ firms even if search effort is zero. There is therefore no reason to incur the search costs necessary to form more than the minimum number of firms. The solution is the same if the planner can choose output in the second stage of the game, but cannot influence search effort: the planner will simply require firms to produce the competitive level of output. Agents, anticipating zero profits, will incur zero search costs, which is the optimal solution.

13. See Cooper and John (1988).

14. The denominator equals $(P' / F) (2F + \rho - 2)$, so the assumption that $F + \rho > 1$ guarantees that the second order condition is satisfied.

15. Since $\pi(F)$ in equation (32) has increased for all F, there will be a fall in the symmetric equilibrium value of e in sector s provided that the left-hand side of (32) is decreasing in e. The left-hand side of (32) is in turn decreasing in e unless there is sufficiently strong strategic complementarity within the sector that the reaction function has slope greater than 1.

References

Basu, S. "Intermediate Goods and Business Cycles: Implications for Productivity and Welfare." *American Economic Review* 85 (1995): 512–531.

Bils, M. "The Cyclical Behavior of Marginal Cost and Price." *American Economic Review* 77 (1987): 838–855.

Blanchard, O. and N. Kiyotaki. "Monopolistic Competition and the Effects of Aggregate Demand." *American Economic Review* 77 (1987): 647–666.

Chatterjee, S. and R. Cooper. "Multiplicity of Equilibria and Fluctuations in Dynamic Imperfectly Competitive Economies." *American Economic Review, Papers and Proceedings* 79 (May 1989): 353–357.

Chatterjee, S., R. Cooper, and B. Ravikumar. "Strategic Complementarity in Business Formation: Aggregate Fluctuations and Sunspot Equilibria." *Review of Economic Studies* 60 (1993): 795–811.

Cooper, R. and A. John. "Coordinating Coordination Failures in Keynesian Models." *Quarterly Journal of Economics* 103 (1988): 441–464.

Davidson, C. *Recent Developments in the Theory of Involuntary Unemployment.* Kalamazoo, Michigan: W. E. Upjohn Institute. 1990.

Davidson, C., L. Martin and S. Matusz. "Search, Unemployment and the Production of Jobs," *Economic Journal* 97 (1987): 857–876.

_____. "The Structure of Simple General Equilibrium Models with Frictional Unemployment." *Journal of Political Economy* 96 (1988): 1267–1293.

_____. "Jobs and Chocolate: Samuelsonian Surpluses in Dynamic Models of Unemployment." *Review of Economic Studies* 61 (1994): 173–192.

Diamond, P. "Aggregate Demand Management in Search Equilibrium." *Journal of Political Economy* 90 (1982): 881–94.

Domowitz, I., G. Hubbard, and B. Petersen. "Market Structure and Cyclical Fluctuations in U.S. Manufacturing." *Review of Economics and Statistics* 70 (1988): 55–66.

Drazen, A. "Involuntary Unemployment and Aggregate Demand Spillovers in an Optimal Search Model." Working Paper No. 32–86, Foerder Institute for Economic Research, 1986.

Hall, R. "The Relation between Price and Marginal Cost in U.S. Industry." *Journal of Political Economy* 96 (1988): 921–947.

Hart, O. "A Model of Imperfect Competition with Keynesian Features." *Quarterly Journal of Economics* 97 (1982): 109–38.

Heller, W. "Coordination Failure Under Complete Markets with Applications to Effective Demand." In *Equilibrium Analysis: Essays in Honor of Kenneth J. Arrow*, Volume 2, edited by W. Heller, R. Starr, and D. Starrett. Cambridge, Massachusetts: Cambridge University Press, 1986.

Hosios, A. "On the Efficiency of Matching and Related Models of Search and Unemployment." *Review of Economic Studies* 57 (1990): 279–298.

Howitt, P. "Business Cycles with Costly Search and Recruiting." In *The Keynesian Recovery: And Other Essays*, edited by P. Howitt. Ann Arbor, MI: University of Michigan Press. 1990.

Howitt, P. and P. McAfee. "Stability of Equilibria with Trade Externalities." *Quarterly Journal of Economics* 103 (1988): 261–278.

Kiyotaki, N. "Multiple Expectational Equilibria under Monopolistic Competition." *Quarterly Journal of Economics* 103 (1988): 695–714.

Mankiw, N.G. and M.D. Whinston. "Free Entry and Social Inefficiency." *Rand Journal of Economics* 17 (1986): 48–58.

Merz, M. "Search Theory Rediscovered: Recent Developments in the Macroeconomics of the Labor Market." This volume.

Mortensen, D. "Job Search and Labor Market Analysis." In *The Handbook of Labor Economics*, Volume II, edited by O. Ashenfelter and R. Layard. Amsterdam: Elsevier, 849–919. 1986.

Rotemberg, J. and M. Woodford. "Oligopolistic Pricing and the Effects of Aggregate Demand on Economic Activity." *Journal of Political Economy* 100 (1992): 1153–1207.

Shapiro, M. "Measuring Market Power in U.S. Industry." Unpublished manuscript. Cowles Foundation, Yale University, 1987.

5

Empirical Search Models

José J. Canals
University of Colorado

Steven Stern
University of Virginia

Abstract

This chapter discusses various methods that have been used to estimate structural models of job search. The focus is mainly on using available data to estimate the parameters of the wage offer distribution, the reservation wage or reservation wage function, the cost of search, the offer arrival rate, and the discount rate. We describe models, estimation procedures, and issues associated with identification. We say relatively little about results. Section 2 presents the classical search model and how to estimate its parameters. Section 3 deals separately with survival analysis because survival models have been used so extensively to look at unemployment spell data. Section 4 discusses empirical equilibrium search models. We present several models, discuss how to estimate their structural parameters, and raise special problems associated with such models.

1. Introduction

This chapter discusses various methods that have been used to estimate structural search and survival models. Most of the focus is on using available data, usually on unemployment spell lengths and accepted wage offers, to estimate the parameters of specific search models. In particular, we focus on estimating the parameters of the wage offer distribution, the reservation wage or reservation wage function, the cost of search, offer arrival rate, and discount rate. There is an added section on survival models because survival models have been used so extensively to look at unemployment spell data.

Throughout we describe actual models, estimation procedures, and issues associated with identification and estimation. There is not as much emphasis on results because we view the literature as still developing methodology. The frontier of the methodology for structural models involves estimating equilibrium search models and allowing for heterogeneity and interesting dynamics. We also think identification issues should receive more attention.

This chapter is divided into three main sections. The next section presents the classical search model and how to estimate its parameters. We begin by presenting early "semi-structural" attempts to estimate this model. Next, there is a discussion on estimating a basic structural search model. We build on the basic model by allowing for measurement error in wages, observed and unobserved heterogeneity, right censoring, continuous time, and observed rejected offers. Next, there is a discussion of models with changing reservation wages.

Section 3 deals with survival analysis. We construct the basic Cox proportional hazards model with unobserved heterogeneity and discuss how to estimate the effects of observed covariates, the parameters of the baseline hazard function and the parameters of the unobserved heterogeneity density function. Then we discuss semiparametric approaches associated with estimating the baseline hazard and unobserved heterogeneity density function.

Section 4 discusses empirical equilibrium search models. A few theoretical models are presented. Then we discuss how to estimate their structural parameters and to deal with special problems associated with such models. Given present data, identification is an important issue. A brief conclusion ends the paper.

2. The Classical Search Model

In this section, we present a simple version of a search model in discrete time. Workers are infinitely lived, wealth maximizing agents who discount the future at a rate $(1+r)^{-1}$. At each moment, a worker can be employed or unemployed. Unemployed workers search actively for job offers. Offers are distributed according to the density $f(w)$ with finite mean. At each period, an unemployed worker incurs a cost of search c and receives a wage offer from one of many firms in the labor market. A wage offer represents a random draw from the time-invariant distribution of wages known to the worker. Once a job is accepted, employment lasts forever. The problem of the worker has the reservation property: there exists a value ξ, called the reservation wage, such that it is optimal for the worker to accept any wage offer if it is not smaller than ξ and to reject it otherwise. Analytically, the reservation wage is the unique solution to

$$(2.1) \qquad\qquad \xi = \frac{1}{r}\int_{\xi}^{\infty}(w-\xi)f(w)dw - c \; .$$

The left-hand side of the equation (2.1) represents the benefit associated with working at the present period for a wage ξ, while the right-hand side represents the expected discounted benefit of one more period of search if wages below ξ are not acceptable to the worker. Consequently, at the reservation wage, the worker is indifferent between accepting the present wage offer or searching one more period. Notice that the left-hand side of equation (2.1) is strictly increasing in ξ, while the right-hand side is decreasing in ξ. Consequently, as long as the cost of search is not too high, there exists a unique positive solution to the last equation. A more rigorous discussion of this model is given by, for example, Lippman and McCall (1976).

2.1 First Attempts

The first attempts to estimate the search model (Kiefer and Neumann, 1979) assumed a wage offer equation

$$(2.2) \qquad\qquad w_i^o = X_t\beta + \varepsilon_i^o$$

and a reservation wage equation

$$(2.3) \qquad\qquad w_i^r = Z_i\gamma + \varepsilon_i^r$$

with X_i and Z_i representing individual characteristics that affect the expected wage offer and the reservation wage, respectively, $\varepsilon_i^0 \sim N(0,\sigma_0^2)$, $\varepsilon_i^r \sim N(0,\sigma_r^2)$, and $E\varepsilon_i^0\varepsilon_i^r = \sigma_{0r}$. Imagine we have data from a sample of workers with information about individual characteristics, the duration of unemployment, and the accepted wage if the worker is employed. Clearly, the distribution of observed wages is truncated because we observe only wages that have been accepted by the workers. Define P_i as the probability that an individual receives an acceptable wage offer at a certain period. Then

$$P_i = \Pr(w_i^o \geq w_i^r)$$

(2.4)
$$= \Pr(X_i\beta + \varepsilon_i^o \geq Z_i\gamma + \varepsilon_i^r)$$

$$= \Pr(X_i\beta - Z_i\gamma \geq \varepsilon_i^r - \varepsilon_i^o)$$

and the probability that an individual searches exactly T periods is

(2.5)
$$(1 - P_i)^{T-1} P_i .$$

P_i can be estimated using data on duration of unemployment for a sample of workers and maximum likelihood estimation (MLE). In particular, the log likelihood function (LLF) is

(2.6)
$$L = \sum_{i=1}^{N} \log(1 - P_i)^{T_i - 1} P_i .$$

Also, we observe accepted wage data. After correcting the wage equation for selection bias as in Heckman (1979), we can estimate

(2.7)
$$w_i^o = X_i\beta + E\left(\varepsilon_i^o \middle| X_i\beta - Z_i\gamma \geq \varepsilon_i^r - \varepsilon_i^o\right) + \varsigma_i$$

$$= X_i\beta + \frac{\phi\left[(X_i\beta - Z_i\gamma)/\sqrt{\sigma_r^2 + \sigma_o^2 - 2\sigma_{or}}\right]}{1 - \Phi\left[(X_i\beta - Z_i\gamma)/\sqrt{\sigma_r^2 + \sigma_o^2 - 2\sigma_{or}}\right]} + \varsigma_i .$$

where φ is the standard normal density function, Φ is the standard normal distribution function, $\phi/(1 - \Phi) = E(\varepsilon_i^o | X_i\beta - Z_i\gamma \geq \varepsilon_i^r - \varepsilon_i^o)$ is the inverse Mill's ratio, and ς_i is the deviation of ε_i^o from its conditional expected value. Equations (2.6) and (2.7) identify β, γ, σ_0^2, σ_r^2, and σ_{or} either by placing restrictions on what variables X_i enter the wage equation and what variables Z_i enter the reservation wage equation or by relying on the nonlinear functional form of the selection bias correction term.

The Kiefer-Neumann approach to estimation of the search model uses the restrictions imposed by equation (2.1) only as a guide for the econometric specification. This presents problems of consistency with the underlying theoretical framework. In particular, the theoretical model predicts that a mean preserving spread transformation of the wage offer distribution will increase the reservation wage, that a decrease in the discount rate will imply a reduction in the reservation wage, and that any anticipated change in future wage offer distributions will affect the reservation wage in the present as well as the future. It is not clear how these restrictions apply in equations (2.2) and (2.3).

2.2 Structural Estimation Without Heterogeneity

More recently, researchers such as Wolpin (1987), Stern (1989), and Christiansen and Kiefer (1991) have pursued a more structural approach in which the estimation is derived explicitly from the theory. This approach incorporates the restrictions given by the condition of optimal search to the empirical work. The econometric specification is then fully consistent with the underlying theoretical framework. In addition, it becomes possible to study parameters such as the discount rate and the cost of search not otherwise present in the econometric specification. In the next paragraphs we analyze the structural estimation of the theoretical search model previously described.

Assume for simplicity that we have data on duration of unemployment and accepted wage offers from a population of homogeneous workers (i.e., there are no observed or unobserved characteristics affecting the wage offer distribution or the reservation wage). Let the distribution of wage offers be $F(\bullet)$ with density $f(\bullet)$ and let the reservation wage that solves equation (2.1) be ξ. Then the probability of observing an individual with a spell of unemployment of t_i periods and accepted wage w_i is

(2.8)
$$F(\xi)^{t_i} \left[1 - F(\xi)\right] \frac{f(w_i)}{1 - F(\xi)} 1(w_i \geq \xi)$$

where $1(w_i \geq \xi)$ is equal to 1 if $w_i \geq \xi$, and it equals 0 otherwise. The first term, $F(\xi)^{t_i} \left[1 - F(\xi)\right]$, is the probability that the first t_i wage offers are rejected. The second term, $f(w_i) / [1 - F(\xi)]$, is the density of a wage conditional on it being acceptable ($w_i \geq \xi$). The last term, $1(w_i \geq \xi)$, ensures that all observed accepted wage offers are greater than the reservation wage. The LLF based on a sample of N individuals is

(2.9)
$$L = \sum_{t=1}^{N} \log \left\{ F(\xi)^{t_i} f(w_i) 1(w_i \geq \xi) \right\}.$$

For this simple specification of the search model, we need to estimate ξ, r, c, and the parameters associated with the distribution of wage offers F. The LLF is increasing in ξ up until it reaches the minimum observed wage. This implies that the MLE of ξ is

(2.10)
$$\hat{\xi} = \min_{i=1,L,N} w_i .$$

Recall that is the first order statistic for the sample $\{w_i\}_{i=1}^{N}$ of observed wage offers,

and its density is equal to $N\left[1 - F\left(w_i \,|w \geq \xi\right)\right]^{N-1} f\left(w_i \,|w \geq \xi\right)$. Observe that the lower limit of the accepted wage offer distribution depends on the reservation wage which is an estimated parameter of the model. For this reason, the standard regularity conditions used to demonstrate the consistency and asymptotic normality of the maximum likelihood estimator do not apply to this problem. However, the parameter estimates are still consistent. In fact, under weak regularity conditions,[1] $\hat{\xi}$ is a superconsistent estimator of ξ; that is $\hat{\xi}$ converges to ξ at a rate faster than $\sqrt{N}$.

The estimation approach in this case consists of substituting $\hat{\xi}$ in the LLF and obtaining estimators of the remaining parameters using standard MLE applied to the resulting function. This technique, described in Christensen and Kiefer (1991), is known as pseudo-maximum likelihood estimation.

Using this approach we can obtain estimators for the reservation wage and the parameters of $f(\bullet)$ for a large class of distributions.[2] Neither the cost of search c nor the discount rate r appears in the likelihood function. As a result, in order to obtain consistent estimators for these parameters, we need to make use of the restrictions implied by equation (2.1). In general, this restriction is not sufficient to independently identify both parameters. To illustrate this point, consider a case where the distribution of wages is exponential with parameter λ: $F(w) = 1-\exp\{-\lambda w\}$ for $w \geq 0$. For this particular specification, the reservation wage satisfies

(2.11)
$$\xi = \frac{1}{r}\frac{e^{-\lambda\xi}}{\lambda} - c.$$

Observe that, for fixed ξ and λ, there is an infinite number of pairs (r, c) that satisfy the last equation. Then, even if we can obtain consistent estimators $\hat{\xi}$ and $\hat{\lambda}$, the restriction implied by equation (2.11) is not enough to independently identify r and c.

The central hypothesis of the structural search model is that agents make optimal choices in a simple environment. From an empirical perspective, the condition of optimal behavior imposes additional restrictions to the econometric model. A test of the search theory will imply a test of these restrictions. Unfortunately, we do not observe fundamental elements of the theory of search like the reservation wage, the cost of search, and the discount rate (to say nothing of parameters measuring heterogeneity) from the data. With this lack of information about fundamental elements of the theoretical model, it becomes difficult to construct meaningful tests of the model. Stern (1989) suggests in a model where r and c are not separately identified that one can construct the set of combinations of r and c hat are consistent with the search behavior equation and then determine whether any elements of the set are "reasonable" values. This provides an informal test of the theory. Nevertheless, the difficulty in testing search models is probably the reason why search theory has been used as a restriction at hand to assist with the identification of the structural models more than as a testable theory.

2.3 Measurement Error

A major criticism of the estimation technique described in equations (2.9) and (2.10) is its sensitivity to measurement error. Observe that the estimator of the reservation wage is the first order statistic from the sample of accepted wage offers. Order statistics are known to be very sensitive to measurement error, even in large samples. All the parameters in the structural model are related to each other, via the restrictions imposed by the theory. Consequently, if measurement error is affecting the estimate of ξ, any other parameter estimated will be affected as well. Several authors have dealt with this problem by explicitly incorporating the possibility of measurement error in the estimation of the structural model. Among the papers that have followed this approach are Wolpin (1987), Stern (1989), and Christensen and Kiefer (1994). All three papers assume that the observed wages are affected by random error in measurement that is normally distributed. Stern argues that there may be two different types of measurement error in the wage-offer data. First, there may be errors in reporting wages, or in imputing tax rates or price levels. Second, the value of a job may deviate from the observed wage because of other factors such as fringe benefits and working conditions. Stern and Christensen and Kiefer present strong evidence that measurement error is an important empirical event.

Assume wages are measured with error where w_i and w_i^* represent the real and the observed wage for individual i, respectively. In particular suppose that $w_i^* = w_i \varepsilon_i$ where ε_i represents a random multiplicative error with distribution $G(\bullet)$, takes a positive value, and is independent of the wage offer. In this case, a wage offer observed without error is equivalent to a situation in which $\varepsilon_i=1$. Notice that, for this specification, it is possible to observe accepted wage offers below the reservation wage without violating the underlying theoretical model. Observe first of all that the existence of measurement error does not violate any assumptions of the theoretical model. Consequently, the structural approach to inference can rely on the restrictions implied by the conditions of optimal search. All of the papers mentioned previously have used MLE to estimate related models. Assume, as in the previous case, that we have data on duration of unemployment and accepted wage offers from a sample of homogeneous workers. The probability that a particular unemployed worker remains unemployed for one more period is still $F(\xi)$. On the other hand, the density of an observed accepted wage offer w_i^* is

(2.12)
$$\left[\int_0^{w_i^*/\xi} f\left(\frac{w_i^*}{\varepsilon} \right) dG(\varepsilon) \right] / \left[1 - F(\xi_i) \right].$$

The upper limit of integration w_i^*/ξ imposes the restriction that or $\xi \le w_i^*/\varepsilon = w_i$.

Consider a sample with N observations of the form (t_i, w_i^*) where t_i represents the length of the unemployment spell and w_i^* represents the accepted wage offer, possibly observed with measurement error, for observation i. The LLF for this sample is

$$(2.13) \qquad L = \sum_{i=1}^{N} \log \left\{ F\left(\xi_i\right)^{t_i} \int_0^{w_i^*/\xi} f\left(\frac{w_i^*}{\varepsilon}\right) dG\left(\varepsilon\right) \right\}.$$

Notice that, due to measurement error, the observed wage w_i^* is not restricted to be above the reservation wage and can take any positive value. For this reason, the first order statistic from the sample of observed wages is not an estimator of the reservation wage. Consequently, the problem of estimation in this case is reduced to standard MLE. Assuming that the distribution of wages F belongs to a certain parametric family, in most cases we will be able to obtain consistent estimators for the reservation wage ξ and the parameters associated with F. However, neither r nor c appear in the likelihood function; estimates of these parameters will have to be obtained from the restrictions imposed by the theory. At this point, the problem is not different from the previous case. As a result, these parameters cannot be independently identified. Stern (1989) presents a extensive discussion of identification in a similar context.

2.4 Sample Heterogeneity

Up to this point, we have considered the case of a sample of homogeneous individuals. In fact, workers with different characteristics may face different wage offer distributions and thus have different reservation wages. Also, in more complex search models in which workers can choose the search intensity, workers with different characteristics may have different costs of search and, as a result, they can optimally choose to search with different levels of intensity as is the case in Stern (1989). We divide our discussion into the effect of observed heterogeneity and the effect of unobserved heterogeneity on estimation.

2.4.1 Observed Heterogeneity. Within our framework it is straightforward to account for heterogeneity. Consider that X_i represents a set of characteristics associated with individual i. Assume also that these characteristics are observed by the econometrician and affect the distribution of wage offers in a known way, $F(\bullet|X_i)$. In this framework, it is simple to define the LLF as an extension of equation (2.13), accounting for observed heterogeneity,

(2.14) $$L = \sum_{i=1}^{N} \log \left\{ F\left(\xi_i \,|\, X_i\right)^{t_i} \int_0^{w_i^*/\xi} f\left(\frac{w_i^*}{\varepsilon} \,\middle|\, X_i\right) dG\left(\varepsilon\right) \right\}$$

where ξ_i represents the reservation wage for a worker with associated characteristics X_i. Wolpin (1987) deals with observed heterogeneity by following the spirit of equation (2.14). In order to reduce the computational burden, he transforms X_i variables, usually considered to be continuous, into dichotomous variables. Some papers divide the sample into different subsamples that contain similar workers. For example, Narendranathan and Nickell (1985) divide the sample into groups of younger and older workers, and Stern (1989) divides the sample by sex and education. This approach allows these papers to solve equation (2.14) for only a small number of individuals each representing a large group of similar individuals. This approach implies strong assumptions that are only justified for reasons of computational complexity. While the cost of computation was a reasonable concern at the time these papers were written, recent advances in computation allow for a much less restrictive treatment of observed heterogeneity.

2.4.2. Unobserved Heterogeneity Another important issue is the existence of omitted variables or unobserved heterogeneity. Even after controlling for the presence of observed characteristics X_i for individual i, there may be relevant characteristics that cannot be observed from the sample, also known as unobserved heterogeneity. Unobserved characteristics are important in explaining the behavior of the worker in the labor market. For example, workers with identical observed characteristics may face different wage offer distributions and have different reservation wages due to differences in relevant unobserved characteristics. Ignoring the problem of unobserved heterogeneity may result in biased estimators of the parameters of the model. Biased estimates can be obtained even if the omitted variables are uncorrelated with the observed ones because of the nonlinearity of the model and the restrictions imposed by the theory that incorporate implicit relations among the parameters. This problem was noticed by Nickell (1979) but has not received much attention in more recent work in this area.

One way to deal with unobserved heterogeneity is to make an explicit assumption about the distribution of the unobserved heterogeneity.[3] In particular, assume that agent i faces a distribution of wage offers $F(\bullet|X_i, v_i)$, with X_i and v_i representing the set of observed and unobserved characteristics, respectively. Even if the function $F(\bullet|X, v)$ is known, this information is not enough to construct the LLF because the value of v for each individual is not observed. Assume that v is distributed according to $G_v(\bullet)$ and is independent of X. Then, the contribution to the LLF of an observation $\left(t_i, w_i^*, X_i\right)$ after the effect of unobserved heterogeneity has been integrated out is

(2.15) $\log \int F\left(\xi_{iv} \mid X_i, v\right)^{t_i} \int_0^{w_i^* / \xi_{iv}} f\left(\frac{w_i^*}{\varepsilon} \mid X_i, v\right) dG_\varepsilon\left(\varepsilon\right) dG_v\left(v\right)$

where $G_\varepsilon(\varepsilon)$ represents the distribution of the measurement error, and represents the reservation wage for an individual with characteristics (X_i, v). This expression can be used to construct the LLF of the sample. As was the case with measurement error, the presence of unobserved heterogeneity does not violate any assumptions of the theoretical model. Consequently, the structural approach to inference can rely on the restrictions implied by the conditions of optimal search. A significant problem with this approach, at least for continuous unobserved heterogeneity distributions, is that the agent conditions on his own unobserved heterogeneity when choosing a reservation wage. Thus, the reservation wage becomes a functional. Essentially, a reservation wage must be computed for each value of v used to compute the integral in equation (2.15). Thus, computation costs increase significantly.

The problem of unobserved heterogeneity has been ignored in most structural models of search. The approach implied by equation (2.15) has been followed in some of the papers that consider estimation of structural search models like Eckstein and Wolpin (1990), Van den Berg and Ridder (1993a) or Engberg (1994).[4] Since the treatment of this issue here will mimic the approach taken in a later section on equilibrium models, we postpone the detailed description of this technique. However, it is appropriate at this point to notice that, in most cases, it is impossible to obtain information about $G_v(\bullet)$. In particular, the search theory does not offer any guidance about $G_v(\bullet)$. It is probably for this reason that most papers that take this problem into consideration, including Nickell (1979), Eckstein and Wolpin (1990), Van den Berg and Ridder (1993a), or Engberg (1994), have adopted a nonparametric approach similar to Heckman and Singer (1984b) which is discussed in Section

2.5 Censoring

A right censored observation is one where the end of the spell has not occurred by the end of the time of observation. For example, consider a sample of newly unemployed people observed between dates τ_1 and τ_2. Any unemployment spells that have not ended by τ_2 are right censored. For those spells, we do not know when, if ever, they would have ended; we know only that the spell had not ended by τ_2. An alternative cause of censoring would occur in unemployment insurance administrative records where the individual is observed until his UI benefits run out. When they run out, the researcher does not know whether the unemployment spell ended in a job or if just the UI coverage ended.[5] The methods for estimation of structural search models described in the previous section can be adapted to handle right censored observations. Consider data of the form (t_i, c_i, w_i, X_i) where t_i is the observed length of the spell, c_i is an indicator of whether spell i is right censored ($c_i = 1$ if spell i is right censored), w_i is the observed accepted wage offer for (uncensored) spell i, and

X_i is a set of observed characteristics of worker i. As long as the censoring process is independent of the process generating the data, the LLF can be modified straightforwardly to account for right censoring. Consider, for example, the structural model with measurement error. The probability of observing $(t_i, c_i = 1, X_i)$ is $F\left(\xi_i | X_i\right)^{t_i}$ (note that no wage offer is observed), while the probability of observing $(t_i, c_i = 0, w_i, X_i)$ is similar to the term in equation (2.14). This information can be incorporated to the LLF as

$$
(2.16) \qquad L = \sum_{i=1}^{N} (1 - c_i) \log \left\{ F\left(\xi_i | X_i\right)^{t_i} \int_0^{w_i^* / \xi_i} f\left(\frac{w_i^*}{\varepsilon_i} \Big| X_i\right) dG(\varepsilon) \right.
$$

$$
\left. + c_i \log \left\{ F\left(\xi_i | X_i\right)^{t_i} \right\} .
$$

Equation (2.16) handles right censoring, but many data sets also have left censored observations. In our context, left censoring appears, for example, if we do not observe the starting time of the unemployment spell. Several authors have tried to avoid this problem by selecting data sets with special characteristics. An early treatment of the left censoring problem can be found in Nickell (1979). Lancaster (1990) provides a good discussion as well. In principle, left censoring should not be a problem for the simple search model described in this section because this model is stationary and the probability of leaving the unemployment state is independent of the time spent in this state. However, there are examples in the literature of models in which this is not the case. Kiefer and Neumann (1979, 1981) consider a specification that accounts for the possibility of decreasing reservation wages. Wolpin (1987) presents a model in which agents search for a certain period of time after which they accept the first wage offered. This feature of the model implies decreasing reservation wages. In addition, if we take into account the possibility of unobserved heterogeneity (Nickell, 1979), left censoring becomes an important problem, even in a stationary environment. Since unobserved characteristics of the agents affect the probability of escape from the unemployment state, a sample with problems of left censoring cannot be assumed random. Consequently, left censoring can produce inconsistent estimators even in stationary models.

2.6 Continuous Time Models With Offer Arrival Rates

In the discrete time search model described in equation (2.1), the theory does not provide any guidance for the choice of the time period length. In this sense, this approach is somewhat arbitrary since it is time unit dependent. In order to overcome this shortcoming some researchers have developed continuous-time versions of the previous model. In this section we present a simple version of a search model in continuous time. The only difference between this model and the discrete time version is in the process of wage offer arrivals. Other than that, this model parallels the structure of the search model in discrete time.

Workers are infinite-lived wealth maximizing agents, and discount the future at a rate r. In order to receive wage offers at a certain time interval Δt, the worker incurs a cost $c\Delta t$. Job offers arrive from a Poisson process with parameter α. The probability of receiving a wage offer in time interval Δt is $\alpha\Delta t + o(\Delta t)$; the probability of receiving two or more offers in time interval Δt is negligible. Offers are distributed according to the time-invariant density $f(w)$ with finite mean. Once a job is accepted, employment lasts forever. The worker's search problem has the reservation wage property. Analytically, the reservation wage ξ is the unique solution to

(2.17)
$$\xi = \frac{\alpha}{r} \int_{\xi}^{\infty} wf(w)\,dw - c.$$

As in the discrete time model, this implicit equation represents the restriction implied by the condition of optimal search.

In order to obtain estimators for the parameters of the structural model in continuous time, it is convenient to start by defining the hazard function associated with the unemployment state. This function represents the instantaneous probability of receiving an acceptable wage offer or equivalently the instantaneous probability of leaving the unemployment state conditional on not having left yet. The hazard in this case is the product of the arrival rate α and the probability that the wage offer is acceptable to the worker $1 - F(\xi)$. The hazard function for leaving unemployment is

(2.18)
$$\lambda = \alpha\left[1 - F(\xi)\right].$$

Observe that the hazard function is time independent which is a result of the stationarity of the model. Given the hazard function λ, the probability of an unemployment spell of length t or less is

(2.19)
$$1 - \exp\{-\lambda t\}.$$

This is an exponential distribution with parameter λ, where λ^{-1} is the average length of an unemployment spell. The associated density function will have the form $\lambda \exp(-\lambda t)$. Also, the probability of observing an accepted wage offer w (with no measurement error) is

(2.20)
$$f(w)\left[1 - F(\xi)\right]^{-1} 1(w \geq \xi).$$

Consider a sample with N observations of the form (t_i, w_i), where t_i represents the length of unemployment spell i and w_i represents the accepted wage offer. The LLF for this sample is

$$(2.21) \qquad L = \sum_{i=1}^{N} \log\left\{\lambda \exp\left\{-\lambda t_i\right\} f\left(w_i\right)\left[1 - F\left(\xi\right)\right]^{-1}\right\}.$$

As in the discrete case, the estimators have to be obtained using Pseudo Maximum Likelihood techniques because no measurement error is assumed.

This expression can be generalized to allow for right censoring and measurement error. Consider a sample of the form $\left\{t_i, c_i, w_i^*, X_i\right\}_{i=1}^{N}$ and measurement error as in the discrete case. In this case, the probability of observing $(t_i, c_i = 1, X_i)$ is $1 - (1 - \exp\{-\lambda(X_i)t_i\}) = \exp\{-\lambda(X_i)t_i\}$ with $\lambda(X_i) = \alpha[1 - F(\xi_i \mid X_i)]$ and ξ_i incorporates the restriction imposed by equation (2.17) given the distribution of wage offers $F(\bullet \mid X_i)$. Meanwhile, the probability of $(t_i, c_i = 0, w_i X_i)$ is

$$(2.22) \qquad \lambda(X_i) \exp\left\{-\lambda(X_i)t_i\right\} \int_0^{w_i^*/\xi_i} f\left(\frac{w_i^*}{\varepsilon} \middle| X_i\right) dG(\varepsilon) / \left[1 - F\left(\xi_i \middle| X_i\right)\right].$$

This information can be incorporated to the LLF to obtain an expression similar to equation (2.14). As in the discrete case, estimation is standard MLE.

2.7 Rejected Offers

With information about unemployment spells and accepted wage offers, it is possible to identify nonparametrically the distribution of accepted wage offers and the reservation wage. The distribution of observed wage offers is equal to the truncated distribution of offers with truncation at point ξ. Since we are primarily interested in the underlying distribution of wages, it is important to know if the distribution of wages can be recovered from the observed distribution of accepted wage offers; this property is known as the recoverability condition. Flinn and Heckman (1982) present a comprehensive discussion of this condition. For example, they show that the Normal and Lognormal distributions, commonly used to describe wage distributions, satisfy the recoverability condition. An example of distribution that does not satisfy this condition is the Pareto distribution.

Flinn and Heckman argue that "most econometric models for the analysis of truncated data are non-parametrically underidentified, and some are parametrically underidentified as well." Obviously, it is possible to choose a parametric family for the distribution of wages such that the recoverability condition is satisfied. A simple example will suffice to explain why this choice is, to a certain extent, arbitrary. Let $F(w)$ be a distribution of wages, and define

$$(2.23) \qquad F_\pi\left(w\right) = \left(1 - \pi\right) F\left(w \middle| w \geq \xi\right) + 1(w \geq \xi) + G\left(w\right) 1\left(w < \xi\right)$$

for any $\pi \in (0, 1)$, and for any distribution $G(w)$ satisfying $G(\xi) = \pi$. Observe that $F_\pi(w)$ is a valid distribution function. In addition $F_\pi(w \mid w \geq \xi) = F(w \mid w \geq \xi)$, and $F_\pi(\xi) = \pi$. This example shows that we cannot identify nonparametrically the underlying distribution of wages from the observed distribution of accepted wage offers in that there is a continuum of other wage offer distributions, $F_\pi(w)$ for all $\pi \varepsilon (0,1)$, with the same accepted wage offer distribution. In other words, given the available data we are unable to distinguish between a labor market with a large availability of job offers and a high probability of rejection from a labor market with a small availability of job offers and a high probability of acceptance. In particular, because we do not know α, the unemployment duration data identifies only $\lambda = \alpha[1- F(\xi)]$ but not $F(\xi)$.[6] Some authors have overcome this identification problem by assuming that the distribution of wages belongs to a specified parametric family satisfying the recoverability property. Wolpin (1987) for example, assumes that the distribution of wages is either normal or lognormal. Other authors have fixed the number of per period offers received by the unemployed worker; once the number of offers per period is fixed, π is identified.

Other authors have considered data sets containing more complete information about the search behavior of the unemployed workers. Lancaster and Chesher (1983) and Van den Berg (1992) for example consider a sample containing a subjective measure of the reservation wage. Jensen, et al. (1987) consider a set of data that contains information about the number of applications and number of offers received. In most cases, subjective information or information that requires a perfect recall of the past by the agents is critiqued for being not reliable.

2.8 Structural Dynamic Models of Search

The search models presented so far have assumed a stationary environment. In such cases, we have observed that the behavior of the workers in the labor market can be described by a constant stopping rule. The stationary search model has serious limitations. For example, Meyer (1990) finds evidence for duration dependence in unemployment spells even after controlling for unobserved heterogeneity (see Section 3); this can not be consistent with a stationary model.

Not many models of search in a nonstationary environment have been estimated. The model we describe, Wolpin (1987), will suffice to illustrate the additional level of complexity added by eliminating the assumption of stationarity from the search model. Wolpin (1987) presents a simple model in discrete time. The two differences of this model relative to a standard stationary model are that a) an unemployed worker is allowed to search for a finite number of periods T, after which, if the worker remains unemployed, he is assumed to accept the first job available and b) offer probabilities change over time; we ignore the second source of nonstationarity. Let V_t denote the value of search in period t conditional on entering period t without a job:

$$(2.24) \qquad V_t + E \max \left[w_t, -c + \left(1+r\right)^{-1} V_{t+1} \right] \qquad \text{if } t=1, \ldots, T-1$$

and $V_T = w_T$. From equation (24), we observe that an unemployed worker at time $t <$ T will accept a job offer if it is at least $\xi_t = \{-c + (1+r)^{-1} V_{t+1}\}$, the reservation wage, and the employed worker at time T will accept any wage offer. Intuitively, the reservation wage after $t-1$ periods of search ξ_t is the expected profit obtained from search the next period. If T is finite, the sequence $\{\xi_t\}_{t=1}^{T}$ is decreasing. Observe that

$$(2.25) \qquad \xi_{T-1} = -c + \left(1+r\right)^{-1} E\left[w\right]$$

and $E\left[w \mid w \geq \xi_{T-1}\right] \geq E\left[w \mid w \geq \xi_T\right] = E[w]$. This implies that

$$(2.26) \qquad \xi_{T-2} = -c + \left(1+r\right)^{-1} E\left[w \mid w \geq \xi_{T-1}\right] \geq \xi_{T-1}.$$

In general, assuming $\xi_{T-i} \geq \xi_{T-i+1}$ for $i=2, \ldots, k-1$, it follows that

$$(2.27) \qquad E\left[w \mid w \geq \xi_{T-k+1}\right] \geq E\left[w \mid w \geq \xi_{T-k+2}\right]$$

which implies that

$$(2.28) \qquad \xi_{T-k} = -c + \left(1+r\right)^{-1} E\left[w \mid w \geq \xi_{T-k+1}\right]$$
$$\geq c + \left(1+r\right)^{-1} E\left[w \mid w \geq \xi_{T-k+2}\right] = \xi_{T-k+1}.$$

This proves by induction that the sequence $\{\xi_t\}_{t=1}^{T}$ is decreasing. In this model, the reservation wage changes through time in a systematic and recursive manner described by equations (2.25) through (2.28).

In order to estimate the model, Wolpin assumes that wage data is observed with measurement error. Assume $\ln w_t^* = \ln w_t + v_t$ where w_t^* represents the observed wage, w_t represents the true wage, and v_t represents measurement error. In order to be consistent with our previous notation, we can consider that $v_t = \ln \varepsilon_t$. By assumption, the distribution of wage offers for an individual i, $F(\bullet|X_i)$ is lognormal,[7] and its median is a function of specific observed characteristics of individual i, X_i; in addition, the distribution of the measurement error $G(\bullet)$ is normal and independent of the distribution of wages. In this case, the contribution to the LLF of an observation $\left(t_i, w_i^*, X_i\right)$ from the sample is

(2.29) $$\sum_{\tau=1}^{t_i-1} \log F\left(\xi_{i\tau}|X_i\right) + \log \int_0^{w_i^*/\xi_{it_i}} f\left(\frac{w_i^*}{\varepsilon}\Big|X_i\right) dG\left(\varepsilon\right).$$

For each guess of the parameters in equation (2.29) and for each observation, the sequence of reservation wages $\left\{\xi_t\right\}_{t=1}^{T}$ is obtained from equations (2.25) and (2.28). The value T is also chosen to optimize the value of the LLF of the sample.

Miller (1984) and Pakes (1986) are both dynamic stopping rule models. Miller uses a special structure to solve an occupational choice problem, and Pakes uses a special case with simulation methods to simulate when firms reject the option to renew a patent. While not the same economic problem as discussed in this chapter, they have a very similar generic structure to dynamic search models.

3. Survival Analysis

The analysis of duration data, also known as survival analysis, was developed to describe the timing of events such as when a person dies (thus the name) or when a machine breaks. These statistical techniques have become a subject of increasing interest in economics, especially labor economics. Numerous empirical papers have addressed such issues as unemployment duration (Lancaster, 1979 and Nickell, 1979), the effects of unemployment benefits on the spells of unemployment (Moffitt, 1985; Solon, 1985; Meyer, 1990; and McCall, 1996), turnover (Burdett, et al., 1984), occupational matching (McCall, 1990), retirement (Diamond and Hausman, 1984), strike length (Kennan, 1985 and Gunderson and Melino, 1990), and job search (Jovanovic, 1984). Sometimes this type of technique is regarded as a reduced form for behavioral economic theories like the theory of job search or the theory of job matching. More appropriately, it is a flexible approximation of behavior or an informative method of describing the data.

Consider a random variable T which takes positive values and describes the length of time until an event of interest occurs. Assume that the distribution of duration T can be specified by a distribution function $F(t)$, with associated density function $f(t)$. Other functions of interest associated with the duration process are the survivor function $S(t)=1-F(t)$ which represents the probability that a spell will last a time period t or longer, and the hazard function $\lambda(t)$ which represents the instantaneous probability of the spell ending at t conditional on it not having ended prior to t. The hazard function can be written as

(3.1) $$\lambda\left(t\right) = \lim_{\Delta t \to 0} \frac{P\left(t \le T \le t + \Delta t | T \ge t\right)}{\Delta t} = \lim_{\Delta t \to 0} \frac{\Delta F\left(t\right)}{\Delta t} S\left(t\right)^{-1} = \frac{f\left(t\right)}{S\left(t\right)}.$$

From the previous definition, it is evident that, given a certain density, we can determine the associated hazard function; as we will show later on, the opposite is also true. The derivative of the hazard function $\partial \lambda(t)/\partial t$ is called the duration dependence. If $\partial\lambda(t)/\partial t>0$, there is positive duration dependence, and if $\partial\lambda(t)/\partial t<0$, there is negative duration dependence. Given the hazard rate for a certain duration process, it is easy to determine the associated survival function. Observe that, $\lambda(t) = -d \ln S(t)/dt$. Then, solving a simple differential equation, we obtain

$$(3.2) \qquad S(t) = \exp\left\{-\int_0^t \lambda(z)dz\right\} = \exp\{-\Lambda(T)\}$$

$$f(t) = \lambda(t)S(t) = \lambda(t)\exp\{-\Lambda(t)\}$$

where $\Lambda(t) = \int_0^t \lambda(z)dz$ is the integrated hazard function.

Up to this point we have considered a simple duration process that does not depend on additional covariates. From an economic perspective, the main concern is usually to study the impact of key exogenous variables on the distribution of T. Consider a data set of the form $\{(t_i, X_i)\}_{i=1}^N$ from a population of individuals where t_i represents the spell of time until an event of interest occurs for observation i and X_i represent a vector of characteristics for i. The distribution of duration for agent i can be specified as $F(t|X_i)$ with associated density function $f(t|X_i)$. Similarly, we can define the survivor function $S(t|X_i)=1-F(t|X_i)$ and the hazard function $\lambda(t|X_i)$. Furthermore, in most data sets we should account for the possibility of right censoring. As we have already mentioned in the previous section, this does not represent a problem as long as the censoring process is independent of the data generating process. Consider a sample of the form $\{(t_i, c_i X_i)\}_{i=1}^N$ where c_i is an indicator of whether spell i is censored ($c_i=1$ if spell i is censored). In this case, the probability of an observation (t_i, c_i, X_i) will be $f(t_i|X_i) = \lambda(t_i|X_i) S(t_i|X_i)$ for $c_i=0$ and $S(t_i|X_i)$ for $c_i=1$. Thus, the log likelihood function is

$$LLF = \sum_{i=1}^N (1-c_i)\log f(t_i|X_i) + c_i \log S(t_i|X)$$
$$(3.3)$$
$$= \sum_{i=1}^N (1-c_i)\log \lambda(t_i|X_i) - \Lambda(t_i|X_i).$$

In empirical applications, it is common to start with the specification of the hazard function. Equations (31) and (32) show how to use $\lambda(t|X)$ to specify the log likelihood function. Consider the following hazard function:

$$(3.4) \qquad \lambda(t|X) = \lambda_0(t)\lambda_1(X,\beta)$$

where $\lambda_0(t)$ is called the baseline hazard. If there is enough variation in the X variables and all of them are observable, $\lambda_0(\bullet)$ and $\lambda_1(\bullet)$ are identified up to a constant. This specification is known as the proportional hazard model. It includes most of the parametric models considered in empirical applications such as Lancaster (1979), Solon (1985), and Narendranathan, Nickell, and Stern (1985). In this case, the function $\Lambda(\bullet)$ can be written as

$$(3.5) \qquad \Lambda\left(t\,\middle|\,X\right)=\lambda_1\left(X,\beta\right)\int_0^t \lambda_0\left(s\right)ds\,.$$

Usually $\lambda_1\left(X,\beta\right)$ is modeled as $\exp\{X\beta\}$.[8] In this case we obtain

$$(3.6) \qquad \lambda\left(t\,\middle|\,X\right)=\lambda_0\left(t\right)\exp\{X\beta\}\,.$$

If $\lambda_0(t)=1$, equation (3.6) becomes the hazard function associated with an exponential distribution with parameter $\exp\{X\beta\}$; $F(t)=1-\exp\{-\lambda_1 t\}$. If $\lambda_0(t)=\alpha t^{\alpha-1}$, equation (3.6) becomes the hazard of a Weibull distribution; $F(t)=1-\exp\{-\lambda_1 t^\alpha\}$. The proportional hazard model does not arise from any theoretical economic model. Its popularity is probably due to the fact that the estimated parameters provide a straightforward interpretation: the estimated coefficients are the derivative of the log hazard with respect to the associated X variable.

Up to this point, we have assumed that all the variables that matter for the duration process are included in X and are observed by the econometrician. Even in early work (Lancaster, 1979 and Lancaster and Nickell, 1980), researchers were aware that ignoring the possibility of omitted variables in a duration model can heavily bias the included parameter estimates and lead to misleading conclusions. To illustrate this point, suppose that the proportional hazard model is the correct specification for the study of unemployment spells. In addition, assume that the econometrician does not observe all the variables affecting the duration of unemployment; i.e., $\lambda(t \mid X) = \exp\{X\beta+\varepsilon\}$ where ε measures the effect of omitted variables. For the sake of concreteness, assume the ε takes on two values, $\varepsilon^+>\varepsilon^-$, and that $\Pr[\varepsilon=\varepsilon^+] = \Pr[\varepsilon=\varepsilon^-] = 2$ at time zero. As the process evolves, people with high values of $\varepsilon(\varepsilon^+)$ will leave the sample faster than people with low values $\varepsilon(=\varepsilon^-)$. This will change the relative proportions of people (with respect to ε) toward people with low values of ε. As time goes by, since the average value of ε is falling, the average hazard rate will fall. Thus, we will observe decreasing hazards, even after controlling for observed heterogeneity (the X's) even though the hazard for each particular worker is constant over time. Consequently, ignoring the problem of omitted variables will lead to negative duration dependence bias. Because of the nonlinearity of the model, it also leads to inconsistent estimates of all of the model's parameters (Flinn and Heckman, 1982).

In order to be able to identify the effects of unobservables and observables, it is necessary to make explicit assumptions about the way in which they interact.[9] Assume then that the true specification of the hazard, for a certain agent i in the sample, is as follows:

(3.7)
$$\lambda\left(t\middle|X_{i},v_{i}\right)=\lambda\left(t\middle|X_{i}\right)v_{i}=\lambda_{0}\left(t\right)\lambda_{1}\left(X_{i},\beta\right)v_{i}$$

where X represents the set of observed variables, and $v_{i}=\exp\{\varepsilon_{i}\}$ summarizes the effect of any other variable that affects the duration process and is not observed (unobserved heterogeneity). Then the survival function is

(3.8)
$$S\left(t\middle|X_{i},v_{i}\right)=\exp\left\{-\int_{0}^{t}\lambda\left(z\middle|X_{i},v_{i}\right)dz\right\}=\exp\left\{-\Lambda\left(t\middle|X_{i},v_{i}\right)\right\}$$
$$=\exp\left\{-\Lambda\left(t\middle|X_{i}\right)v_{i}\right\},$$
$$f\left(t_{i}\middle|X_{i},v_{i}\right)=\lambda\left(t\middle|X_{i},v_{i}\right)S\left(t\middle|X_{i},v_{i}\right)$$

In this case, the LLF for the sample $\left\{t_{i},c_{i},X_{i}v_{i}\right\}_{i=1}^{N}$ is

(3.9)
$$\sum_{i=1}^{N}\left(1-c_{i}\right)\log f\left(t_{i}\middle|X_{i},v_{i}\right)+c_{i}\log S\left(t_{i}\middle|X_{i},v_{i}\right)$$

In principle, this expression cannot be used to estimate the model because the values of $\left\{v_{i}\right\}_{i=1}^{N}$ are not observed. This problem can be overcome if the distribution generating the unobserved heterogeneity is known. Then we can define a LLF based on the marginal probabilities once the unobserved heterogeneity has been integrated out. More precisely, assume that v_{i} represents a particular realization from a distribution $G(\bullet)$ independent of X_{i}. It is usual in this case to choose the normalization $E(v)=1$.[10] We can define

(3.10)
$$S\left(t\middle|X\right)=\int S\left(t\middle|X,v\right)dG\left(v\right)$$
$$=\int \exp\left\{-\Lambda\left(t\middle|X\right)v\right\}dG\left(v\right)$$
$$=M_{v}\left[-\Lambda\left(t\middle|X\right)\right]$$

and

$$f(t|X) = \frac{-\partial S(t|X)}{\partial t}$$

(3.11)

$$= \lambda(t|X) \int v \exp\{-\Lambda(t|X)v\} dG(v)$$

$$= \lambda(t|X) M_v^{(1)} \left[-\Lambda(t|X)\right]$$

where $M_v[\bullet]$ and $M_v^{(1)}[\bullet]$ represent the moment generating function of v and its derivative, respectively.[11] We can now specify the LLF for the sample $\{t_i, c_i, X_i\}_{i=1}^N$ using the integrated, or marginal probabilities:

$$LLF = \sum_{i=1}^N (1 - c_i) \log f(t_i|X_i) + c_i \log S(t_i|X_i)$$

(3.12)

$$= \sum_{i=1}^N (1 - c_i)\left\{\log \lambda(t|X) + \log M_v^{(1)}\left[-\Lambda(t|X)\right]\right\} + c_i \log M_v\left[-\Lambda(t|X)\right].$$

Lancaster (1979) lets

(3.13) $$\lambda(t|X_i, v_o) = \alpha t^{\alpha-1} \mu_i v_i$$

where $\mu_i = \exp\{X_i\beta\}$ and the unobserved heterogeneity has a density $g(v) \propto v^{\sigma-1} \exp\{-v\sigma\}$. In this case, $M_v[z] = [1-(z/\sigma)]^{-\sigma}$ and we obtain:

(3.14) $$S(t|X) = M_v\left[-\Lambda(t|X)\right] = \left(1 + \frac{\mu((t)}{\sigma}\right)^{-\sigma}$$

where $\mu_i = \exp\{X_i\beta\}$ and $I(t) = \int_0^t \alpha t^{\alpha-1} dt$. From this expression, it is straightforward to obtain $f(t|X)$ and to construct the LLF of the sample. Using MLE, we can obtain consistent estimators of the parameters associated with the duration process (α, β, σ).

It is important to recognize the significance of controlling for unobserved heterogeneity. The true hazard for an individual with unobserved heterogeneity v is

(3.15) $$\lambda(t|X, v) = \alpha t^{\alpha-1} \mu v.$$

By controlling for unobserved heterogeneity, we consistently estimate the expected hazard

(3.16) $$\lambda\left(t\,|\,X\right)=E_{v}\left\{\lambda\left(t\,|\,X,v\right)\right\}=\alpha t^{\alpha-1}\mu\,.$$

On the other hand, if we control just for the observed characteristics X, the survival function of the duration process is given in equation (3.14) with associated hazard

(3.17) $$\lambda^{*}\left(t\,|\,X\right)=\frac{\partial\log S\left(t\,|\,X\right)}{\partial t}=\alpha t^{a-1}\mu S\left(t\,|\,X\right)^{1/\sigma}=\lambda\left(t\,|\,X\right)S\left(t\,|\,X\right)^{1/\sigma}$$

If we do not control for unobserved heterogeneity, we obtain a consistent estimator for $\lambda^{*}(\bullet)$ in equation (3.17). As t increases, the survival probability goes to zero and the hazard $\lambda^{*}(t|X)$ decreases over time with respect to the true hazard $\lambda(t|X)$; this confirms our previous intuition. This argument can be generalized easily by observing that

(3.18) $$\lambda^{*}\left(t\,|\,X\right)=E\left(\lambda(t|X,v)\,|\,T>t\right)=\lambda(t|X)\,E\left(v|T>t\right)$$

where T represents the time of employment and $E(v|T>t)$ represents the expected value of the unobserved heterogeneity among the remaining unemployed workers at time t. Under the assumption that v is independent of the observed heterogeneity, this expectation should be decreasing over time.

We have learned that it is important to take into account the possibility of unobserved heterogeneity. This is especially true in many applications of duration analysis to labor economics in which the concern has been to study the effect of unemployment benefits or the behavior of the unemployed workers over the spell of unemployment. In this sense, we have shown that by ignoring the existence of unobserved heterogeneity in the sample, we are potentially estimating more negative duration dependence than actually exists.

In the previous example, given data on spell duration and observed characteristics of the workers, it was possible to estimate the distribution of unobserved heterogeneity, the baseline hazard, and the effect of observed characteristics on the probability of leaving the unemployment state. In order to achieve that goal, it was necessary to make strong parametric assumptions about the form of the hazard function and the distribution of unobserved heterogeneity. In most cases, we may have little prior information about the correct distribution of unobserved heterogeneity, and we therefore may produce misleading results by misspecifying this distribution. It is then pertinent to ask to what extent the available data can provide a nonparametric identification of each one of the relevant functions separately. Lancaster and Nickell (1979) find that "it seems in practice very difficult to distinguish between the effects of heterogeneity and the effect of pure time variation in the hazard function." Elbers and Ridder (1982) show that, at least for the proportional hazard specification, it is possible to identify nonparametrically the distribution of unobserved heterogeneity independently of the other components of the duration process as long as there is enough variation in the observed characteristics. The intuition for this result is that changes in the duration variable and the covariates allow us to trace out the different components of the hazard. This result depends crucially on the form of the proportional hazard model, in particular, the separability of the hazard into one function of the duration, another of the covariates, and the independence of the unobserved characteristics with respect to the observed ones.[12] Gurmu, Rilstone and Stern (1996) present a similar result for the proportional hazard model allowing for the possibility of interactions between t and some of the covariates. The identification result of Elbers and Ridder (1982) and Heckman and Singer (1984a) opens the possibility of nonparametric estimation of the distribution of the unobserved heterogeneity.

Authors like Lancaster (1979) and Heckman and Singer (1984b) have shown that ignoring unobserved heterogeneity can lead to biased estimates of the parameters of the hazard function. In addition, Heckman and Singer (1984b) have shown that different specifications for the distribution of the unobserved heterogeneity can lead to very different estimates. This finding led them to propose a flexible nonparametric method to control for unobserved heterogeneity. In this paper we pursue a heuristic description of this method. Readers interested in a more technical description should refer to the original paper. From equation (41), we obtain

$$(3.19) \quad LLF = \sum_{i=1}^{N} (1-c_i) \left\{ \log \lambda (t|X) + \log M_v^{(1)} \left[-\Lambda (t|X) \right] \right\} + c_i \log M_v \left[-\Lambda (t|X) \right]$$

where

$$(3.20) \quad \begin{aligned} M_v \left[-\Lambda (t|X) \right] &= \int \exp \left\{ -\Lambda (t|X) v \right\} dG(v) \\ M_v^{(1)} \left[-\Lambda (t|X) \right] &= \int v \exp \left\{ -\Lambda (t|X) v \right\} dG(v). \end{aligned}$$

The Heckman and Singer approach consists of approximating the unknown distribution of unobserved heterogeneity $G(v)$ with a discrete distribution with positive probability mass at a finite number of points. Consider then the set of points $\{v_1, v_2,..., v_k\}$ with probability mass $\pi_j > 0$ associated to v_j, $j = 1, ..., k$ and $\sum_{j=1}^{k} \pi_i = 1$. Substituting the discrete approximation of $G(v)$ in equation (3.20), we obtain

$$(3.21) \quad \begin{aligned} \hat{M}_v \left[-\Lambda (t|X) \right] &= \sum_{j=1}^{k} \pi_j \exp \left\{ -\Lambda (t|X) v_j \right\} \\ \hat{M}_v^{(1)} \left[-\Lambda (t|X) \right] &= \sum_{j=1}^{k} \pi_j v_j \exp \left\{ -\Lambda (t|X) v_j \right\} \end{aligned}$$

where $\hat{M}_v[\cdot]$ and $\hat{M}_v^{(1)}[\cdot]$ represent the approximations to the true functions, $M_v[\cdot]$ and $\hat{M}_v^{(1)}[\cdot]$ respectively. Substituting of the approximations, $\hat{M}_v[\cdot]$ and $\hat{M}_v^{(1)}[\cdot]$ for the true functions, $\hat{M}_v[\cdot]$ and $\hat{M}_v^{(1)}[\cdot]$ in equation (3.19), we obtain an approximation for the LLF,

(3.22)
$$LLF_k = \sum_{i=1}^{N}(1-c_i)\left\{\log\lambda(t|X)+\log\hat{M}_v^{(1)}\left[-\Lambda(t|X)\right]\right\}$$
$$+c_i\log\hat{M}_v\left[-\Lambda(t|X)\right].$$

The method proceeds by obtaining estimators of $\{v_j,\pi_j\}_{j=1}^{k}$ and estimators of the parameters of the hazard function. These estimators will be the values that maximize equation (3.22). Observe that this problem is not a standard MLE problem because the number of parameters necessary to estimate the approximate distribution of unobserved heterogeneity, $2k$, can be in principle infinite and the asymptotics rely on $k \to \infty$. In practice, the estimation strategy consists of choosing the k for which LLF_k stops growing in k. Sometimes researchers use a criterion such as the Akaike number; most of the time researchers increase k until the LLF stops growing (Card and Sullivan, 1988; Gunderson and Melino, 1990; and Gritz, 1993) or fix k ahead of time (Heckman and Walker, 1990; Behrman, Sickles, and Taubman, 1990; and Johnson and Ondrich, 1990). One major criticism of this approach is the lack of asymptotic distribution theory for the parameters estimated. In practice, the results of the estimation will depend on the parameters of the unobserved heterogeneity.

Some authors, as for example Han and Hausman (1990) and Meyer (1990), have shown that a nonflexible specification of the baseline function $\lambda_0(t)$ can bias the estimates of the other parameters. They suggest to estimate $\lambda_0(t)$ semi-parametrically assuming that it can be represented as a step function. Furthermore, these authors have argued that the biases in the proportional hazard model may be larger for misspecification of the baseline hazard than for misspecification of heterogeneity distribution. For a similar model, Sueyoshi (1992) presents Monte Carlo evidence indicating that estimates are sensitive to misspecification of the unobserved heterogeneity distribution. In addition, this type of misspecification yields biased estimates of the baseline function $\lambda_0(t)$. In conclusion, the literature on this subject shows that both types of misspecification are important and should be taken into account when estimating a proportional hazard model.[13]

4.   Empirical Equilibrium Search Models

The theoretical search models described in section two assume that unemployed workers search sequentially for a job. The worker accepts the first offer above his reservation wage and remains in that job forever. These models are formally inconsistent because each (homogeneous) firm acting optimally will offer a wage which depends upon only the distribution of reservation wages. If all firms face the same distribution of reservation wages, each will offer the same wage, and there will be a degenerate distribution of wage offers. Also, there is no search because either the worker's reservation wage is above the common wage offer and the first wage offer received is always accepted or the worker's reservation wage is below the common wage offer and he does not search. These implications are at odds with the phenomena that these models try to explain, the search behavior of the agents as well as the variation in wages. This inconsistency was first pointed out by Diamond (1971).

In order to respond to Diamond's critique, several authors have developed theoretical models that depict wage (or price) dispersion and search as an equilibrium outcome (Reinganum, 1979; Albrecht and Axell, 1984; Burdett and Judd, 1983; and Mortensen, 1990). These equilibrium models are variations of the more simple models presented in Section 2. An important difference is the incorporation of the optimal behavior of firms into the models. Several options have been suggested in order to obtain a nondegenerate distribution of wages at equilibrium. For example, some models assume that workers may face several job offers simultaneously. In this case, workers with more than one job offer are able to bargain for a wage above the reservation wage (Burdett and Judd, 1983). Others depict a framework with heterogeneous agents. For example, Albrecht and Axell (1984) assume that the firms in the market differ in their productivity and the agents, searching sequentially for a job, differ in their valuation of leisure. In this scenario, it may be optimal for firms that differ in their productivity to have different wage policies.[14] Mortensen (1990) models agents searching sequentially for a job when unemployed and when employed, moving from a job to a new one offering a higher wage. In this framework, firms face a tradeoff between short run and long run profits. A firm offering high wages keeps workers for a longer period of time than a firm offering lower wages but extracts a smaller surplus per period from each worker. Intuitively, different wage policies can be optimal for the firms. As a result, the equilibrium in this model is characterized by a nondegenerate continuous distribution of wage offers where each wage in the support of this distribution represents an optimal wage policy for the firm.

Equilibrium models of search have not been incorporated to the empirical literature until recently. Eckstein and Wolpin (1990) estimate a generalization of the Albrecht and Axell model. Eckstein and Wolpin note that "estimating equilibrium labor market models does not require data on both workers and firms, although it does require assumptions about the structure of the distributions of preferences and technology." More recently, several other authors have estimated the Mortensen model with homogeneous agents, or different generalizations of this model with heterogeneous agents.

We begin this section with a description of the Eckstein and Wolpin model. Next, we present several attempts to estimate the Mortensen model. We conclude the section pointing out some of the shortcomings of the existing literature and some possible avenues for future research.

4.1 Eckstein and Wolpin

Eckstein and Wolpin (1990) represents the first attempt to estimate an equilibrium model. Individuals work in a market where firms differ in their productivity. All workers have the same productivity at the same firms, i.e., they are homogeneous with respect to their market skills, but are heterogeneous with respect to their nonmarket productivity, or preferences for leisure. Individual preferences and firm productivity are private information, although the distribution of preferences over individuals and the distribution of wage offers are known to all agents. There are $n+1$ types of individuals with many people of the same type and many firms with heterogeneous productivities. The problem of the worker is as described in Section 2, and each firm maximizes intertemporal profits.

A Nash equilibrium wage offer distribution is shown to exist. Wage dispersion arises due to heterogeneity in worker tastes for leisure and differences in productivity across firms. Different worker types have different reservation wages. In addition values between two adjacent reservation wages are not optimal wage offers for the firms. Consequently, the distribution of wages in equilibrium has a discrete support that corresponds to the reservation wages of the different worker types. More productive firms offer high wages, attracting high reservation wage types in addition to the low reservation wage types. The model also predicts that an average high reservation wage worker spends more time looking for a job and eventually obtains a higher wage; this contradicts other theoretical models that rely on unobserved heterogeneity to generate a negative correlation between unemployment spell length and accepted wage offer.

In order to be able to estimate the model, the authors introduce several parametric assumptions about the distribution of productivity among firms and the distribution of workers types. The model is estimated first just using information on duration of unemployment and then using information on duration of unemployment and accepted wage offers. In order to be able to fit the wage data to a discrete distribution with $n+1$ points of support, the authors assume that wages are measured with errors. A novel feature of this paper is that the restrictions imposed by the equilibrium are incorporated to the estimation procedure. However, any heterogeneity in productivity across workers, whether observed or unobserved, would cause the distribution of wage offers to have more than $n+1$ points of support. Thus, their implementation of the model relies upon an unreasonable assumption about individuals. Both estimated equilibrium models perform poorly. In fact, measurement error accounts for almost all of the dispersion in observed wages. Nevertheless, the model estimated with duration data is used to simulate the effects of alternative levels of the minimum wage on unemployment and wages.

4.2 Mortensen Model

In this section, we present a simple version of the equilibrium model described in Mortensen (1990). The economy consists of a continuum of homogeneous workers and homogeneous firms. Firms set wages and unemployed and employed workers search for wage offers among firms.

Workers are infinite-lived wealth maximizing agents. Unemployment income net of search cost is given by b. Job offers arrive from a Poisson process with parameter α_u if the worker is unemployed and α_e if employed. When employed, a worker is laid off at rate δ. Assume that each worker faces a known, stationary, nondegenerate distribution of wages $F(w)$ with a finite mean. Mortensen and Neumann (1988) show that the problem of the worker can be characterized by a reservation wage ξ. Analytically, the reservation wage is the unique solution to

$$(4.1) \qquad \xi = b + \left(\alpha_u - \alpha_e \right) \int_\xi^\infty \frac{1 - F(w)}{\delta + \alpha_e \left[1 - F(w) \right]} dw.$$

An unemployed worker accepts any wage offer above the reservation wage, and an employed worker accepts any wage offer that exceeds his current wage.

In this framework, there is a flow of workers between different states, employment and unemployment, and among different jobs. Let m denote the measure of workers in the economy and u denote the measure of them that are unemployed. The instantaneous flow of workers from unemployment to employment is $\alpha_u [1 - F(\xi^-)]u$,[15] the product of the offer arrival rate, the acceptance probability, and the measure of unemployed workers. Similarly, the instantaneous flow of workers from employment to unemployment is equal to $\delta(m - u)$. If the economy is at its steady state, these two flows should be equal implying

$$(4.2) \qquad u = \frac{m}{\delta + \alpha_u \left[1 - F(\xi^-) \right]}.$$

Let $G(w)$ represent the fraction of all unemployed workers who earn wage w or less. An expression for $G(w)$ can be obtained at the steady state. Observe that the measure of workers with wage less or equal to w is $G(w)(m - u)$ and should be constant in steady state. On the one hand, the flow of workers into this group, that is those unemployed workers that accept a wage less than or equal to w, is $\alpha_u[F(w) - F(\xi^-)]u$. On the other hand, the flow of workers out of this group is the sum of those in the group who become unemployed, $\delta G(w)(m - u)$ and those who receive a job offer that exceeds w, $\alpha_e[1-F(w)]\,G(w)(m-u)$. Since the inflow and outflow should be equal in steady state,

(4.3) $$G(w)=\frac{F(w)-F(\xi^-)}{\left[1-F(\xi^-)\right]}\frac{\delta}{\delta+\alpha_e\left[1-F(w)\right]}.$$

The distribution in equation (4.3) is useful to determine the supply of labor to firms. Observe that $F(w)-F(w-\varepsilon)$ is a measure of the percentage of wage offers within the range $(w-\varepsilon, w)$. On the other hand, $[G(w)-G(w-\varepsilon)](m-u)$ is a measure of the number of workers with wages within the range $(w-\varepsilon, w)$. Consequently, the steady state number of workers per firm offering a wage w can be defined as

(4.4) $$l(w)-\lim_{\varepsilon\to 0}\frac{\left[G(w)-G(w-\varepsilon)\right](m-u)}{F(w)-F(w-\varepsilon)}.$$

The steady-state profit flow earned by a firm who offers a wage w is

(4.5) $$\pi(w;p)=(p-w)l(w),$$

the product of the per-worker profit times the steady state number of workers. Firms maximize the steady state level of benefits.

In this framework, a steady-state market equilibrium is a reservation wage ξ for the workers and a market wage offer distribution $F(\bullet)$. The equilibrium conditions are that the reservation wage maximizes the expected wealth for each worker, i.e., it satisfies equation (4.1) given $F(\bullet)$, and every wage offer in the support of $F(\bullet)$ maximizes the steady state level of profits of the firm, i.e. it satisfies equation (4.5).

Observe that firms are allowed to make profits. All firms should earn the same amount of profits in equilibrium. Consequently $\pi(w;p)$ should be constant for any wage in the support of $F(\bullet)$, the distribution of wage offers in equilibrium. A nice feature of this model is that a closed form solution for $F(\bullet)$ is obtained (see Mortensen, 1990):

(4.6)
$$F(W)=\left[\frac{1+k_e}{k_e}\right]\left[1-\left[\frac{p-w}{p-\xi}\right]^{1/2}\right]\forall w\in[\xi,h],$$
$$\text{with } h=p-\left[\frac{1}{(1+k_e)}\right]^2(p-\xi),\text{ and } k_e=\frac{a_i}{\delta}.$$

$F(\bullet)$ is continuous with connected support.[16] It can be shown that the distribution of wage offers $F(\bullet)$ and the distribution of earnings $G(\bullet)$ have increasing densities $f(\bullet)$

and $g(\bullet)$, respectively. Also, a firm never offers wages below the reservation wage; consequently all wage offers are accepted. In addition, transitions from one job to another should result in an increase in the wage of the worker, and wage growth on the job is not allowed.[17]

4.2.1 Fit of the Model. Several authors have estimated Mortensen's equilibrium model or generalizations of it. A rigorous analysis of the estimation and identification of the model with homogeneous agents has been conducted by Christensen and Kiefer (1994). They show that the model can be estimated, using MLE techniques, with a data set containing unemployment duration, reemployment wage, and job duration from a random sample of workers.

The probability of a spell of unemployment of duration t_i^u is equal to $\alpha_u \exp\{-\alpha_u t_i^u\}$. Since firms never post offers below the reservation wage, offers from any firm to an unemployed worker are always accepted. In addition, the probability of a wage offer w_i is equal to $f(w_i)$. The probability of a spell of employment of duration t_i^e, given that the wage at the present job is w_i, can be defined as,

$$(4.7) \qquad \left(\delta + \alpha_e \left[1 - F(w_i)\right]\right) \exp\left\{-\left(\delta + \alpha_e \left[1 - F(w_i)\right]\right) t_i^u\right\}$$

The contribution to the likelihood function of an observation $\left(t_i^u, w_i, t_i^e\right)$ is the product of these three probabilities:

$$(4.8) \qquad \begin{aligned} L_i(\theta) &= \alpha_u \exp\left\{-\alpha_u t_i^u\right\} \bullet f(w_i) \bullet \\ &\left(\delta + \alpha_e \left[1 - F(w_i)\right]\right) \exp\left\{-\left(\delta + \alpha_e \left[1 - F(w_i)\right]\right) t_i^u\right\} \end{aligned}$$

where $\theta = (\alpha_u, \alpha_e, \delta, p, b)$ represents the parameters of the structural model to be estimated.

The restrictions imposed by equilibrium are implicitly stated in equations (4.1) and (4.5) and give rise to the closed form solution for the distribution of wages described in equation (4.6). Observe that equation (4.6) implies that any observed wage w_i belongs to the interval $[\xi, h]$. Using the same arguments presented in Section 2.2, we can consider the estimators $\hat{\xi} = w_{min}$ and $\hat{h} = w_{max}$ for ξ and h, where w_{min} and w_{max} represent the minimum and maximum wage observed in the sample, respectively. Assuming wages are observed without measurement error, these estimators are consistent and converge at a rate faster than $\sqrt{n}$. As explained in Section 2.2, the estimators, $\hat{\xi}$ and $\hat{h}$, can be substituted directly in the likelihood function. After this, we obtain an expression that depends only on α_u, α_e, and δ. These remaining parameters can be estimated using MLE. Christensen and Kiefer (1994) present a more exhaustive description of these issues.

A different way to approach this problem is to assume that wages are measured with error. This approach is essentially the same that we summarized in Section 2.3 with the main distinction being that the distribution of wages is obtained here endogenously. This technique has been applied to this framework by Van den Berg and Ridder (1993b).

In order to improve the fit of the model to the data, it is necessary to introduce changes in the basic model allowing for the possibility of heterogeneous agents. Bowlus, Kiefer and Neumann (1995a, b) consider the case of homogeneous workers and a finite number of firm types differing in productivity. Koning, Ridder and Van den Berg (1995) present a model in which the labor market is segmented and consists of a large number of separate submarkets within which workers and firms are homogeneous.

Bowlus, Kiefer and Neumann (1995a, b) assume that there are Q types of firms with productivity $p_1 < p_2 < ... < p_Q$, and let π_j, $j=1, ..., Q$, represent the fraction of firms having productivity p_j or less. This generalization of the homogeneous model is described in Mortensen (1990).[18] The equilibrium in this case is defined as in the homogeneous case with the distinction that here firms of the same productivity should have the same profits but firms of different productivities may have different profits. Mortensen shows that the equilibrium wage distribution is

(4.9) $$F(w) = F_j(w) \qquad\qquad \forall w \in \left[w_{lj}, w_{hj} \right]$$

where

(4.10) $$F_j = (w) = \frac{1+k_e}{k_e} \left[1 - \frac{1+k_e\left[1 - \pi_{j-1} \right]}{1+k_e} \right] \left[\frac{p_j - w}{p_j - w_{hj-1}} \right], \forall w \in \left[w_{lj}, w_{hj} \right],$$

and the equilibrium implies that $w_{l1} = \xi$, and $w_{hj-1} = w_{lj} \forall j$; that is, firms with higher productivity offer higher wages. The set of pairs $\left\{ p_j, \pi_j \right\}_{j=1}^{Q}$ have to be estimated with the rest of parameters of the model. The wage policies of different firm types create discontinuities in the wage offer distribution; for this reason, non standard techniques have to be used to estimate the model.

Koning, Ridder and Van den Berg (1995) address the problem of unobserved heterogeneity from a different perspective. They assume that there is a large number of separate markets in which workers and firms meet. Within each market workers and firms are homogeneous, and an equilibrium wage distribution of the form presented in equation (4.6) exists. The productivity of firms among different segmented markets follows a continuous distribution. They effectively have a continuum of submarkets which differ in the value of productivity of workers.

The econometrician observes a mixture of the information generated in different markets. In particular, the value of productivity p at a certain market is not observed by the econometrician and varies among different markets. In this case, assuming that $p \sim H(\bullet)$, the contribution to the likelihood function of an observation $\left(t_i^u, w_i, t_i^e\right)$ is

$$(4.11) \qquad\qquad \int L_i(\theta)\, dH(p)$$

with $L_i(\theta)$ defined as in equation (4.8). The authors assume that $H(p)$ follows a lognormal distribution. The parameters associated with this distribution have to be estimated jointly with the rest of the parameters of the model. Van den Berg and Ridder (1993b) follow a similar approach.

4.3 Policy Implications

The most common policy application of the equilibrium search models has been the study of the labor market effects of an increase in the minimum wage. Eckstein and Wolpin (1990) simulate the effect of different values of the minimum wage finding that an increase in the minimum wage increases the unemployment rate as well as the expected duration of unemployment. In particular, an increase in the minimum wage reduces the number of employers by expelling from the market the less productive ones. This produces a reduction in the rate of job offer arrival per worker and consequently increases the expected duration of unemployment per-worker. Intuitively, the same result should hold in the model presented by Bowlus, Kiefer and Neumann (1995a, b). Taking into account the poor fit of the model to the data, Eckstein and Wolpin recommend caution when interpreting their quantitative results.

Koning, Ridder and Van den Berg (1995) use data from the Netherlands to estimate their model with only between market heterogeneity. Intuitively, this can be interpreted as a situation in which workers with the same productivity interact in the same market and do not have the option of moving to markets with higher productivity. Thus, an increase in the minimum wage will result in the closure of the markets with the lower productivity. Consequently, workers in these markets will become unemployed without any chance of getting a job in the future. Koning, Ridder and Van den Berg use the estimated model to examine the effect of changes in the mandatory minimum wage on the magnitude of structural unemployment. They find that "a 10 percent increase in the minimum wage increases structural unemployment from 5.2 percent to 10.1 percent."

While in Eckstein and Wolpin (1990) and Bowlus, Kiefer and Neumann (1995a, b) an increase in the minimum wage produces an increase in the average length of unemployment spells, in Koning, Ridder and Van den Berg (1995) or Van den Berg and Ridder (1993b) it produces an increase in the number of workers that are permanently unemployed. This difference is due to differences in the theoretical models; thus the data provides no information about which is correct.[19] These different implications about the effect of an increase in the minimum wage are relevant for policy analysis.

The efforts of several authors in estimating equilibrium models of search represent the most recent contributions to the empirical search literature. The equilibrium models with homogeneous agents produce a bad fit of the data. Once the hypothesis about homogeneous productivity on the model of Mortensen is removed, there are several generalizations that, in principle, are not distinguishable and that can fit the data similarly. We see this as an unpleasant feature of the existing literature; this is an issue to be addressed in future research. One possible way to deal with this problem is to exploit richer data sets, possibly including also information about firm behavior. Another possible avenue of research consists of investigating the nonparametric identification of equilibrium models.

5. Conclusions

The field of empirical search models is an important and growing field. There has been significant progress made in developing models to deal with measurement error, observed and unobserved heterogeneity, dynamics, and equilibrium conditions. While we have much hope for this field, we believe there to be two significant problems to overcome in working with these models. The first is the need for powerful computers. This need is being met over time although no faster than models become more demanding of computer time. In particular, handling observed and unobserved heterogeneity and many nonparametric and semiparametric methods require very large computer resources.

The other problem is limited data. Presently, we are using essentially spell length data and accepted wage data to identify all of the parameters of a search model. In even the simplest model, such data can not separately identify a search cost and discount rate. Allowing for important other functions implied by unobserved heterogeneity or equilibrium may be asking too much of the limited data available. We feel it would be useful to identify other potential (possibly new) sources of data with direct information on possibly search cost, rejected offers, or firm behavior.

Nevertheless, we enthusiastically encourage others to pursue this field. In particular, we think there is significant work to be done on identification, testing, nonparametrics, and data acquisition. We are also excited about empirical implementation of equilibrium models though we see significant identification issues not yet addressed.

Notes

1. If the wage offer distribution is twice continuously differentiable, then $f(\xi) > 0$ is a sufficient condition.

2. In order to be able to identify the distribution of wages from the distribution of accepted wage offers certain regularity conditions are needed. We will elaborate on this topic in the section about rejected offers. Flinn and Heckman (1982) present an extensive discussion of this issue.

3. Ignoring unobserved heterogeneity is equivalent to assuming that the distribution is degenerate. This is a much stronger assumption than needs to be made.

4. Eckstein and Wolpin (1990) and Engberg (1994) evaluate the reservation wage for each value of unobserved heterogeneity. Van den Berg and Ridder (1993a) have closed form solutions to equation (2.15) that preclude evaluating the reservation wage conditional on v.

5. This problem could be mitigated by linking UI administrative data with wage data. However, this is not done typically.

6. Note that even if we assume $\alpha=1$, there is too much freedom in choice of $G(\bullet)$ to nonparametrically identify $F(\bullet)$.

7. Observe that, in principle, the assumption that agents accept any offer after T implies that the distribution of wage offers can be identified nonparametrically by observing the accepted wage offers and spell lengths after this time.

8. In particular, this specification is equivalent to the one introduced by Cox (1972).

9. See Heckman (1991) for an illuminating review of this issue.

10. Observe that this is not a restriction because a constant is included in $X_i\beta$, and any $E(v) \neq 1$ would be captured in the constant.

11. For some distributions G, the moment generating function does not exist. More generally $M_v[-\Lambda(t \mid X)]$ is the Laplace transform of G.

12. A similar result in the context of risk models can be found in Heckman and Honore (1989).

13. Papers that use this approach are Holt, Merwin, and Stern (1996) and McCall (1996).

14. Burdett and Judd (1994) show that the model in Albrecht and Axell (1984) works only if there is a finite mass of people with zero search costs. One might consider this to be an unreasonable assumption.

15. The wage offer distribution $F(\bullet)$ might have a discontinuity at ξ. Thus, we use the notation ξ^- to indicate a wage infinitesimally less than ξ.

16. Notice that, if there are a mass of employers offering the same wage in equilibrium, then it is optimal for each of these employers to increase its wage offer by a small amount in order to attract workers from other employers.

17. The model does not consider the possibility of entry of new firms into the market. If we allow for this possibility, entry will occur until the point in which profits are not possible for new entrants. In this case, the most one can do is to choose a cost of entry consistent with the model, that is $c = \pi^* / r$ where π^* represents the flow of profits at the steady state equilibrium.

18. The informational structure is important in order to compute the equilibrium. Here workers and firms know the distribution of wage offers but they have no information about each other's type.

19. A nonnested testing procedure would be necessary to test these models against each other.

References

Albrecht, J. W. and B. Axell. "An Equilibrium Model of Search Unemployment." *Journal of Political Economy* 92 (1984): 824–840.

Behrman, J. R. Sickles, and P. Taubman. "Age-Specific Death Rates with Tobacco Smoking and Occupational Activity: Sensitivity to Sample Length, Functional Form, and Unobserved Fraility." *Demography* 27 (1990): 267–284.

Bowlus, A. J., N. M. Kiefer, and G. R. Neumann. "Estimation of Equilibrium Wage Distributions with Heterogeneity." *Journal of Applied Econometrics* 10 (1995): S119–S131. (a)

——. "Fitting Equilibrium Search Models to Labor Market Data." Unpublished manuscript, University of Iowa, 1995 (b).

Burdett, K. and K. Judd. "Equilibrium Price Dispersion." *Econometrica* 51 (1983): 955–970.

Burdett, K., N. Kiefer, D. Mortensen, and G. Neumann. "Earnings, Unemployment and the Allocation of Time over Time." *Review of Economic Studies* 51 (1984): 559–578.

Card, D. and D. Sullivan. "Measuring the Effect of Subsidized Training Programs on Movements In and Out of Employment." *Econometrica* 56 (1988): 497–531.

Christensen, B. J. and N. M. Kiefer. "The Exact Likelihood Function for an Empirical Job Search Model." *Econometric Theory* 7 (1991): 464–486.

———. "Measurement Error in the Prototypal Job-Search Model." *Journal of Labor Economics* 12 (1994): 618–639.

Cox, D. R. "Regression Models and Life Tables." *Journal of the Royal Statistical Society*, Series B, 34 (1972): 187–220.

Diamond, P. "A Model of Price Adjustment." *Journal of Economic Theory* 3 (1971): 156–168.

Diamond, P. and J. Hausman. "Individual Retirement and Savings Behavior." *Journal of Public Economics* 23 (1984): 81–114.

Eckstein, Z. and K. I. Wolpin. "Estimating a Market Equilibrium Search Model from Panel Data on Individuals." *Econometrica* 58 (1990): 783–808.

Elbers, C. and G. Ridder. "True and Spurious Duration Dependence: The Identifiability of the Proportional Hazard Model." *Review of Economic Studies* 49 (1982): 403–410.

Engberg, J. B. "Search Duration, Accepted Wages and Selection Bias." Unpublished manuscript, Heinz School, Carnegie Mellon University, 1994.

Flinn, C. and J. J. Heckman. "New Methods for Analyzing Structural Models of Labor Force Dynamics." *Journal of Econometrics* 18 (1982): 115–168.

Gritz, M. "The Impact of Training on the Frequency and Duration of Employment." *Journal of Econometrics* 57 (1993): 21–51.

Gunderson, M. and A. Melino. "The Effects of Public Policy on Strike Duration." *Journal of Labor Economics* 8 (1990): 295–317.

Gurmu, S., P. Rilstone, and S. Stern. "Nonparametric Hazard Rate Estimation." Unpublished manuscript, University of Virginia, 1996.

Han, A. and J. A. Hausman. "Flexible Parametric Estimation of Duration and Competing Risk Models." *Journal of Applied Econometrics* 5 (1990): 1–28.

Heckman, J. J. "Sample Selection Bias as a Specification Error." *Econometrica* 47 (1979): 153–161.

———. "Identifying the Hand of Past: Distinguishing State Dependence from Heterogeneity." *American Economic Review*, Papers and Proceedings, 81 (1991): 75–79.

Heckman, J. J. and B. Honore. "The Identifiability of the Competing Risks Model." *Biometrika* 76 (1989): 325–330.

Heckman, J. J. and B. Singer. "The Identifiability of the Proportional Hazard Model." *Review of Economic Studies* 51 (1984): 231–241. (a)

————. "A Method of Minimizing the Impact of Distributional Assumptions in Econometric Models for Duration Data." *Econometrica* 52 (1984): 271–320. (b)

Heckman, J. J. and J. Walker. "The Relationship Between Wages and Income and the Timing and Spacing of Births: Evidence from Swedish Longitudinal Data." *Econometrica* 58 (1990):1411–1443.

Holt, F., E. Merwin, and S. Stern. "The Length of Psychiatric Hospital Stays and Community Stays." Unpublished Paper, University of Virginia, 1996.

Jensen, P. and N. C. Westergard-Nielsen. "A Search Model Applied to the Transition from Education to Work." *Review of Economic Studies* 54 (1987): 461–472.

Johnson, W. and J. Ondrich. "The Duration of Post-Injury Absences from Work." *The Review of Economics and Statistics* 72 (1990): 578–586.

Jovanovic, B. "Wages and Turnover: a Parameterization of the Job Matching Model." In *Studies in Labor Market Dynamics*, edited by G.R. Neumann and N.C. Westergaard-Nielsen. Berlin: Springer-Verlarg, 1984.

Kennan J. F. "The Duration of Contract Strikes in U.S. Manufacturing." *Journal of Econometrics* 28 (1985): 5–28.

Kiefer, N. M. and G. R. Neumann. "An Empirical Job Search Model with a Test of the Constant Reservation Wage Hypothesis." *Journal of Political Economy* 87 (1979): 89–107.

————. "Individual Effects in a Nonlinear Model: Explicit Treatment of Heterogeneity in the Empirical Job Search Model." *Econometrica* 49 (1981): 965–979.

————. "Wage Dispersion with Homogeneity: The Empirical Equilibrium Search Model." In *Proceedings of the Third Symposium on Panel Data and Labour Market Dynamics*, edited by N.C. Westeergard-Nielsen and P. Jensen. New York: North-Holland, 1994. Pp. 57–74.

Koning, P., G. Ridder, and G. J. Van den Berg. "Structural and Frictional Unemployment in an Equilibrium Search Model with Heterogeneous Agents." *Journal of Applied Econometrics* 10 (1995): S133–S151.

Lancaster, T. "Econometric Methods for the Duration of Unemployment." *Econometrica* 47 (1979): 939–956.

————. *The Econometric Analysis of Transition Data*. New York: Cambridge University Press, 1990.

Lancaster, T. and A. Chesher. "An Econometric Analysis of Reservation Wages." *Econometrica* 51 (1983): 1661–1776.

Lancaster, T. and S. Nickell. "The Analysis of Reemployment Probabilities for the Unemployed." *Journal of the Royal Statistical Society*, Series A, 143 (1980): 141–152.

Lippman, S. A. and J. J. McCall. "The Economics of Job Search: A Survey." *Economic Inquiry* 14 (1976): 155–189 and 347–368.

McCall, B. "Occupational Matching: A Test of Sorts." *Journal of Political Economy* 98 (1990): 45–69.

———. "Unemployment Insurance Rules, Joblessness, and Part-Time Work." *Econometrica* 64 (1996): 647–682.

Meyer, B. D. "Unemployment Insurance and Unemployment Spells." *Econometrica* 58 (1990): 757–782.

Miller, R. "Job Matching and Occupational Choice." *Journal of Political Economy* 92 (1984): 1086–1120.

Moffitt, R. "Unemployment Insurance and the Distribution of Unemployment Spells." *Journal of Econometrics* 28 (1985): 85–101.

Mortensen, D. T. "Equilibrium Wage Distributions: A Synthesis." In *Panel Data and Labor Market Studies*, edited by J. Hartog, G. Ridder, and J. Theeuwes. New York: North-Holland, 1990. Pp. 279–296.

Mortensen, D. T. and G. R. Neumann. "Estimating Structural Models of Unemployment and Job Duration in Dynamic Econometric Modeling." In *Dynamic Econometric Modeling*, Proceedings of the Third International Symposium in Economic Theory and Econometrics, edited by W.A. Barnett, E. Berndt, and H. White. Cambridge: Cambridge University Press, 1988. Pp. 335–357.

Narendranathan, W. and S. Nickell. "Modeling the Process of Job Search." *Journal of Econometrics* 28 (1985): 29–49.

Narendranathan, W., S. Nickell and J. Stern. "Unemployment Benefits Revisited." *Economic Journal* 95 (1985): 307–329.

Nickell, S. "Estimating the Probability of Leaving Unemployment." *Econometrica* 47 (1979): 1249–1266.

Pakes, A. "Patents as Options: Some Estimates of the Value of Holding European Patent Stocks." *Econometrica* 54 (1986): 755–784.

Reinganum, J. F. "A Simple Model of Equilibrium Price Dispersion." *Journal of Political Economy* 87 (1979): 851–858.

Solon, G. "Work Incentive Effects of Taxing Unemployment Benefits." *Econometrica* 53 (1985): 295–306.

Stern, S. "Estimating a Simultaneous Search Model." *Journal of Labor Economics* 7 (1989): 348–369.

Sueyoshi, G. "Semi-parametric Proportional Hazards Estimation of Competing Risks Models with Time-Varying Regressors." *Journal of Econometrics* 51 (1992): 25–58.

Van den Berg, G. J. "A Structural Dynamic Analysis of Job Turnover and the Cost Associated with Moving to Another Job." *Economic Journal* 102 (1992): 1116–1133.

Van den Berg, G. J. and G. Ridder. "On the Estimation of Equilibrium Search Models from Panel Data." *Labor Demand and Equilibrium Wage Formation*, edited by J.C. Van Ours, G.A. Pfann, and G. Ridder. New York: North-Holland, 1993. Pp. 227–245. (a)

———. "An Empirical Equilibrium Search Model of the Labour Market." Unpublished manuscript, Free University of Amsterdam, 1993. (b)

Wolpin, K. "Estimating a Structural Search Model: The Transition from School to Work." *Econometrica* 55 (1987): 801–818.

6

Variation in the Impact of Benefit Exhaustion on Unemployment Duration

John B. Engberg
Carnegie Mellon University

Abstract

Search theory predicts that individuals will be more likely to exit unemployment as they approach the exhaustion of their unemployment benefits. Theory also predicts that individuals are likely to differ in the magnitude of their response to benefit exhaustion. The first prediction has been repeatedly verified. The second prediction has not been systematically tested but a close examination of the empirical literature provides some support. Building on this theoretical and empirical basis, I develop a parsimonious specification to examine variation in the impact of benefit exhaustion. The estimator can be implemented with standard statistical packages. An empirical example indicates that less educated workers have a much lower response to benefit exhaustion than more educated workers.

1. Introduction

Over the past two and a half decades, job search theory has been a guiding force for empirical models of unemployment duration.[1] A primary implication of most sequential search models is the use of a reservation wage as an optimal stopping rule. Individuals formulate search strategies based on their expectations regarding the frequency and distribution of potential job offers and costs and benefits of continued unemployment, ending their search when they receive a wage offer greater than their reservation wage. Over the course of an unemployment spell, an individual will plan to change his or her search intensity and reservation wage, adjusting to foreseen changes in the search environment. As exhaustion of unemployment benefits approaches, search theory predicts that individuals will search more intensively and lower their reservation wage.

Hazard function specification and estimation provides a convenient method for empirically modeling the change in the probability of exiting unemployment as the unemployment spell continues. The hazard rate can be specified as a function of the characteristics of the individual, the search environment and of the accrued duration of the unemployment spell. Once the impact of these factors on the hazard function is understood, the implied impact on the distribution of unemployment spells can be calculated. For example, if the hazard functions for old and young individuals are known, differences in mean or median duration of unemployment between these groups can be calculated.

Search theory makes specific predictions about the impact of finite duration unemployment benefits on the hazard rate (Mortensen, 1977). The hazard will increase at an increasing rate as the remaining benefit entitlement declines. Starting with Moffitt (1985), several studies have provided empirical evidence of this entitlement effect.[2]

I build on this theoretical and empirical foundation to examine variation in the impact of benefit exhaustion on the hazard rate. Although a few studies have reported variation in the impact, there has not been a systematic investigation of variation or an attempt to link estimated variation to search theoretic predictions. I develop a parsimonious specification that combines benefit amount and remaining entitlement in a form that mirrors the theoretical prediction. Interacting the measure of remaining benefits with individual characteristics permits the analysis of variation in the effect of benefit exhaustion on unemployment duration.

The following section of the paper reviews the search theoretic implications for the shape of the hazard function when benefit entitlement has a limited duration. Next, I review previous empirical examinations of the entitlement effect. I then develop a reduced-form specification of the variation in the entitlement effect and provide estimates using a sample of men from the Trade Adjustment Assistance survey. The concluding remarks contain suggested extensions of the research and implications for program design.

2.   Theory

To understand the entitlement effect on unemployment duration from a search theoretic perspective, it is most straightforward to assume that the limited duration of benefits is the only source of nonstationarity. This model has been examined in detail elsewhere (Mortensen, 1977, 1986; van den Berg, 1990). Therefore, I will forego a rigorous development of the theory and focus on the underlying concepts.[3]

The fundamental principle of sequential search theory is that the value of a job offer, usually represented by the present value of the job's wage stream, will be compared to the value of remaining unemployed. The value of remaining unemployed includes the value of leisure and unemployment benefits in the immediate future plus the "option value" of continuing to wait for a higher offer. The option value reflects not only the expected value of future acceptable offers but also the possibility of continued unemployment. If the value of the job is greater than the value of remaining unemployed, then the job is accepted.

The reservation wage is the threshold value that separates acceptable and unacceptable job offers. In a stationary environment (i.e., the probability of an offer, the distribution of wages, and the value of leisure and benefits are unchanging) the reservation wage is constant. Likewise, the individual will have no reason to change the intensity of search. Therefore, the hazard rate also will be constant. The stationary model is a useful approximation of the search environment after the exhaustion of unemployment benefits.

Prior to benefit exhaustion, the option value of continued unemployment declines over time, reflecting the upcoming loss of benefits. As the remaining weeks of benefit entitlement diminish, the optimal strategy is to search more intensively (which is presumed to be costly) and to reduce the reservation wage. At the beginning of the unemployment spell, the reduction of remaining entitlement (appropriately discounted) is sufficiently small that the search strategy will not change very much from week to week. However, as exhaustion approaches, the rate of decrease of the reservation wage and the rate of increase in the search intensity both increase, leading to a sharp rise in the hazard rate immediately before exhaustion. The change in the hazard rate as exhaustion approaches is referred to as the entitlement effect. Figure 6.1 illustrates the shape of the hazard function in this stylized model.

Figure 6.1 also illustrates the impact of variation in the benefit amount on the hazard function. Individuals with high benefit amounts initially have lower hazard rates. However, as benefit exhaustion approaches, both hazard rates increase at an

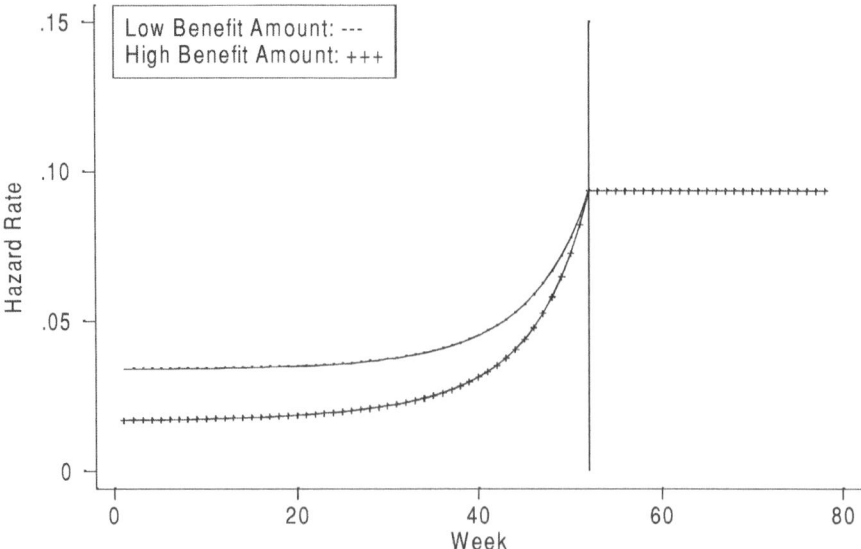

Figure 6.1. Impact of benefit amount on hazard function.

increasing rate to the stationary level. Therefore, the magnitude of the entitlement effect depends on the benefit amount.

Figure 6.2 illustrates the impact on the hazard function of variation in several of the underlying parameters of the search model, holding benefit amount constant. The value of the hazard rate at any time is determined by the characteristics of the individual and the search environment. These characteristics include the distribution of wage offers, the value of leisure, the ease with which an offer can be generated by increasing search intensity, the discount rate, and the parameters of the unemployment benefit system. The difference between the hazard rates increases as exhaustion approaches if there is variation in the mean wage offer, the discount rate, or the value of leisure. On the other hand, variation in the variance of the wage offer distribution produces hazard rates which get closer together as exhaustion approaches. Variation in the cost of search can produce hazard functions that cross with the approach of benefit exhaustion. A low search cost implies that workers can greatly increase their offer probability with a small increase in search intensity. Such workers will not begin intensive search until shortly before benefit exhaustion. On the other hand, workers with a high cost of increasing search intensity will search at a relatively constant intensity throughout their unemployment spell.

Figure 6.2 provides an important insight. We can measure the entitlement effect as the difference between the hazard rate in a specific week of benefit receipt (say, 12 weeks prior to exhaustion) and the hazard after exhaustion. Clearly the magnitude of the effect varies depending on the values of the search parameters. Unemployment benefits have a greater impact for individuals with a high discount rate, a high offer

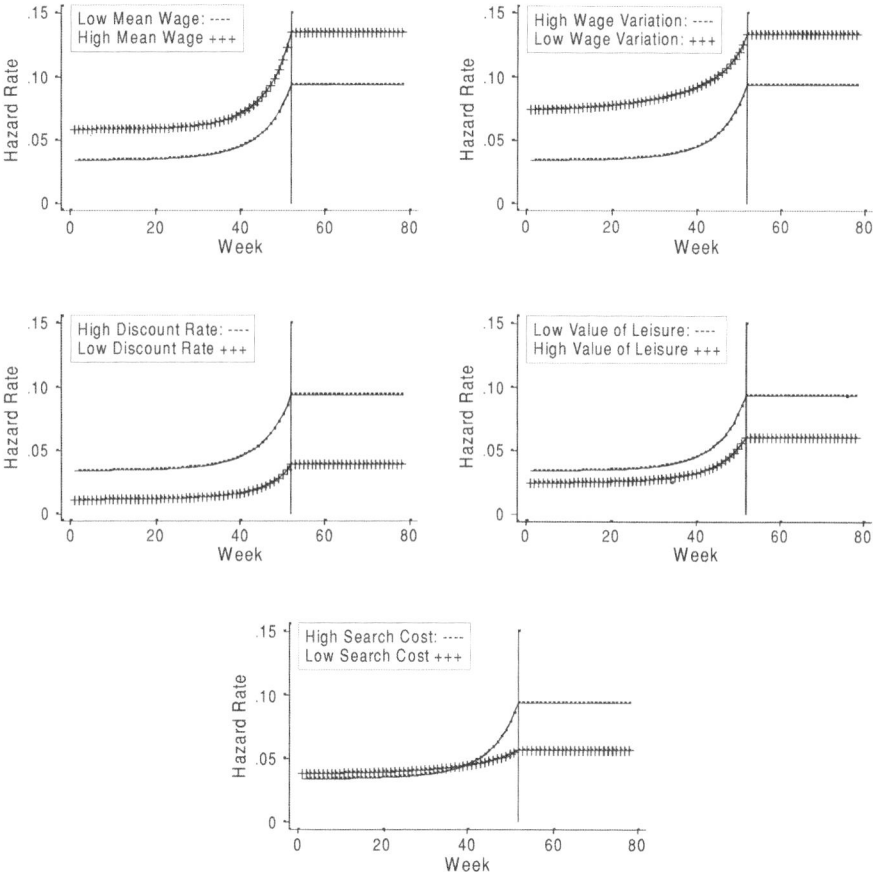

Figure 6.2. Impact of search parameter variation on hazard.

variance, a low value of leisure, a high mean wage offer, or a high search cost. Individual characteristics represent differences in the parameters of individual search problems, and will have differing impacts depending on the amount of benefits or the time until exhaustion.

3.   Related Empirical Work

3.1 Structural Estimation

One possibility for capturing the complex interaction of unemployment benefits and individual characteristics is to estimate the underlying parameters of the search problem. (See van den Berg, 1990, and Engberg, 1994a, for structural estimation of the entitlement effect.) The search parameters are expressed as functions of observed (and, possibly, of unobserved) individual characteristics. The search parameters determine search behavior (the choice of search intensity and reservation wage) as a function of the stream of benefits. The search strategy implies a probability distribution for unemployment spell lengths and accepted wages. The dependence of the search parameters on demographic characteristics is estimated by maximum likelihood or generalized method of moments using sample distributions of unemployment spells and wages conditional on individual characteristics and benefit streams.

Although these exercises can be informative, they come at a high cost. Structural estimation requires many functional form assumptions and the computational requirements, both in terms of programming and computer power, are forbidding. It is useful, therefore, to develop reduced form methods which benefit from theoretical restrictions without incurring these high costs.

3.2 Reduced Form Estimation

Reduced form estimation specifies the hazard rate as a function of individual characteristics and the search environment, but does not attempt to recover the underlying behavioral parameters that define the search problem. A common starting point is the proportional hazard model:

(1) $$h(t \mid X) = \exp(\gamma(t))\exp(X\beta)$$

In this simple form, the proportional specification imposes that changes in the hazard rate over the duration (t) of the unemployment spell are the same manner for everyone and that individual characteristics (X) only shift the hazard up or down proportionally. As demonstrated by the illustrations in Figure 6.2, the theoretical predictions suggest that this specification is not appropriate. If differences in X correspond to differences in the structural parameters of the search problem, then it is necessary to modify equation 1 to allow a non-proportional effect of X on the hazard function.

The non-proportional relationship between X and the hazard function can be modeled by allowing some of the components of the hazard to change over the duration of the unemployment spell. The ability of a hazard function specification to capture time-varying covariates and time-varying effects of covariates is one of the features that has led econometricians to prefer hazard estimation over regression estimation of average spell length. (Another feature is the ease with which it appropriately incorporates censored spells.) A more general hazard specification takes the following form:

(2) $$h(t \mid X_t) = \exp(\gamma(t))\exp(X_t\beta_t)$$

The observed characteristics, X_t, are indexed by time to indicate that they can be allowed to vary during the spell. Likewise, the impact of these characteristics, represented by the parameter vector β_t can change during the course of the spell. For example, the entitlement effect can be captured by including the number of weeks until exhaustion as a covariate in the model. A changing impact of the benefit amount can be captured by allowing the coefficient on benefits to change over the course of the spell.[4]

The remaining portion of the hazard function, $\exp(\gamma(t))$, captures the true duration dependence. After controlling for measured changes in the environment through $X_t\beta_t$, other changes in the hazard can be estimated as a parametric (e.g., Lancaster, 1979) or nonparametric (e.g., Meyer, 1990) function of duration. A third option is to estimate a partial likelihood function which eliminates this portion of the hazard (Cox, 1975).

Several authors have used variations of equation (2) tailored to detect the decrease in the impact of unemployment benefits as exhaustion approaches. Moffitt (1985) estimated a proportional hazard analysis with a non-parametric baseline hazard on administrative data from the Continuous Wage and Benefit History. He found that the non-parametric estimates of the baseline hazard showed sharp increases immediately prior to the times at which many individuals in the sample faced benefit exhaustion.

Moffitt's efforts to capture this apparent entitlement effect with a parametric form provide a notable example of using theoretical predictions to refine reduced form model specification. When he included remaining entitlement as a linear term in X_t, he found that the hazard *decreased* as exhaustion approaches, counter to theoretical prediction. This led to the addition of a series of splines that allowed for a change in the impact of declining entitlement as exhaustion becomes imminent. The coefficients on the splines indicate that the hazard rate declined early in the spell, but as predicted by theory the hazard increased at an increasing rate when less than ten weeks of benefits remained. Moffitt found that benefit amount was inversely related to the hazard, but did not explicitly examine the relationship between the benefit amount and the change in the hazard as exhaustion approached.

Ham and Rea (1987) estimated a model similar to Moffitt's using Canadian data. Instead of a nonparametric baseline hazard, they used a sixth-order polynomial in duration. They also controlled for unobserved heterogeneity with a parametric random effect. They represented entitlement as a quadratic function of the weeks until exhaustion. Both the linear and quadratic terms were significant and had signs that indicate that the hazard increases at an increasing rate with the approach of exhaustion as predicted by theory. They did not find evidence that the benefit amount had an impact on the hazard nor of an interaction between the benefit amount and remaining weeks. They attributed this to the small independent variation of benefit amount in their data.

Ham and Rea were the first to explicitly investigate whether the entitlement effect varied by demographic characteristics. They interacted age with benefit amount, but not with entitlement. The interaction of age with benefit amount was not significant. Again, the absence of substantial variation in benefit amount could account for this result.[5]

Meyer (1990) extended Moffitt's analysis of CWBH data using a different nonparametric baseline specification and controlling for unobserved heterogeneity. Like Moffitt, he estimated splines that indicate that the hazard increased with the approach of exhaustion and that higher benefits decreased the hazard rate. Katz and Meyer (1990) extended Meyer (1990) by including some interaction terms to loosen the proportional hazard restriction. They found that the impact of benefits diminished as exhaustion approached, as predicted by theory. They also interacted benefit amount with age and found that the hazard rate for men 24 years and younger was more than twice as responsive to the benefit amount than was the hazard for older men.

In a recent paper, Hunt (1995) examined the impact of policy changes in Germany that altered the duration and amount of benefits for particular demographic groups. She used a Cox (1975) partial likelihood estimator to provide flexibility in the baseline hazard. Although she does not include remaining entitlement, her estimates reveal variation in the entitlement effect by interacting age group dummies with dummies for programmatic change. Similar to Katz and Meyer (1990), she finds that older workers are less responsive to increased entitlement. Although no single study has systematically examined variation in the impact of changes in both the duration and amount of benefits, the cumulative evidence supports the theoretical implication that benefit amounts and duration act jointly to produce an entitlement effect and that this effect varies with individual characteristics.

In addition to the direct evidence that individuals differ in their responses to benefit exhaustion, there is indirect evidence that this may be important. For example, any evidence that the impact of individual characteristics on the hazard is non-proportional is consistent with a differential entitlement effect. Referring back to Figure 6.2, it appears that differences in search cost have an effect which is particularly non-proportional. Evidence of differences in search method by demographic group (e.g., Holzer, 1988) suggests that the cost of increasing search intensity may vary greatly, leading to considerable differences in the ability to increase the hazard sharply as entitlement declines.

4. Estimation Method

Given the empirical evidence that the entitlement effect exists and the theoretical prediction that it varies among individuals, the goal is to design a reduced form specification that captures these differences. I take advantage of the theoretical and empirical observation that benefit amount and remaining entitlement do not have separate effects on the hazard, but enter the search problem jointly. I combine benefit amount and remaining entitlement to create the present value of remaining benefits (*PVRB*). Then by allowing demographic characteristics to enter the hazard both as proportional shifters and interacted with the present value of remaining benefits, the specification can capture variation in the entitlement effect. This uses search theory and earlier empirical evidence to restrict the reduced form specification, achieving greater power to examine differences among individuals. Without this restriction, interactions of demographic characteristics with benefit amount, remaining entitlement and their interaction would lead to three times as many coefficients.

The benefit amount, as captured by the replacement rate (RR),[6] and the remaining entitlement (RE_t) are combined to form a time-varying covariate representing the present value of remaining benefits:

(3) $$PVRB_t = RR * \left(1 - \delta^{RE_t}\right), t = 1, 2, ...$$

where t indexes the duration of the unemployment spell and δ is a parameter which captures the degree to which future benefits are discounted. For values of δ between zero and one, the term inside the parentheses will approach zero at an increasing rate as the remaining weeks of entitlement approaches zero. Prior to exhaustion, this form imposes the search theoretic implication that the entitlement effect will vary directly with the amount of benefits. Smaller values of δ imply a steeper increase in the hazard rate near the time of benefit exhaustion.[7]

The estimated hazard takes the following form:

(4) $$h(t \mid X, RE_t, RR) = \exp(\gamma(t))\exp(X\beta_1 + (PVRB_t * X)\beta_2)$$

The parameter vector β_1 captures the proportional shift in the hazard function due to variation in individual characteristics X. Figure 6.3A graphs the effect of a change in X due to a nonzero value of β_1 on the relative hazard function, $\exp(X\beta_1 + (PVRB * X)\beta_2)$. (The complete hazard function is obtained by multiplying this function by $\exp(\gamma(t))$, the nonparametric baseline hazard.) The parameter vector β_2 determines how entitlement effects vary with individual characteristics (Figure 6.3B). Together, these parameters permit the hazard function to vary with X in a way that accommodates the search theoretic predictions (Figure 6.3C). For any element in X, various values of β_1 and β_2 can reproduce the patterns in Figure 6.2.

Since theory implies that individuals with a greater present value of remaining benefits will have a lower hazard rate, we expect the impact of $PVRB_t$, as captured by $X\beta_2$, to be negative. Significant differences in the entitlement effect due to variation in individual characteristics will be detected by significant values of elements of β_2.

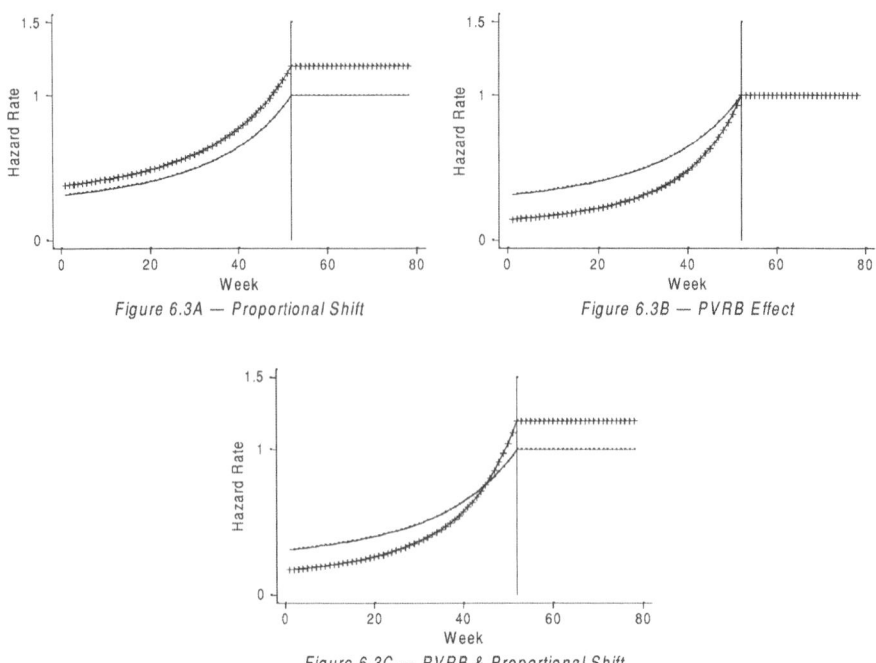

Figure 6.3A — Proportional Shift

Figure 6.3B — PVRB Effect

Figure 6.3C — PVRB & Proportional Shift

Figure 6.3. Reduced form specification of relative hazard.

For a given value of δ, this specification can be easily estimated using maximum likelihood estimators of proportional hazard models available in many commercial statistical packages (e.g., STATA, SAS, LIMDEP, GAUSS, etc.). The best value of δ can be chosen by comparing the maximum likelihood over a range of values for δ.[8]

To ease interpretation of the coefficient on *PVRB* and to provide a basis for comparisons across specifications, the value for *PVRB* is standardized by dividing the value defined in equation (3) by the quantity obtained when (3) is evaluated twelve weeks prior to exhaustion at the average replacement rate in the sample: *RR* $*(1-\delta^{12})$. This allows the coefficient on *PVRB* to be interpreted as the proportional decrease in the hazard between the time after exhaustion and twelve weeks earlier, given the average replacement rate.

This specification of the entitlement effect is more parsimonious than splines (Moffitt, 1985; Meyer, 1990; Katz and Meyer, 1990). By capturing the entitlement effect in a single term, it provides a convenient way to allow for the theoretically predicted interaction between the entitlement effect and demographic characteristics. It is more consistent with theory than a linear or quadratic function of remaining entitlement (Ham and Rea, 1987). Entering the number of weeks until benefit exhaustion a linear term in the log hazard (i.e., $h(t|X,RE_t)=\exp(X\beta_1+\beta_2 RE_t)$) is inappropriate because a value of β_2 sufficiently negative to imply a steep increase in the hazard function as benefit exhaustion approaches will also imply that the hazard is approximately zero in the early weeks of the spell. Adding a quadratic term permits a steep increase in the hazard prior to exhaustion, but implies a theoretically inappropriate non-monotonic form for the entitlement effect. For example, Ham and Rea's (1987) quadratic estimates imply that the eventual exhaustion of benefits drive a decreasing hazard rate early in the unemployment spell. The monotonic form of *PVRB* avoids this problem.

5. Empirical Example

The estimator is illustrated on a sample of 211 men from the Trade Adjustment Assistance (TAA) Survey.[9] This sample includes individuals who received high benefits for an extended period because they were deemed to have lost their jobs due to import competition, as well as a comparison group who only received unemployment insurance. The large resulting variation in *PVRB* provides power in estimating the entitlement effect. A dummy variable for TAA participation is included to detect average differences in search behavior unrelated to benefit duration or amount. In order to focus on search behavior, individuals who retired or were recalled to their previous job were eliminated from the sample.[10] The first column of Table 6.1 provides the means and standard deviations of variables used in estimation.

First the hazard is estimated including *PVRB* and its components, the replacement rate and the discounted remaining weeks of entitlement (column 2 of Table 6.1). The coefficients on the two components are not significant individually or jointly, although a joint test on all three variables has a *p*-value of 0.014. The coefficient on *PVRB* is negative and significant at the .01 level. This suggests *PVRB* is an adequate representation of the entitlement effect. (*P*-values for all tests are provided in the notes to Table 6.1).

The third column of Table 6.1 presents estimates from a specification which drops the two components. The coefficient on *PVRB* is significant at the .01 level. The magnitude of the entitlement effect twelve weeks before exhaustion is given by the percentage difference in the hazard rates: $ee_{12}=[h(PVRB_{12})-h(PVRB_0)]/h(PVRB_0)$, where $PVRB_0$ equals zero. Using equation (4) and setting X equal to a constant gives $ee_{12}=1-\exp(PVRB_{12}\beta_2)$. The point estimate indicates that the hazard twelve weeks prior to exhaustion is 30 percent less than its value after exhaustion.

The specification presented in the fourth column adds interactions of *PVRB* with individual characteristics. The set of coefficients on variables containing *PVRB* is jointly significant at a 5 percent level. A test on just the interactions is also significant at a 5 percent level, suggesting that there are differences in the entitlement effect among individuals. The coefficients on the individual interactions suggest that differing education is primarily responsible for differences in the entitlement effect.

Table 6.1. Unemployment Hazard Function Estimates.

Variable	Means (std. Dev.) (1)	Estimated Hazard Coefficients (std. error)			
		(2)	(3)	(4)	(5)
Age (years)	32.2 (12.0)	–0.018** (0.007)	–0.018** (0.007)	–0.006 (0.011)	–0.024 (0.034)
Education (years)	11.8 (2.93)	0.025 (0.026)	0.028 (0.026)	0.118^{**} (0.040)	0.172 (0.118)
White	0.782 (0.414)	0.096 (0.200)	0.117 (0.198)	0.314 (0.315)	0.323 (1.02)
TAA participant	–0.284 (0.452)	–0.509** (0.190)	–0.470** (0.189)	–0.419 (0.306)	–2.05 (1.24)
Replacement Rate: (RR)	1 (0.432)	0.618 (0.344)			
Discounted Remaining Entitlement: $(1-\delta^{RE})$	1 0	0.523 (0.449)			
PV Remaining Benefits: $PVRB=RR * (1-\delta^{RE})$	1 (0.432)	–0.991** (0.334)	–0.348** (0.128)	1.45* (0.647)	1.27 (0.693)
$PVRB$ * Age				–0.014 (0.012)	–0.010 (0.014)
$PVRB$ * Education				–0.118** (0.041)	-0.123^{**} (0.046)
$PVRB$ * White				–0.171 (0.322)	–0.104 (0.394)
$PVRB$ * TAA				–0.127 (0.313)	0.187 (0.412)
ln(duration) * Age					0.004 (0.008)
ln(duration) * Education					–0.016 (0.030)
ln(duration) * White					–0.015 (0.251)
ln(duration) * TAA					0.403 (0.292)
δ		.893	.945	.821	.808
Log likelihood		–863.737	–865.337	–861.404	–859.525

Notes: ** $p < .01$ * $p < .05$ Sample size: 211.
All specifications also include state dummies. Estimation uses Cox partial likelihood proportional hazard model. Discounted remaining entitlement is standardized to equal unity twelve weeks prior to exhaustion. Replacement rate is standardized to have a mean of unity. Present value of remaining benefits is standardized to have a mean of unity twelve weeks prior to exhaustion. Standard errors are conditional on estimated value of δ.

Table 6.1. *(continued)* Unemployment Hazard Function Estimates.

Notes to Table 6.1 (continued):

Joint Hypothesis Tests:

Column 2:

χ^2 test of RR, $(1-\delta RE)$ and PVRB:	*p*-value=0.014
χ^2 test of RR and $(1-\delta RE)$:	*p*-value=0.163

Column 4:

χ^2 test of PVRB and interactions with PVRB:	*p*-value=0.012
χ^2 test of interactions with PVRB:	*p*-value=0.045
χ^2 test of Age and interaction of Age * PVRB:	*p*-value=0.022
χ^2 test of Education and interaction of Education * PVRB:	*p*-value=0.009
χ^2 test of White and interaction of White * PVRB:	*p*-value=0.586
χ^2 test of TAA and interaction of TAA * PVRB:	*p*-value=0.025

Column 5:

χ^2 test of PVRB and interactions with PVRB:	*p*-value=0.016
χ^2 test of interactions with PVRB:	*p*-value=0.039
χ^2 test of interactions with ln(duration):	*p*-value=0.483

A potential concern is that the estimated differences among individuals in the entitlement effect really reflect differences in the shape of the hazard function that arise from other sources of non-stationarity in the search environment.[11] For example, if duration dependence varies by education level due to differences in savings, then our specification which omits an interaction of education and duration would yield biased coefficient estimates. The interactions of the demographic variables with the present value of remaining benefits are particularly susceptible to such a bias because of the strong time trend in *PVRB*.

To examine this possibility, the last column of Table 6.1 provides estimates from an additional specification which adds interactions of the demographic variables with the natural log of duration.[12] The coefficients on these interactions are not individually or jointly significant but the interactions with *PVRB* remain significant. This provides evidence that the coefficients on the interactions with *PVRB* are estimating differences in the entitlement effect rather than differences in duration dependence due to other sources of non-stationarity.

Table 6.2 presents the entitlement effect at twelve weeks prior to exhaustion for a range of individual characteristics, using the coefficient estimates from the fourth column of Table 6.1. The median worker in the sample is white, 29 years old, does not participate in TAA, has 12 years of schooling, and has benefits which replace 48 percent of his pre-unemployment earnings. When X and $PVRB_{12}$ take these values, the entitlement effect at twelve weeks is 42 percent: $ee_{12} = 1-\exp(PVRB_{12}X\beta_2) = 1-\exp(-.550) = 0.42$. The effect increases to 57 percent for a 50-year old worker, to 63

Table 6.2. Effect of Benefits on Hazard Function.

	$PVRB_{12}X\beta_2$ (1)		ee_{12} (2)
Median	−0.550**	(0.203)	0.42
Black Worker	−0.380	(0.342)	0.32
Young (19 years old)	−0.406	(0.230)	0.33
Low Education (8 years of school)	−0.080	(0.231)	0.08
Low Replacement Rate (*RR*=0.24)	−0.275**	(0.101)	0.24
TAA Recipient	−0.678*	(0.331)	0.49
Old (50 years old)	−0.853**	(0.323)	0.57
High Education (16 years of school)	−1.021**	(0.288)	0.63
High Replacement Rate (*RR*=0.71)	−0.814**	(0.300)	0.55

Notes: ** $p < .01$ * $p < .05$
Column (1) shows the estimated impact (and standard error) of the present value of remaining benefits ($PVRB_{12}(X\beta_2)$) on the hazard function twelve weeks prior to exhaustion. *PVRB* is standardized so that the value $X\beta_2$ is equivalent to the proportional difference between the hazard rate after benefit exhaustion and the hazard rate twelve weeks prior to benefit exhaustion. Column (2) shows the proportion by which the hazard rate is diminished by the entitlement effect: $ee_{12}=1-\exp(PVRB_{12}X\beta_2)$. Calculated from specification in column 4 of Table 6.1. Median individual is white, 29 years old, 12 years of school, and does not participate in TAA, and has a 48 percent benefit replacement ratio. Range in age, education and replacement rate is equivalent to the 10th and 90th percentiles.

percent for a worker with a college education, and to 49 percent for a TAA participant. All of the entitlement effects described above are significantly different from zero at a 5 percent level. The effect is smaller for black, younger or less educated workers and is not significantly different from zero at the 5 percent level.

The benefit amount has a large impact on the entitlement effect. The last row of Table 6.2 presents the entitlement effect at the 10th and 90th percentiles of replacement rate. A low replacement rate (24 percent) for a worker with median characteristics reduces the entitlement effect to 24 percent but a high replacement rate (71 percent) increases it to 55 percent. By way of comparison, a ten percentage point increase in the replacement rate increases the entitlement effect by the same amount as adding one year to educational attainment or eight years to the worker's age.

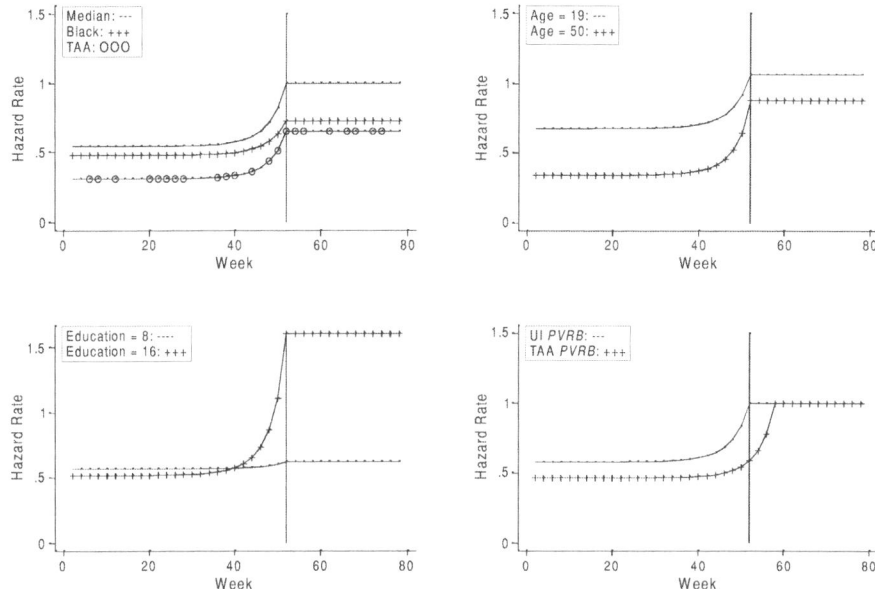

Figure 6.4. Estimated relative hazard functions.

Figure 6.4 presents these differences in the hazard functions graphically.[13] The figures show the ratio of the hazard rate for specified individuals relative to the hazard rate of an individual who receives no benefits but otherwise has the median characteristics. In addition to the differences in the entitlement effect, the figures portray the shifts in the hazard functions suggested by the estimates of β_1. The smooth function in the upper left panel shows the relative hazard function for a worker with median characteristics and an average replacement rate. As indicated in Table 6.2, the hazard rate twelve weeks prior to exhaustion is 48 percent below the post-exhaustion hazard rate.

The upper left panel also provides the relative hazard for a black worker with otherwise identical characteristics to the median worker. Although the difference is not significant, the point estimates indicate that the hazard is always lower than the hazard for the white worker and exhibits a smaller entitlement effect. The lower hazard is consistent with the hypothesis that black workers face a wage distribution with a lower mean and the smaller entitlement effect could reflect a higher cost of generating additional offers (see Figure 6.2). Alternatively, the difference in hazard functions could reflect a higher value of leisure for black workers. Although these alternatives cannot be distinguished using only unemployment duration data, an examination of wages on the accepted jobs would provide a test. The first alternative implies that black workers would have lower wages on new jobs than comparable white workers, with the reverse being true for the second alternative.

The upper left panel also provides the relative hazard function for a TAA recipient who has the median value of other characteristics, including the average replacement rate and benefit duration. A joint test of the two TAA coefficients is significant at the 5 percent level, though neither coefficient is individually significant. Although TAA recipients have a slightly lower entitlement effect, the largest part of the impact of TAA participation is the shift in the hazard function rather than in differences in the entitlement effect. One possible interpretation of the shift is that TAA participants have skills for which the wage offer distribution exhibits a larger variance. The increased import competition that led to TAA certification could cause the workers to search in unfamiliar sectors of the economy. A higher wage offer variance leads to a lower hazard, as indicated by Figure 6.2, because of the greater possible payoff from waiting for an unusually high offer.

The combined impact of age through the entitlement effect and the proportional shift of the hazard are jointly significant at the 5 percent level. In contrast with the effect of TAA status, the older individuals have a lower hazard function but have a greater entitlement effect. Therefore, the effect of age on the hazard rate is greater in the early weeks of search than in the weeks after exhaustion. The lower hazard of the older workers is consistent with having a higher value of leisure, a lower wage offer variance, and a lower discount rate. The cumulative impact of these apparently is sufficient to offset the presumably higher mean wage offer received by older workers. Furthermore, Figure 6.2 implies that lower hazards are usually accompanied by smaller entitlement effects. This contrasts with the larger entitlement effect exhibited by the older workers. The higher entitlement effect could be the result of more efficient job search strategies perhaps using larger social and occupational networks that reduce the cost of search.

As shown in the lower left corner of Figure 6.4, the most dramatic differences in the hazard function are due to education. Initially, highly educated workers have slightly lower hazards than poorly educated workers. As exhaustion approaches, the hazard for highly educated workers increases sharply but the hazard for poorly educated workers remains virtually constant. The similarity between this figure and the panel depicting the impact of search cost in Figure 6.2 suggests that more educated workers have a lower cost to increasing search intensity as exhaustion approaches. Less educated workers presumably must continue to searching at the same intensity throughout their unemployment spell.

In spite of the sharp similarity between the cost of search panel in Figure 6.2 and the education panel in Figure 6.4, it is not appropriate to conclude that education only affects unemployment duration through its impact search costs. Since more educated workers draw from a higher wage offer distribution, they should have a higher hazard function from the beginning of the unemployment spell onward. The similarity in hazard rates during the early weeks of search suggest that the higher wage distribution is offset by other factors—perhaps a negative relationship between discount rates and education. It should be noted that the estimated positive relationship between age the and entitlement effect stands in contrast to the negative relationship found earlier by Katz and Meyer (1990) and Hunt (1995). These earlier studies, however, did not control for entitlement effect differences due to education. Given the typical negative correlation between education and age, it is possible that the earlier studies were picking up the strong positive impact of education on the entitlement effect.

The final panel of Figure 6.4 shows the impact of the higher replacement rates and longer benefit duration provided by the TAA program. The TAA recipients had an average replacement rate of 60 percent and an average benefit entitlement of 58 weeks. The non-TAA individuals in the sample had an average replacement rate of 43 percent for an average of 52 weeks. These differences lead to a hazard function that is shifted to the right and has greater entitlement effect. To obtain the total estimated effect of being a TAA recipient, it is necessary to combine the downward shift in the hazard depicted in the upper left panel and impact of program benefits in the lower right panel. Both components lead to longer unemployment spells for TAA recipients with program benefits representing a slightly smaller portion. In addition to these two components, the TAA recipients had demographic characteristics that led to longer unemployment spells—TAA recipients were older, had less education, and were more likely to be black.

6.   Suggested Extensions

6.1 Timing of the Entitlement Effect

Although the functional form introduced for *PVRB* allows for the magnitude of the entitlement effect to vary among individuals, it appears that the timing of the effect is constrained to be the same for everyone. As shown in Figure 6.4, the hazard rate for all subjects is virtually constant until approximately ten weeks prior to exhaustion. This restriction could be removed by parameterizing δ as a function of the explanatory variables. This would allow the timing of the entitlement effect to vary among individuals. Unfortunately, the parameters could no longer be estimated using "canned" survival routines that are available with many commercial software packages. Furthermore, although the non-linear nature of the specification suggests that the impact of individual characteristics on entitlement timing can be separately identified from the impact on entitlement magnitude, whether existing data have the power to precisely distinguish these effects is an empirical question.

6.2 Unobserved Heterogeneity

Although the unemployment duration analysis presented above extends usual practices by allowing the entitlement effect to vary among individuals, it ignores the issue of unobserved heterogeneity. Ever since the introduction of hazard specifications to unemployment duration analysis, there has been concern about biases due to the improper treatment of omitted variables (Lancaster, 1979; Nickell, 1979). Omitted variables can lead to biased coefficient estimation and improper inferences. Unlike the case of linear regression, bias will exist even if the omitted variables are uncorrelated with the included explanatory variables. Therefore, the hazard specification frequently includes a "random effect"—a factor which represents unobserved heterogeneity and is assumed to be distributed independently of the other explanatory variables. Maximum likelihood estimation of the coefficients of the hazard specification requires integrating the implied distribution of spell lengths with respect to the assumed (or approximated) distribution of this unobserved factor.

In practice, however, many researchers have concluded that a sufficiently flexible functional form for the baseline hazard ($\gamma(t)$ in equation 1) eliminates the need to control for unobserved heterogeneity (e.g., Han & Hausman, 1990; Meyer, 1990). In spite of theoretical identification results, most data sets do not provide sufficient power to precisely estimate the impact of an unobserved factor with an unknown distribution in the presence of a baseline hazard of unknown shape.

The introduction of variation among individuals in the entitlement effect raises a new dimension to the debate regarding unobserved heterogeneity. Virtually without exception, previous empirical work has imposed the assumption that the unobserved factor leads to a proportional shift in the hazard function. This is consistent with the treatment of observed characteristics as having a proportional impact on the hazard. However, the theoretically motivated inclusion of interactions between the entitlement effect and observed individual characteristics suggests a similar treatment of unobserved heterogeneity:

$$(5) \qquad h(t \mid X, RE_t, RR, v) = \exp(\gamma(t))\exp(X\beta_1 + v\alpha_1 + PVRB_1 * (X\beta_2 + v\alpha_2))$$

where v is distributed independently of X. The distribution of v can be estimated jointly with the coefficients and the baseline hazard function $\gamma(t)$.

It remains to be determined whether existing data has the power to precisely estimate the coefficients of v and the distribution of v, allowing for a flexible baseline hazard. However, it is possible that the difficulty in precisely estimating the impact of unobserved heterogeneity jointly with the shape of the baseline hazard has been due partly to the inappropriate assumption of proportionality. If adding the present value of remaining benefits and appropriate interactions to the hazard specification removes confounding noise, then tighter estimates of the baseline hazard and the effect of the unobserved factor might be obtained.

7. Conclusion

Earlier reduced form empirical work has confirmed the search theoretic prediction that (1) the hazard rate increases at an increasing rate as exhaustion approaches (Moffitt, 1985; Ham and Rea, 1987; Katz and Meyer, 1990); (2) higher benefits reduce the hazard (Moffitt, 1985; Katz and Meyer, 1990); (3) there is an interaction between benefit amount and entitlement duration (Katz and Meyer, 1990); (4) and the effect of benefits on the hazard rate varies with demographic characteristics (Katz and Meyer, 1990; Hunt, 1995). This paper builds on the first three findings in order to further investigate the fourth.

Although many empirical studies of unemployment duration have examined the impact of unemployment benefits, the frequently used proportional hazard specification contains important violations of the restrictions implied by search theory. The exhaustion of unemployment benefits represents an important source of nonstationarity in the search problem. Individual differences in the fundamental parameters of the searcher's dynamic optimization problem will have different impacts on the hazard before and after benefit exhaustion. Benefit duration and amount affect the hazard though the composite term representing the present value of remaining benefits, rather than as individual linear terms.

Estimates using a sample with large variation in benefit duration and amount indicate that the entitlement effect can be captured by a function which appropriately combines benefit duration and amount into the present value of remaining benefits (*PVRB*). The variation among individuals in the entitlement effect is captured by interactions of demographic characteristics with the time-varying *PVRB*. The entitlement effect increases dramatically with education. The estimated hazard rate triples with the approach of benefit exhaustion for college graduates but remains virtually constant for high school drop-outs. One additional year of education has the equivalent impact on the entitlement effect of a ten percentage point increase in the benefit replacement rate.

Although the sample used in this analysis has an unusual amount of variation in benefits, its small size limits the precision of the estimates. However, the use of a single variable to capture benefit duration and amount in a single variable implies that a similar analysis can be performed on samples that contain variation in only one dimension of benefits—either duration or amount. Variation in either duration or amount leads to variation in *PVRB* that is independent of the duration of the spell. This permits the use of a flexible baseline hazard while estimating the impact of unemployment benefit exhaustion.

If the inferences from these data are confirmed by other samples, they have important implications for the design of efficient benefit policies. The distortionary impact of the benefit system depends on the size of the entitlement effect. A large entitlement effect suggests that a worker is waiting until benefit exhaustion to look for work, whereas a small benefit effect suggests a constant search intensity. The large increase in the entitlement effect with educational attainment suggests that it would be more efficient to make the replacement rate an inverse function of education.

Tying benefits to demographic characteristics, however, may not be politically feasible. However, the positive relationship between the entitlement effect and both education and age, combined with the positive relationship between previous wages and these worker characteristics suggests a more progressive replacement schedule will have less distortionary effects. If higher replacement rates are provided for workers with lower previous wages, then the observed entitlement effects (i.e., $RR*(1-\delta^{RE})*PVRB*X\beta_2$) for will converge for young and old and for more and less educated.

Notes

1. Mortensen (1986) reviews the development of job search theory. Seminal works include McCall (1970), Mortensen (1970), and Gronau (1971). Devine and Kiefer (1991) provide an exhaustive review of the empirical literature.

2. Although I focus on the impact of benefit entitlement on unemployment duration, many other effects of the unemployment insurance system on labor market dynamics have been identified theoretically and empirically. See Atkinson and Micklewright (1991) for a review.

3. There are other models of non-stationary search. Examples include search which provides information about job opportunities (Lippman and McCall, 1976) or search while learning about characteristics of the match at the current job (Mortensen, 1986). These examples differ from the case of limited duration benefits in that the non-stationarity is anchored by the starting time rather than the identifiable date of benefit exhaustion later in the spell. We will briefly return to these examples in the empirical section of the paper.

4. An additional modification of the hazard function involves the correction for unobserved heterogeneity, usually by adding a time-invariant "random-effect" to the hazard function. We will return to the issue of unobserved heterogeneity in the final section.

5. Narendranathan, et. al. (1985) found significant differences among age groups in the impact of benefit amounts on the hazard rate, but they did not model the impact of benefit exhaustion.

6. See Mortensen (1986) for a theoretical justification for using the replacement rate to capture benefit amounts. Meyer (1990) notes that his estimates of the impact of previous wages and of benefits are of equal magnitude and opposite sign, providing empirical support for using the replacement rate.

7. Engberg (1994b) uses a similar functional form to capture the entitlement effect.

8. The examples provided below were estimated using the Cox partial likelihood procedure of STATA. By imbedding the COX command in a STATA program that loops through values of δ, the maximum likelihood with respect to all parameters can be found quickly.

9. Corson and Nicholson (1981) provide more detail on the TAA program and the data set.

10. This sampling strategy is appropriate if individuals knew at the time of separation that they would accept recall or retirement. If, instead, all laid-off workers engaged in job search and only retired or accepted recall if they did not receive an acceptable offer, then it would be appropriate to enter recall and retirement dates as censoring times for unsuccessful spells of search. If retrospective survey data is to be believed, members of the sample were quite accurate in predicting future recall (Corson and Nicholson, 1981).

11. Although the Cox estimator allows the baseline hazard, $\gamma(t)$, to assume any shape, the proportional form of equation (4) constrains the shape of the baseline hazard to be the same for all individuals.

12. This moves out of the proportional class of hazard functions. The interactions allow the time-invariant observed attributes to change the shape of the hazard function, rather than just shifting the hazard proportionately. See McCall (1994) for a discussion of estimation and testing of the proportional hazard assumption.

13. As with Figure 6.3, the figures only present the relative hazard. The complete hazard function is obtained by multiplying the relative hazard times the baseline hazard, $\exp(\gamma(t))$.

References

Atkinson, A. B. and J. Micklewright. "Unemployment Compensation and Labor Market Transitions: A Critical Review." *Journal of Economic Literature* 29 (1991): 1629–1727.

Corson, Walter and Walter Nicholson. "Trade Adjustment Assistance for Workers: Results of a Survey of Recipients Under the Trade Act of 1974." *Research in Labor Economics* 4 (1981): 417–469.

Cox, D. R. "Partial Likelihood." *Biometrika* 62 (1975):269–276.

Devine, T. and N. Kiefer. *Empirical Labor Economics: The Search Approach.* New York: Oxford University Press, 1991.

Engberg, John. "The Impact of Unemployment Benefits on Job Search: Structural Unobserved Heterogeneity and Spurious Spikes." Heinz School Working Paper, 1994(a).

_____. "Search Duration, Accepted Wages, and Selection Bias." Heinz School Working Paper, 1994(b).

Gronau, R. "Information and Frictional Unemployment." *American Economic Review* 61 (1971): 290–301.

Ham, John and Samuel Rea, Jr. "Unemployment Insurance and Male Unemployment Duration in Canada." *Journal of Labor Economics* 5 (1987): 325–353.

Han, Aaron and Jerry Hausman. "Flexible Parametric Estimation of Duration and Competing Risk Models." *Journal of Applied Econometrics* 5 (1990): 1–28.

Holzer, Harry. "Search Method Use by Unemployed Youth." *Journal of Labor Economics* 6 (1988): 1–20.

Hunt, Jennifer. "The Effect of Unemployment Compensation on Unemployment Duration in Germany." *Journal of Labor Economics* 13 (1995): 88–120.

Katz, L. and B. Meyer. "The Impact of Potential Duration of Unemployment Benefits on the Duration of Unemployment." *Journal of Public Economics* 41 (1990): 45–72.

Lancaster, Tony. "Econometric Methods for the Duration of Unemployment." *Econometrica* 47 (1979): 939–956.

Lippman, S. A. and J. J. McCall. "Job Search in a Dynamic Economy." *Journal of Economic Theory* 12 (1976): 365–390.

McCall, Brian P. "Testing the Proportional Hazards Model in the Presence of Unmeasured Heterogeneity." *Journal of Applied Econometrics* 9 (1994): 321–334.

McCall, J.J. "Economics of Information and Job Search." *Quarterly Journal of Economics* 84 (1970): 113–126.

Meyer, Bruce D. "Unemployment Insurance and Unemployment Spells." *Econometrica* 57 (1990): 757–782.

Moffittt, Robert. "Unemployment Insurance and the Distribution of Unemployment Spells." *Journal of Econometrics* 28 (1985): 85–101.

Mortensen, Dale T. "Job Search, the Duration of Unemployment, and the Phillips Curve." *American Economic Review* 60 (1970): 505–517.

_____. "Unemployment Insurance and Job Search Decisions." *Industrial and Labor Relations Review* 30 (1977): 505–517.

_____. "Job Search and Labor Market Analysis." In *Handbook of Labor Economics*, Volume II, O. Ashenfelter and R. Layard, eds. Amsterdam: Elsevier Science Publishers, 1986.

Narendranathan, W., S. Nickell and J. Stern. "Unemployment Benefits Revisited." *Economic Journal* 95 (1985): 307–329.

Nickell, S. "Estimating the Probability of Leaving Unemployment." *Econometrica* 47 (1979): 1249–1266.

van den Berg, G. J. "Nonstationarity in Job Search Theory." *Review of Economic Studies* 57 (1990): 255–277.

7

Offer Arrivals Versus Acceptance

Theresa J. Devine
Congressional Budget Office

Abstract

This paper uses the basic job search model to study demographic variation in the rate at which workers become reemployed. The model implies that the transition rate into employment equals the product of the instantaneous probability that an offer will be received—the arrival rate—and the probability that an offer will be accepted when received—the acceptance probability. By applying estimation methods that require replication to grouped data from the Survey of Income and Program Participation, the paper investigates the relative importance of these two factors. In short, the results suggest that variation in reemployment rates—and thus time spent jobless between jobs—reflects variation in the arrival rate across groups.

1. Introduction

The structure of the stationary job search model is now familiar. The unemployed worker searches each period for wage offers from some distribution. With some probability, an offer is secured. The worker knows both the distribution of offers and the probability of receiving an offer. Uncertainty exists because the worker does not know which firms are making which offers. When an offer is received, the worker must choose between employment at the offered wage and continued search. Suppose that the worker's objective is maximization of the discounted value of lifetime income and that unemployment income net of search costs does not change as a spell continues. The optimal policy for the worker is acceptance of the first offer that exceeds his or her *reservation wage*, which is simply the wage that equates the marginal cost and marginal benefit of continued search.

Given the model's simplicity, it seems unreasonable to expect it to provide a precise description of any individual worker's experience. Complicating the model— by adding structure to the worker's environment or behavior—thus seems an appropriate strategy when attempting to explain demographic variation in the transition rate into employment. Suppose, however, that the objective is to explain variation across major groups that comprise the labor force. One might maintain the simple structure of the model at the individual worker level, but allow for the existence of only a few worker types, *i.e.*, stop somewhere between the macro and micro levels of aggregation and see if the simple model is useful for explaining observed variation across major groups in the labor force. This is the approach taken here.

The basic search model implies that the length of an unemployment spell is determined by the rate that acceptable offers are received—the *transition rate*. This factors into two components: the rate that a worker receives offers—the *arrival rate*—and the probability that a worker will accept an offer once received—the *acceptance probability*. My objective is to determine the relative contributions of offer arrivals versus acceptance to variation in the transition rate across major demographic groups in the U.S.[2]

Others have studied the relative importance of arrival rates and acceptance probabilities. In most cases, researchers have specified parametric functions of *individual* demographic characteristics and local labor market conditions, and then used parametric restrictions or unusual data (numbers of offers or reported reservation wages) to identify the arrival rate and acceptance probability upon estimation. In general, the results of these studies are not encouraging—poor fits are obtained with individual-level data. Since my interest is variation across *groups* of workers, I carry out estimation using *grouped* duration and accepted wage data, treating workers within each subsample as a random sample from a homogeneous population. Grouping the data allows me to estimate the transition rate, arrival rate, and acceptance probability for each group using methods that require replication (but do not require unusual data on reservation wages or actual frequency of offer receipt). Relationships between the key variables are then studied using the results for all groups together. The sample partition basically plays the role of the identifying restriction necessary to determine the relative roles of arrivals versus acceptance.[3]

Offer arrival rates might differ due to discrimination on the demand side of the labor market, for example, or variation in search networks, skills, and effort on the supply side. The acceptance probability depends on the wage offer distribution, which may vary due to differences in human capital, search strategies, or discrimination. It also depends on the reservation wage, which depends on all factors on both the demand and supply sides of the labor market.

Section 2 sets out the basic search model more formally and establishes notation. Section 3 describes the grouped data estimation approach. Section 4 presents a description of the data source—the 1984 Panel of the Survey of Income and Program Participation (SIPP). Section 5 presents a summary of results. Section 6 concludes.

The results presented here suggest that the acceptance probability varies little across demographic groups, but the arrival rate varies substantially—and this variation in the receipt of offers produces almost all variation in exits out of joblessness.

2. The Model

The labor force is treated here as consisting of distinct groups of workers. Within each group, workers are assumed homogeneous. Whether this assumption is reasonable depends on the definition of groups. Obviously, this assumption holds when groups are individuals, perhaps not when the group is the total labor force. The idea here is to locate a reasonable middle ground. At the individual level within a group, I adhere to the standard theoretical job search framework. An individual's labor market history is therefore modeled as a stochastic process which moves the worker among labor market states in response to random events—job offers and layoffs for unemployed and employed workers, respectively.[4]

Letting groups be indexed by c, an individual worker in group c seeks to maximize expected lifetime income, discounted to the present over an infinite horizon at some constant positive rate r_c. When unemployed, the worker searches for job offers and offers arrive according to a time-homogeneous Poisson process with parameter δ_c, referred to as the *arrival rate*.[5] A job offer is summarized by a wage rate w that will be received continuously over tenure of employment, if accepted, and successive job offers are independent realizations from a known wage offer distribution with finite mean μ_c, distribution function $F_c(w)$, and density $f_c(w)$. Once employed, a worker may be laid off; the occurrence of these layoffs follows a

Poisson process with parameter a_c. Finally, the income flow while unemployed (net of any search costs) is fixed over the course of a given spell at rate b_c and there is no on-the-job search. Under these assumptions, the optimal acceptance/rejection strategy for the worker is a time-invariant reservation wage policy: accept if $w \geq w_c^r$, where the reservation wage w_c^r is defined by equating the expected present value of employment and the expected present value of continued search.

My interest is the empirical implications of this simple model. Let τ_c denote the instantaneous probability that an individual of type c will become reemployed, $i.e.$, the $transition\ rate$. This is simply the instantaneous probability that an acceptable offer will be received by this individual,

$$\tau_c = \delta_c \, \pi_c \left(w_c^r \right).$$

The first term δ_c is the $arrival\ rate$. The second term $\pi_c \left(w_c^r \right)$ is the conditional probability that an offer, once received, will be accepted under the worker's optimal policy,

$$\pi_c \left(w_c^r \right) \;=\; \int\limits_{w_c^r}^{\infty} dF_c(w)$$

$$=\; 1 - F_c \left(w_c^r \right).$$

This is the $acceptance\ probability$.

In this model, the transition rate between the states of unemployment and employment, τ_c (also referred to as the instantaneous reemployment probability, reemployment rate, or hazard rate) does not depend on elapsed duration, nor does it depend on calendar time—because neither the preferences of the worker, nor the environment depends on these measures of time. This has implications for the distribution of unemployment spell durations T_c. Completed durations have an exponential distribution with parameter τ_c and mean $1/\tau_c$.[6] Thus, variation in mean unemployment spell lengths among groups may be discussed in terms of variation in transition rates τ_c—and variation in transition rates across types c may be attributed to variation in arrival rates δ_c or acceptance probabilities $\pi_c(w_c^r)$. The simple model implies nothing about the relative roles of these two variables. The model renders this an empirical question.

The assumptions of this model are clearly restrictive, but fairly standard in $structural$ empirical search studies.[7] The assumptions may not be relaxed too far without greatly affecting the basic empirical implications of the model. For example, with any source of variation in τ_c over time—such as variation in b_c or δ_c—we lose the exponential distribution for durations. This likely serves to limit the success of attempts to fit stationary search models to individual-level data. Of course, replacements for the assumptions that deliver stationarity are also assumptions—and additional assumptions (that may have unclear or questionable economic bases or implications) are consequently required for estimation of more complex models. In light of this situation, this study questions whether the simple search model can be useful for understanding average experience within major groups in labor force.

3.   The Empirical Approach

A few previous studies have attempted to sort out arrival rates and acceptance probabilities (*e.g.,* Mortensen and Neumann 1984, Narendranathan and Nickell 1985, Ridder and Gorter 1986, Blau and Robins 1986). These studies all focus on experience at the individual worker level. Accordingly, their econometric approaches involve parameterization of each structural element in the model. That is, functions defined over individual characteristics, income variables, and labor market conditions are specified for the arrival rate, parameters of the offer distribution, etc. A number of somewhat arbitrary restrictions are then suggested for identification. In some cases, unusual data are used for identification (numbers of offers in the study by Blau and Robins, for example, and reported reservation wages and minimum wage offers in the study by Ridder and Gorter). In general, consistency checks on such data are not favorable to the interpretation used in estimation, which calls their use into question.

My approach to the data involves working directly with a partition of a sample from the labor force based on demographic characteristics. Specifically, for each group c within a partition of the labor force, there exists a set of basic search parameters $\{\tau_c, \delta_c, F_c(w), w_c^r\}$. I estimate these parameters using data on accepted wages and spell durations for the sample of workers of type c, alone, and then interpret the results as representative for all individuals having the characteristics that define the group. Beyond specification of a partition, the only parameterization required at the empirical stage is specification of a parametric family of wage offer distributions $\{F(w \mid \theta_c), \theta_c \in \Theta\}$. This is unavoidable in the absence of complete data on *rejected* offers. This is the usual situation—and it is the situation faced here.

With estimates of the arrival rate and acceptance probability for each group, I can consider whether observed variation in transition rates across groups reflects systematic variation in arrival rates or acceptance probabilities or both. The precise strategy I follow to estimate the elements of the vector $\{\tau_c, \delta_c, [F(w \mid \theta_c), \theta_c \in \Theta], w_c^r\}$ for each group c follows:

3.1 The Transition Rate

The search model set out above implies that completed unemployment spell lengths of all workers in group c are independently and identically distributed according to an exponential distribution with parameter τ_c. The maximum likelihood estimate of the transition rate for group c therefore involves a straightforward calculation using data on spell durations for the group c sample. Let $d_{ci} = 1$ if spell observation t_{ci} for person i in the group c sample is censored, and let $d_{ci} = 0$ otherwise. Let N_c denote the group c sample size. Then the maximum likelihood estimator is given by

$$\tau_c^* = \sum_{i=1}^{N_c} d_{ci} \bigg/ \sum_{i=1}^{N_c} t_{ci} \ .$$

Note that the maximum likelihood estimator for mean duration is simply $1/\tau_c^*$.

3.2 The Reservation Wage

Assuming that the wages observed for individuals in group c are realizations of independently and identically distributed random variables with distribution function $F_c(w \mid w \geq w_c^r)$, a number of consistent estimators w_c^{r*} for w_c^r based on accepted wages are available. In particular, any of the first m order statistics, m fixed, and their averages represent strongly consistent estimators. I use the average of the first two order statistics.[8]

3.3 The Offer Arrival Rate

With estimates of the reservation wage and the transition rate for group c, if I know the distribution $F_c(w)$, then I need only assume that the arrival rate and offer distribution are stochastically independent to calculate a consistent estimate of the arrival rate. That is, since $\tau_c = \delta_c \pi_c(w_c^r)$, I can use

$$\delta_c^* = \tau_c^* / \pi_c\left(w_c^{r*}\right),$$

as an estimator. I do not know $F_c(w)$ or, equivalently $\pi_c(w) = 1 - F_c(w)$, but must estimate this instead. I turn to this next.

3.4 The Offer Distribution

Specification of a parametric family of wage offer distributions is unavoidable for two reasons if identification of the arrival rate δ_c is desired. First, economic theory says very little about the true offer distribution. Second, the true offer distribution $F_c(w)$ faced by the type c workers cannot be determined uniquely from my sample wage data using nonparametric methods alone—regardless of the group c sample size—because only *accepted wages* are observed. That is, observed wages are drawn from distributions truncated at the reservation wage w_c^r with density

$$f_c\left(w \mid w \geq w_c^r\right) \;=\; f_c(w)/\pi_c\left(w_c^r\right), \qquad w \geq w_c^r$$
$$=\; 0, \qquad\qquad\qquad \text{otherwise.}$$

Nonparametric estimation clearly requires data on $w < w_c^r$, *i.e.*, information regarding the mass below the reservation wage.

Given this situation, I assume that $F_c(w)$ is a member of a parametric family $\{F(w \mid \theta_c),\ \theta_c \in \Theta\}$ and use the observations from the truncated distribution to estimate the parameters θ_c. Obviously, the set from which this parametric family may be chosen has one key restriction. The vector of parameters must be estimable from the data on the accepted wages, which means that no element of θ_c can depend on anything below w_c^r.[9] The gamma represents a candidate family, given this restriction, and it is attractive because it is a two-parameter family. It is also nonnegative, which seems sensible for a wage distribution.[10]

The parameters θ_c are estimated using the method of moments. Precisely, theoretical moments $m(\theta_c)$ and sample moments S_c for the truncated distribution are equated, yielding a system of k nonlinear simultaneous equations in θ_c

$$S_c = m(\theta_c),$$

where the choice of k satisfies $k \geq p$, the dimension of θ_c. Consistent estimates are then obtained by solving the minimum distance problem

$$\min_{\substack{\theta \\ \theta \in \Theta}} \; D(\theta) = \left[S_c - m(\theta)\right]' \, A \, \left[S_c - m(\theta)\right]$$

where A is a consistent estimate for the inverse of the asymptotic covariance matrix for S_c.[11] By working with more than two moments of the accepted offer distribution, the system of equations is overidentified. A specification check—in the form of a Chi-square test of the overidentifying restriction—is therefore available under each distributional assumption.

As with any identification method, there is a price involved with taking a grouped data approach. I cannot infer the effects of heterogeneity remaining within each group at each level of aggregation. Marginal effects of particular variables on turnover (such as the effect of a one-year increase in age) are not ascertained. As noted, however, results obtained by others suggest that pushing the stationary job search model to explain varied behavior at the individual level may be pushing it too far.[12] The usefulness of the grouped data method is examined here for a simpler objective—casting light on variation across major groups, as opposed to variation across individual workers.

4. Data

The data are taken from the Public Use Files for the 1984 Panel of the Survey of Income and Program Participation (SIPP), a nationwide longitudinal multi-panel survey conducted by the Bureau of the Census since 1984. SIPP is an attractive data source for empirical labor economics for several reasons. Labor force activity and income data are available in finer detail than that offered by alternative sources for the U.S. The data are also collected more frequently (every four months, as opposed to annually). SIPP samples are also relatively large and representative for the U.S. The most undesirable feature of the SIPP data is the relatively complex structure of the survey design and the microdata files that contain complete information collected in the survey. For example, respondents report labor force activity information on a week-by-week basis for each four-month reference period, and the data for each four-month reference period are provided in a separate microdata file.[13] Merging data for individuals across reference periods is less than straightforward, but necessary to fully exploit SIPP's longitudinal features.[14]

I work with data from the first four interviews of the survey (*i.e.*, sixteen months) for a sample of 5,214 workers who: (i) experienced an initialized spell of joblessness (new entrants are thus excluded), (ii) did not report having a job in either an agricultural occupation or an agricultural industry, (iii) either worked full-time hours or reported part-time hours were due to economic reasons when employed, (iv) remained age 64 or less at the end of the first completed spell of joblessness or the end of the sixteen month period considered, and (v) were neither disabled nor self-employed during the survey period. Table 7.1 presents a summary of the sample.[15]

The two key variables in my analysis are accepted wages and unemployment spell lengths.[16] Neither is reported directly in SIPP, but numerous related items are reported. In turn, using the data for research requires a number of decisions. In this paper, durations are measured as weeks of *joblessness*, where being *with a job* is defined as having an arrangement with an employer for regular work.[17] Responses to a direct question about the hourly wage are used for hourly workers. For salaried workers, average hourly earnings must be used. These are based on monthly earnings, weeks employed, and usual weekly hours.[18]

Table 7.1. Data Summary.

Variable	Mean	Standard Deviation
Proportion White	0.84	
Proportion Male	0.47	
Proportion Married	0.45	
Age	32.46	13.64
Years of Education	12.72	3.08
Jobless Spell Durations (Weeks):		
All Spells	14.96	13.74
Uncensored	9.83	8.14
Wage (accepted Hourly Wage or Average Hourly Earnings)	5.88	4.37

Note: The total number of jobless spell duration observations is 5,214. Of these, 4,112 are completed during the survey reference period, and accepted hourly earnings can be measured for 3,396 of the accepted jobs. See text for discussion of additional sample restrictions.

Table 7.2. Demographic Group Definitions.

Characteristic	Partition			
Age	16–19	20–24	25–44	45–64
Race	White		Nonwhite	
Sex	Male		Female	

5. Results

Results are presented here for a partition by race, sex, and age. Table 7.2 provides a complete summary of the classification scheme which produces sixteen groups.

Table 7.3 presents estimates of the transition rate between unemployment and employment τ_c for each group and the expected jobless spell lengths based on these estimates (Expected Duration). Note that these estimates do not depend on a distributional assumption for offers, but do rely on the exponential specification for durations. The number of duration observations and number of wage observations are reported, since these vary across groups. Obviously more confidence can be placed in results for white workers and younger workers.

Some clear age and race patterns appear in the estimates for the group transition rates. First, older workers become reemployed much more slowly than younger workers. Nonwhite workers also leave joblessness more slowly than their white

Table 7.3. Group Transition Rates.

Group	Number of Observations		Estimated τ_c	Expected Duration
	Wage	Spells		
White Males:				
Ages 16–29	296	360	0.073	13.69
Ages 20–24	404	516	0.069	14.49
Ages 25–44	556	801	0.068	14.70
Ages 45–64	187	392	0.036	27.77
Nonwhite Males:				
Ages 16–29	44	57	0.059	16.94
Ages 20–24	66	88	0.064	15.62
Ages 25–44	89	150	0.048	20.83
Ages 45–64	25	73	0.020	50.00
White Females:				
Ages 16–29	240	293	0.067	14.92
Ages 20–24	363	527	0.063	15.87
Ages 25–44	598	1005	0.051	19.60
Ages 45–64	226	484	0.033	30.30
Nonwhite Females:				
Ages 16–29	40	47	0.064	15.62
Ages 20–24	63	103	0.042	23.80
Ages 25–44	129	233	0.039	25.64
Ages 45–64	36	85	0.023	43.47

Notes: Data collected in 1984 Panel of the Survey of Income and Program Participation (SIPP).

counterparts, although the contrast is less sharp for female teens (16–19) and young adult males (20–24). As for gender differences, white males within each age group tend to move out more quickly than their female counterparts, but the difference is substantial only for prime-age workers (25–44). Among nonwhite workers, on the other hand, this gender difference appears only for the young adult and prime-age nonwhite groups and, even for these age groups, the nonwhite gender differences are relatively small.

The general demographic pattern exhibited in the transition rate estimates is roughly consistent with those based on CPS gross flow data (*e.g.*, Ehrenberg 1981). My interest is in determining which of the two potential factors—the arrival rate or the acceptance probability—plays the greater role in producing this pattern. Table 7.4 presents estimates of the search model parameters $\{\tau_c, \delta_c, \pi_c(w_c^r)\}$ under the gamma specification for the family of offer distributions, with the average of the first two order statistics serving as the reservation wage estimator.[19] Overall, the arrival rate

Table 7.4. Results for Gamma Famly of Distributions.

Group	N	w_r^c	$E\left(w \mid w \geq w_f^c\right)$	τ_c	$\pi_c\left(w_r^c\right)$	δ_c	χ^{2a}
White Males:							
Ages 16–29	296	1.054	4.067	0.073	0.999	0.073	4.152
Ages 20–24	404	1.054	5.640	0.069	0.995	0.070	1.763
Ages 25–44	556	1.684	8.261	0.068	0.980	0.069	1.097
Ages 45–64	187	1.364	9.857	0.036	0.984	0.037	1.081
Nonwhite Males:							
Ages 16–29	44	2.249	3.667	0.059	0.956	0.061	2.132
Ages 20–24	66	1.169	4.445	0.064	0.997	0.064	3.646
Ages 25–44	89	1.634	6.849	0.048	0.966	0.049	2.518
Ages 45–64	25	2.464	8.739	0.020	0.968	0.020	1.974
White Females:							
Ages 16–29	240	1.054	3.792	0.067	0.998	0.068	1.038
Ages 20–24	363	1.064	4.493	0.063	0.990	0.064	1.480
Ages 25–44	598	1.029	5.842	0.051	0.984	0.052	5.518
Ages 45–64	226	1.539	6.043	0.033	0.968	0.034	7.269
Nonwhite Females:							
Ages 16–29	40	2.125	3.602	0.064	0.974	0.066	9.295
Ages 20–24	63	3.059	4.355	0.042	0.906	0.046	15.588
Ages 25–44	129	1.484	5.911	0.039	0.964	0.041	1.166
Ages 45–64	36	1.579	4.655	0.023	0.982	0.023	1.102

[a] The critical values for the chi-square statistic with one degree of freedom are 0.000982 and 5.02 at the 5 percent level, and 0.0000393 and 7.88 at the 1 percent level.

Notation:

w_r^c	=	reservation wage
$E\left(w \mid w \geq w_f^c\right)$	=	mean of accepted offer distribution
τ_c	=	transition rate
$\pi_c\left(w_c^r\right)$	=	acceptance probability
δ_c	=	arrival rate
χ^2	=	Chi-Square value

appears to be the dominant factor. This can be gathered most easily from the plots of the estimates for the transition rates τ_c against the arrival rate δ_c estimates in Figure 7.1 and against the acceptance probability $\pi_c(w_c^r)$ estimates in Figure 7.2. The positive, essentially linear relationship in Figure1 suggests that groups with higher transition rates are groups with higher arrival rates. The simple correlation between the τ_c and δ_c estimates is 0.998 under the gamma specification. In contrast, there is little evidence of a systematic relationship between the transition rate and acceptance probabilities estimates. The simple correlations between the τ_c and $\pi_c(w_c^r)$ estimates is 0.412.[20]

Note that estimated *levels* of the group acceptance probabilities do exhibit sensitivity to the specification of the offer distribution family. Under the gamma specification, the results imply that all groups accept essentially all offers. But experimentation with the family of normal distributions produces very different results.

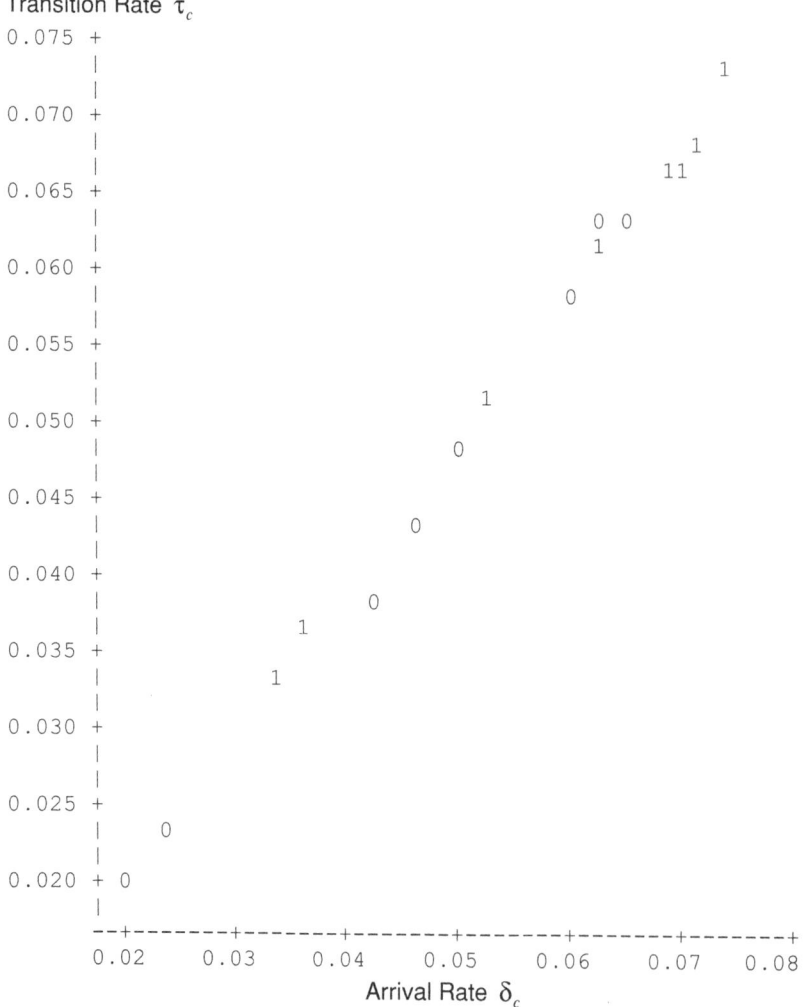

Figure 7.1. Plot of Estimated Transition Rate against Estimated Arrival Rate.

Notes: Symbols indicate race, with White=1 and Nonwhite=0.

Acceptance probability estimates are about one-half the size of the gamma probability estimates when the normal family is specified, and arrival rate estimates reach higher levels accordingly.[21] Overall, the gamma distributions do seem to fit the data better, however. Although chi-square statistics for the test of the over identifying restrictions (reported for the gamma distribution in the last column of Table 7.4), which provide a measure of overall fit of a distribution to the data, are similar for the two families, distribution parameter estimates are more precise for the gamma distributions. Moreover, the gamma distribution estimates make more sense than the

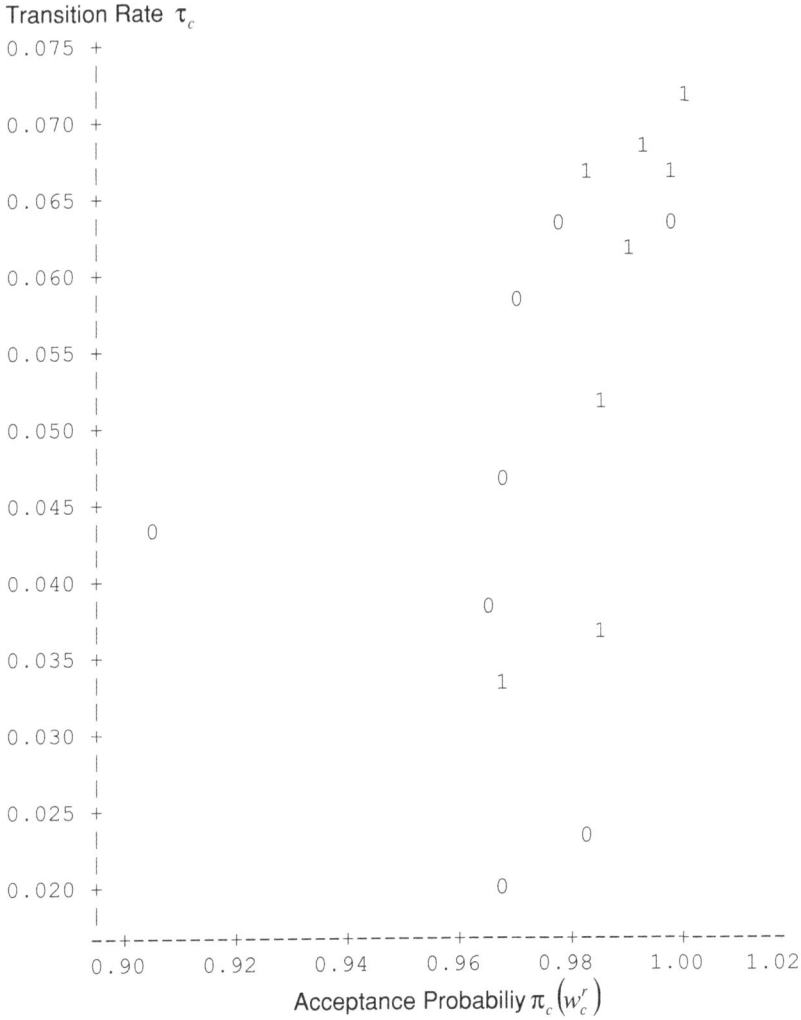

Notes: Symbols indicate race, with White=1 and Nonwhite=0.

Figure 7.2. Plot of Estimated Transition Rate against Estimated Acceptance.

normal distribution estimates. The normal wage offer distribution estimates center roughly at a mean wage offer of zero for all groups, which imply negative offers. On balance, it appears that the data to want to force half-normal distributions (*i.e.,* something close to a gamma).[22] Note, also, that relatively little variation appears in the offer probability estimates for different groups when the normal distribution. Thus, the results for the normal specification also imply that demographic variation in the offer arrival rate produces demographic variation in transition rates and spell lengths.

As a second check on the results, estimation was also carried out using the first and the second order statistics under both the gamma and normal offer distribution specifications. The levels of the acceptance probabilities vary slightly for individual groups—as expected, given slightly different truncation points—but there is little difference in fit. Most important, the results for arrival rates versus acceptance probabilities are consistent with those reported above.[23]

6.   Concluding Remarks

The results presented here suggest that offer arrival rates vary substantially across major demographic groups in the U.S. labor force. They further suggest that variation in the transition rate into employment is related directly to this arrival rate variation. This finding appears robust to variation in the specification of a parametric family for the offer distributions and choice of estimator for the reservation wage.

The estimated level of the acceptance probability for each demographic group appears sensitive to the specification of the offer distribution, but it is close to one when a sensible specification is chosen—and there is virtually no evidence of a systematic relationship between the transition rate and the acceptance probability.

Throughout this analysis, the arrival rates and offer distributions are treated as exogenous. Given that the acceptance probability estimates are not far from unity, one might conclude that all variation in transition rates across groups reflects bad luck for some and good luck for others.[24] However, on the basis of my findings alone, we cannot rule out the possibility of variation in search intensity or "systematic search," *i.e.,* that workers apply for jobs that they will almost certainly accept if offered. Under either interpretation, choice on the part of individual workers represents the source of variation in arrival rates and thus transition rates—with or without variation in the acceptance probability. Studies of systematic search by young workers have generally found evidence of its importance (*e.g.,* Jensen and Westergaard-Nielsen, 1987, and Stern, 1989). The findings reported here suggest that further investigation—for prime-age and older workers, in particular—could yield interesting results. More generally, the results suggest the importance of search technology. Although there have been hundreds of empirical search studies, our current understanding of the actual search process remains limited.[25]

Additional assumptions of the model serve primarily to ensure the stationarity of the worker's environment and preferences. It is not clear that structural analysis can be done in a nonstationary framework without extraordinary data or at least some fairly arbitrary assumptions.[26] This remains an area of active research. Of course, the arrival rate estimator used here is basically *residual* inter-group variation in the transition rate after controlling for variation in acceptance probabilities.[27] This means that unavoidable measurement error in the accepted wage data can affect all results. Modeling this error formally represents one way to deal with this issue, although this approach requires extensive assumptions.

These concerns make the findings presented here tentative. Nevertheless, the basic finding that the arrival rate is the main source of variation in time spent jobless is quite striking—particularly given the emphasis of the search literature on reservation wages and acceptance probabilities. Offer arrival rates can vary due to discrimination on the demand side of the labor market. Alternatively, variation may be due to differences in networks, search skills, and search effort across groups. Sorting out the contributions of these sources represents an important avenue for future research.

Notes

1. Principal Analyst, Health and Human Resources Division, Congressional Budget Office. The views expressed in this paper are those of the author and should not be interpreted as those of the Congressional Budget Office. The author thanks Nick Kiefer, George Jakubson, and David Easley for many helpful discussions and comments on this work. Ken Burdett, Alberto Martini, Lars Muus, Derek Neal, George Neumann, Geert Ridder, Mark Roberts, Steve Woodbury, members of the Cornell Labor Workshop, and participants in the Midwest Economics Association meetings are also thanked for comments and suggestions along the way. Remaining errors are mine alone. The data were obtained from ICPSR through CISER at Cornell and most of the computing was done at the Cornell National Supercomputer Facility. Support from the National Science Foundation (SES 90-23-776, SES 90-103-07), Cornell Center for Analytic Economics, and the American Bar Foundation is gratefully acknowledged.

An earlier paper, "Interpreting Reemployment Patterns in the 1980s," used the same estimation approach as this paper and used data from the January 1984 Displaced Worker Survey (DWS) supplement to the January CPS. Unfortunately, serious limitations of the 1984 DWS duration data (namely, reported nonemployment spell durations are aggregated over an unknown number of spells) required a change of data source. My thanks extend to the BLS staff for bringing the DWS problems to my attention—and to many colleagues who made comments on the earlier paper. For the record, the results are qualitatively the same.

2. The relationship between transition rates among labor market states and levels of unemployment rates has been well-documented—and a source of concern—for decades. Studies by Hall (1972), Perry (1972), Ehrenberg (1981), and Bailey (1982), for example, used CPS gross flow data to calculate transition rates among unemployment, employment, and nonparticipation that together produce observed variation in unemployment rates across demographic groups. Consistent with most of the empirical search literature, this paper

focuses only on variation in the transition rate into employment. See Devine and Kiefer (1991) for a survey and critique of the empirical search literature.

3. The structural studies of Flinn and Heckman (1982) and Wolpin (1987) also use this replication principle, but focus exclusively on a single group (young white U.S. men) and use different estimation approaches. The principle is also applied to single demographic groups by Lancaster and Chesher (1983) using data for U.K. men and Stern (1989) using data for young U.S. men, but these studies both rely on very unusual data. Devine and Kiefer (1991) discuss these studies in detail.

4. The model of individual behavior used here is a simple extension of the first sequential search model set out by McCall (1970) and Mortensen (1970). See Lipmann and McCall (1976) and Mortensen (1986) for a summary of basic and more elaborate theoretical search models. Consistent with nearly all of the search literature, it is "partial-partial" equilibrium in its treatment of employer behavior as passive and all other markets as exogenous. Equilibrium search is an active area of current research.

5. The probability of receiving at least one offer within a short interval h is thus $\tau_c h + o(h)$, where $o(h)$ is the probability of receiving more than one offer in the interval h and $(o(h)/h) \Rightarrow 0$ as $h \Rightarrow 0$.

6. Under the Poisson layoff assumption, employment durations for a type c worker also have an exponential distribution (with parameter a_c). This assumption is not used in the core empirical analysis of this paper. See Devine and Kiefer (1991) for studies of employment exits.

7. The term *"structural"* here refers to studies that attempt to identify parameters of a tight theoretical structure. See Devine and Kiefer (1991) for discussion of the cited studies and many other structural search studies.

8. Since the reordering of the individuals in the sample of group c workers does not change the information content of the sample, by assumption (*i.e.,* the subscript i serves only as a label), the individuals are "exchangeable" in the statistical sense. This allows one to treat the sample as if it were an independently and identically distributed sample from some distribution (diFinetti 1975). This property of each type c sample is exploited at all stages of estimation.

A practical problem with using order statistics for accepted wages is their sensitivity to errors in measurement; all order statistics will be inconsistent if there is measurement error. As checks on my results, I estimated the model using each of the first two order statistics and calculated a variety of informal tests. In general, the results were sensible. These results are presented in appendices (E and F) which will be provided upon request. Note, also, that Flinn and Heckman (1982) use the first order statistic as a reservation wage estimator in their study of male youth.

9. The Pareto family, for example, with density

$$f\left(w; w_{oc}, \alpha_c\right) = \alpha w_{oc}^\alpha w^{-\alpha-1}, \, w_{oc}, \alpha > 0,$$

is excluded on this basis, since the lower bound $w_{oc} \leq w_c^r$ cannot be identified.

10. Since my estimator for the arrival rate δ_c^* may be sensitive to choice of family, experimentation with alternatives seems an appropriate approach. Results reported below are restricted to the gamma family estimates, but the full set of parameters was also estimated for the normal family. The normal family shares the first two required characteristics of the gamma family, but not the third desirable characteristic—normal distributions have negative mass. See Devine (1988).

11. This estimation procedure is described in greater detail in an appendix (Appendix C), which is available from the author upon request.

12. See, for example, Ridder and Gorter (1986). Devine and Kiefer (1991) critique this and other structural search studies.

13. Data from all interviews for each Panel are now available in single data files. However, these longitudinal data files only include data aggregated to the monthly level. Weekly labor market data are not available. See Devine (1991, 1993) for discussion.

14. Discussion of SIPP and the approach used here to merge the data is provided in an (Appendix D), which the author will provide upon request. For details on available labor market data, survey improvements (from the labor economist's perspective), and problems remaining in SIPP data for Panels started after 1984, see Devine (1991, 1993).

15. A restriction to the nonstudent population is desirable, but infeasible for the 1984 SIPP Panel. Only enrollment beyond high school is reported, it is reported for the entire four month reference period preceding a given Wave interview, and there is no indication of the type of education program the person attends. Thus, it is impossible to distinguish high school dropouts from those enrolled in high school or college students from those enrolled in job training programs. No exclusion is used here. Twenty-eight percent of the sample analyzed here reported enrollment at some time in the sixteen month period followed. For both whites and nonwhites, this translates into enrollment of forty to fifty percent of persons less than 25 years of age, about twenty percent for those between 25 to 44, and five to nine percent for older workers. In all cases, these proportions are implausibly large and suggest ambiguity on the part of respondents. These school enrollment data problems are not present for 1985 and subsequent Panels of SIPP.

16. Using both reported hourly wage rates and average hourly earnings, I have observations for 3,396 persons. As expected, the average hourly earning data show clear signs of measurement error. In the analysis reported here, I restrict my sample to wage rates at or above one dollar, which excludes 34 observations. Obviously, this level is arbitrary, but alternative levels yielded qualitatively similar results.

17. This concept is distinct from the standard BLS definition of *unemployment* (*i.e.,* either temporary layoff or no employment arrangement with an employer *and* actively searching). It is also distinct from being *out of work* (which may include paid or unpaid absence due to illness, a labor dispute, or vacation). Data for the 1986 Panel of SIPP allow one to get closer to the standard BLS definitions, but not without a lot of human effort and computer time. At present, I am developing a data set that consists of week-by-week histories based on better

employer identification and work status data available for the 1986 and subsequent SIPP Panel. See Devine (1991, 1993) for discussion.

18. Observation on accepted earnings (used for estimation of the reservation wages and parameters of offer distributions) are not used if earnings or hours were imputed by the Census Bureau or earnings in accepted jobs could not be distinguished. The latter problem of incomplete data was the more important problem (imputations rates are low in SIPP) and it resulted from problems in the design of the Core questionnaire for the 1984 Panel (which partially corrected for subsequent Panels of SIPP). See Devine (1988, 1991, 1993) for discussion.

19. Corresponding estimates of the distribution parameters θ_c and their standard errors are presented below in the appendix. Note that the sample sizes for all nonwhite groups are significantly smaller than sample sizes for the white groups. This may explain the higher estimates for the reservation wage; the positive bias of the order statistics can be shown to be decreasing with sample size. Note that this will decrease the acceptance probability estimate and thus push up the estimates for the arrival rates. Consequently, the white-nonwhite differential in the arrival rates is probably understated by the numbers presented here.

Also, as noted, the duration data pertain to time spent *jobless*, versus *unemployed* as measured by the Bureau of Labor Statistics. Empirical evidence on the importance of distinguishing nonparticipation and unemployment is limited, but it appears that the distinction is perhaps more relevant for adult males than for other groups. See Devine and Kiefer (1991).

20. Regressions of τ_c on δ_c yield coefficients of 0.995 (s.e. 0.015) under the gamma when all group observations included and 0.993 (s.e. 0.012) when only the twelve observations with χ^2 less than 5.02 are included. Regressions of τ_c on $\pi_c(w_c^r)$ yield coefficients of 0.309 (s.e. 0.183) under the gamma with all group observations included and 0.645 (s.e. 0.338) when only the twelve observations with χ^2 less than 5.02 are included.

21. Limited variation in the acceptance probability across groups should not be confused with a lack of variation in the offer distributions across groups. As shown below in the appendix, the offer distributions vary substantially.

22. Wolpin (1987) reports that he obtains negative estimates for mean offers when he attempts to fit a normal distribution to wage data for young male workers. His results might also be interpreted as suggesting half-normal distributions.

23. Results for the normal distribution are presented in an appendix (Appendix E), which the author will provide upon request. Note, also, that experimentation with the lognormal family (which also rules out negative wages) yielded estimates of unity for the acceptance probability.

24. When looking at the roles of arrivals versus acceptance probabilities in producing variation across individuals, Mortensen and Neumann (1984) maintain this assumption and accordingly describe the two factors as *"chance"* and *"choice"*, respectively.

25. Holzer (1988), for example, provides descriptive evidence on the search process of low-income youth in the U.S. See Devine and Kiefer (1991) for discussion of additional direct

evidence. Davidson (1990) reviews alternative theoretical models of unemployment, including search theories, and empirical evidence. Bridging these literatures at the empirical level seems an appropriate response to the limited empirical performance of the individual theoretical frameworks.

26. In his analysis of young males in the U.S., Wolpin (1987) relaxes stationarity by imposing a finite search horizon, which is defined as a date after which all offers are accepted. At the empirical stage, this horizon is a parameter that must be assigned. See Devine and Kiefer (1991) for discussion of this and other structural studies.

27. Taking logs of the equation that defines the estimator, $\delta_c = \tau_c / \pi_c(w_c^r)$, makes this clear.

References

Bailey, Martin. *Workers, Jobs, and Inflation*. Washington, DC: The Brookings Institution, 1982.

Blau, David *M*. and Philip *K*. Robins. "Job Search, Wage Offers, and Unemployment Insurance." *Journal of Public Economics* 29 (1986): 173–197.

Davidson, Carl. *Recent Developments in the Theory of Involuntary Unemployment*. Kalamazoo, MI: Upjohn Institute, 1990.

Devine, Theresa J. "Interpreting Reemployment Patterns in the Search Framework." Unpublished Ph.D. Dissertation, Cornell University, 1988.

_____. "Job Exits and Job-to-Job Transitions: The Potential of SIPP for Empirical Analysis." In *1991 Annual Research Conference Proceedings*, U.S. Bureau of the Census, 1991.

_____. "Measurement of Job Exits: What Difference Does Ambiguity Make?" In *Labour Market Dynamics*, edited by Niels Westergaard-Nielsen, Henning Bunzel, and Peter Jensen. Amsterdam: North Holland, 1993. Pp. 75–105.

Devine, Theresa J. and Nicholas *M*. Kiefer. *Empirical Labor Economics: The Search Approach*. Oxford, UK: Oxford University Press, 1991.

diFinetti, Bruno. *Theory of Probability*, vol. 2. New York: Wiley, 1975.

Ehrenberg, Ronald G. "The Demographic Structure of Unemployment Rates and Labor Market Transition Probabilities." In *Research in Labor Economics*, volume 3, edited by Ronald G. Ehrenberg. Greenwich, CT: JAI Press, 1981. Pp. 241–291.

Flinn, Christopher and James Heckman. "New Methods for Analyzing Structural Models of Labor Force Dynamics." *Journal of Econometrics* 18 (1982): 115–68.

174   Theresa J. Devine

Hall, Robert. "Turnover in the Labor Force." *Brookings Papers on Economic Activity* (1972): 709–756.

Holzer, Harry. "Search Method Use by Unemployed Youth." *Journal of Labor Economics* 6 (1988): 1–20.

Jensen, Peter and Westergard-Nielsen, Niels. "A Search Model Applied to the Transition from Education to Work." *Review of Economic Studies* 54 (1987): 461–72.

Lancaster, Tony and Andrew Chesher. "An Econometric Analysis of Reservation Wages." *Econometrica* 51 (1983): 1661–1176.

Lipmann, Steven A. and John J. McCall. "The Economics of Job Search: A Survey." *Economic Inquiry* 14 (1976): 155–189 and 347–368.

McCall, John J. "The Economics of Information and Job Search." *Quarterly Journal of Economics* 84 (1970): 113–126.

Mortensen, Dale T. "Job Search, the Duration of Unemployment, and the Phillips Curve." *American Economic Review* 60 (1970): 505–517.

_____. "Job Search and Labor Market Analysis." In *Handbook of Labor Economics*, volume 2, edited by O. Ashenfelter and R. Layard. Amsterdam: North-Holland, 1986.

Mortensen, Dale T. and George R. Neumann. "Choice or Chance? A Structural Interpretation of Individual Labor Market Histories." In *Studies in Labor Market Dynamics*, edited by George R. Neumann and Neils Westergard-Nielsen. Heidelberg: Springer-Verlag, 1984. Pp. 98–131.

Narendranathan, Wiji, and Stephen Nickell. "Modeling the Process of Job Search" *Journal of Econometrics* 28 (1985): 29–49.

Perry, George L. "Unemployment Flows in the U.S. Labor Market." *Brookings Papers on Economic Activity* (1972): 245–292.

Ridder, Geert and Kees Gorter. "Unemployment Benefits and Search Behavior: An Empirical Investigation." Manuscript, Cornell University, May 1986.

Stern, Steven. "Estimating a Simultaneous Search Model." *Journal of Labor Economics* 7 (1989): 348–69.

U.S. Department of Commerce, Bureau of the Census. *Survey of Income and Program Participation - 1984 Panel, Rectangular Core and Topical Modules, Technical Documentation*, 1985–1987.

Wolpin, Kenneth. "Estimating a Structural Search Model: The Transition from School to Work." *Econometrica* 55 (1987): 801–818.

Appendix

Parameter Estimates for the Offer Distribution

Table 7.A1 presents parameter estimates for the gamma family using the average of the first order two statistics as the estimator for the reservation wage, corresponding to the search parameter estimates reported in Section 4. The implied mean and variance for the gamma are also reported (GMU and GVAR, respectively).

The size of the maximum of the absolute value of the gradient at the reported estimates is reported along with the parameter estimates and their asymptotic standard errors. For some groups, the parameters did not converge under the gradient convergence criterion of 10^{-4}. However, experimentation with alternative starting values and alternative step sizes failed to produce any change in the parameter values from those reported for these cases and the distance appeared to be at a minimum.

The standard errors for the parameter estimates are quite small in statistical terms for both distributions, with the exception of the mean of the offer distribution under the normal specification. As for the relative fits of the two distributions, the values of chi-square statistic are only slightly more likely to lead to a rejection of the overidentifying restriction under the gamma than under the normal.

Obviously, variation in sample size across groups should be considered in interpreting the results. While the overall sample size is quite large, the sample sizes for some of the nonwhite groups are quite small. By the same token, it appears that no alternative data source provides larger samples for these groups, while providing observations on the variables required.

Table 7A.1. Gamma Distribution: Parameter Estimates.

Group	N	ALPHA α_c	BETA β_c	GMU $E_c(w)$	GVAR $\mathrm{Var}(w)$	CCHI[a] χ^2	MAX F[b]
White Males:							
Ages 16–29	296	14.253	0.279	3.978 (1.713)	1.110 (0.035)	4.152	0.000
Ages 20–24	404	4.471	1.234	5.520 (0.389)	6.817 (0.121)	1.736	0.000
Ages 25–44	556	3.338	2.400	8.014 (0.230)	19.236 (0.175)	1.097	0.000
Ages 45–64	187	2.664	3.457	9.211 (0.407)	31.846 (0.564)	1.081	0.000

Table 7A.1 *(continued)*. Gamma Distribution: Parameter Estimats.

Group	N	ALPHA α_c	BETA β_c	GMU $E_c(w)$	GVAR $Var(w)$	CCHI[a] χ^2	MAX F[b]
Nonwhite Males:							
Ages 16–29	44	17.835	0.199	3.553 (1.171)	0.707 (0.013)	2.123	0.647
Ages 20–24	66	7.997	0.508	4.064 (2.287)	2.066 (0.151)	3.646	0.003
Ages 25–44	89	3.331	1.908	6.357 (0.693)	12.130 (0.424)	2.518	0.001
Ages 45–64	25	3.992	2.100	8.387 (1.554)	17.621 (0.737)	1.974	0.002
White Females:							
Ages 16–29	240	9.101	0.402	3.662 (1.616)	1.473 (0.073)	1.038	0.000
Ages 20–24	363	4.882	0.886	4.329 (0.873)	3.839 (0.165)	1.480	0.000
Ages 25–44	598	3.221	1.716	5.527 (0.273)	9.485 (0.160)	5.518	0.000
Ages 45–64	226	3.756	1.472	5.532 (0.502)	8.147 (0.210)	7.269	0.000
Nonwhite Females:							
Ages 16–29	40	18.999	0.185	3.519 (2,886)	0.662 (0.026)	9.295	6.184
Ages 20–24	63	41.500	0.091	3.817 (30.930)	0.351 (0.121)	15.588	21.447
Ages 25–44	129	3.427	1.615	5.535 (0.525)	8.940 (0.263)	1.166	0.000
Ages 45–64	36	6.578	0.671	4.416 (3.273)	2.965 (0.328)	1.102	0.000

Average of first two order statistics used as estimator for reservation wage.

[a]The critical values for the chi-square statistic with one degree of freedom are 0.000982 and 5.02 at the 5 percent level and 0.0000393 and 7.88 at the 1 percent level.

[b]MAX F is the maximum absolute value of the gradient at the reported estimates. In some cases, this value exceeds the desired value for convergence. In such cases, the sum of squares and reported parameter values were unchanging.

8

Optimal Unemployment Insurance with Risk Aversion and Job Destruction

Carl Davidson
Michigan State University

Stephen Woodbury
Michigan State University and
W. E. Upjohn Institute

Abstract

This paper extends earlier research on optimal unemployment insurance (UI) by developing an equilibrium search model that encompasses simultaneously several theoretical and institutional features that have been treated one-by-one (or not at all) in previous discussions of optimal UI. In particular, the model developed determines both the optimal potential duration of UI benefits and the optimal UI benefit amount, assumes (realistically) that not all workers are eligible for UI benefits, allows examination of various degrees of risk aversion by workers, models labor demand so that the job destruction effects of UI are taken into account, and treats workers as heterogeneous. The model suggests that the current statutory replacement rate of 50 percent provided by most states in the United States is close to optimal, but that the current potential duration of benefits (which is usually 26 weeks) is probably too short. This main result—that the optimal UI system is characterized by a fairly low replacement rate and a long potential duration—conflicts with most of the existing literature on optimal UI. However, the result is consistent with a large literature on optimal insurance contracts in the presence of moral hazard.

1. Introduction

Expenditures in the United States on unemployment insurance (UI) amount to about 0.75 percent of GDP. In Canada, France, Germany, and the United Kingdom, expenditures on UI are about 2 percent of GDP; in Japan, just 0.3 percent of GDP (OECD 1995, Table T). These differences reflect differences in both labor markets and in the generosity of UI across the countries. In all cases, however, the primary intent of these expenditures was to provide a safety net for workers facing employment risk who were unable to self-insure by saving enough while employed to smooth consumption across jobless spells. Because workers are unable to purchase UI in the private sector due to moral hazard and adverse selection, insurance is provided publicly. But governments cannot monitor perfectly the effort put forth by the unemployed to find new jobs, and by providing benefits to the unemployed, the government reduces the incentives workers face to seek reemployment. Thus, there is a tradeoff—if too much public insurance is provided, the unemployed will not work hard enough to find new jobs, but if too little insurance is provided, the unemployed will bear too much employment risk. In devising an optimal UI program, the government must find a way to provide adequate insurance without substantially reducing the incentive to seek new jobs.

Existing UI programs are diverse in the benefits they provide. In the United States, UI is a collection of state-federal programs that differ in the replacement rate paid to workers and in the potential duration of benefits. Nevertheless, the most common characterization of the UI program in the United States is that it provides a benefit equal to roughly 50 percent of the wage earned on the previous job for one-half of a year after a worker loses her job.[1] Similar programs exist in Canada, the United Kingdom, and most other developed countries. In many cases the replacement rate is higher and in most cases the potential duration of benefits is longer.

Recently a large literature has developed that investigates whether existing UI programs are optimal in a variety of senses. Some papers focus on replacement rates (are they too high or too low?), some focus on the time path of benefits (should benefits be constant, rise, or fall over the spell of unemployment?), some focus on the welfare effects of these programs (what is the deadweight loss associated with current programs when compared with optimal programs or no program at all?), and some focus on the potential duration of benefits (should benefits be offered for shorter or longer time periods?). The prevailing view offered by these papers is that current programs are poorly designed and overly generous.

The policy implications of the existing literature on optimal UI are often tenuous because the assumptions underlying the models used are often very strong. For example, most of the studies that attempt to measure the welfare loss from current UI programs assume that workers are risk neutral, so that there can be no welfare gain from the insurance provided by the government. Studies that address the adequacy of current replacement rates often make the unrealistic assumption that the potential duration of benefits is infinite, which leads to conclusions that may be misleading (see below). Articles that have investigated the optimal time path of benefits usually do not address the issue of overall program adequacy.

This paper offers some new results on optimal unemployment insurance programs when the benefit rate is constant over the spell of unemployment. These results can be viewed as an extension of earlier work (Davidson and Woodbury 1997), but they also provide some insights concerning the robustness of the findings of the existing literature.

Section 2 begins with a brief description of the approach that has been adopted in this literature and a critical review of several important contributions in the optimal UI literature. Section 3 develops an extended version of the model developed in Davidson and Woodbury (1997). Section 4 presents the results of this extended model and compares them with results in the existing literature. This comparison illustrates the fragility of some previous results—minor changes in assumptions often dramatically alter conclusions. The comparison also reveals that the key parameter in determining whether current programs are too generous is the degree of worker risk aversion. For example, if the degree of relative risk aversion is low (less than one-half), then current UI programs in the United States are too generous. If, however, the degree of relative risk aversion is high (greater than one-half), then current UI programs in the United States are not generous enough.

2.   Optimal UI: Strengths and Weaknesses of Previous Research

Most work on optimal UI is based on a search model of the labor market in which unemployed workers choose search effort to maximize expected utility. More generous UI increases the insurance offered to the unemployed but also lowers optimal search effort, thereby triggering an increase in unemployment. Although most papers adopt a similar approach, they often differ in the questions that are addressed, the complexity of the models, and the assumptions that are used to simplify the analysis. Attention is restricted to papers that assume the replacement rate to be constant over the spell of unemployment. This assumption is used in subsequent analysis (Section 3) and is consistent with most actual UI programs.[2]

The two pioneering papers on optimal unemployment insurance appeared in the same 1978 issue of the *Journal of Public Economics*. These papers, by Martin N. Baily and J.S. Flemming, are so similar in approach and conclusions that they carried almost identical titles. Both authors use a search model of the labor market in which unemployed workers choose search effort to maximize expected lifetime utility. Workers are risk averse, so that insurance is desired, and an equilibrium model is used in order to capture the impact of UI on unemployment. However, neither author explicitly models firm behavior so that neither is able to capture the impact of UI on the number of job opportunities available to workers. Accordingly, the entire increase in unemployment from UI is due to its impact on search effort.

The papers differ in the time horizons considered (Baily uses a two-period model while Flemming uses an infinite horizon approach), the manner in which the capital market (and thus, saving) is handled, and the utility function used. Nevertheless, as discussed below, they derive remarkably similar results.

Both authors have the same goal—to determine the optimal replacement rate assuming that the rate remains constant over the spell of unemployment. The results are then compared with replacement rates offered in the U.S. and the U.K. to determine whether current UI programs are too generous. Briefly, Baily and Flemming both find that if agents cannot save the optimal replacement rate lies in the 60 to 70 percent range. This result is robust because it does not depend on the time horizon or the manner in which the authors calibrate their models. There is one exception—the result does depend on the degree of risk aversion. Baily assumes that the Arrow-Pratt measure of *relative* risk aversion is constant and equal to one, while Flemming assumes that the Arrow-Pratt measure of *absolute* risk aversion is constant and equal to one. For lower measures of risk aversion, they find lower optimal replacement rates.

When agents can save but capital markets are imperfect (so that workers can only partially self-insure), Baily and Flemming find that the optimal replacement rate falls by about 25–30 percentage points. Thus, they conclude that the optimal replacement rate is below 50 percent and that the current U.S. unemployment insurance program is too generous. Similar conclusions have been reached by Gruber (1994) who used Baily's framework to investigate benefit adequacy in the United States.

In earlier work (Davidson and Woodbury 1997), we extended the work of Baily and Flemming by dropping two of the assumptions used in their analysis—that all unemployed agents are eligible for UI benefits and that they receive such benefits for as long as they remain unemployed. In fact, fewer than 50 percent of unemployed U.S. workers are eligible for UI benefits (Blank and Card 1991), and roughly 70 percent of unemployed U.K. workers are eligible (Layard, Nickell, and Jackman 1991). In addition, benefits are usually limited to 26 weeks in most U.S. states and have duration limits in almost every other country. In Section 4, we review these earlier results, which suggest that the conclusions reached by Bailey and Flemming are sensitive to these two assumptions. Section 4 then further extends the Baily-Flemming analysis by explicitly modeling firm behavior and making the wage rate and the number of active firms endogenous. This allows the impact of UI on aggregate job opportunities to be captured.

In addition to Baily and Flemming, several macroeconomists have criticized the generosity of current labor market policies. For example, Layard, Nickell, and

Jackman (1991) and Ljungqvist and Sargent (1998) argue that the disincentive effects of UI are so strong that they have significantly increased the unemployment rate throughout Europe. There have also been claims that the existing U.S. unemployment insurance program generates a large welfare loss for the economy (for example, Mortensen 1994).

Layard, Nickell and Jackman (1991) trace much of the European experience with unemployment over the last two decades to changes in UI programs. They argue that the gradual increase in the "natural rate" of unemployment in several European countries can be explained by increased UI program generosity. In addition, they argue that differences in UI programs are an important determinant of cross-country differences in unemployment. They estimate that roughly 91 percent of the variation in the average 1983–1988 unemployment rate across the major OECD industrial countries can be explained by differences in the generosity of labor market policies and the extent of collective bargaining coverage. Based on their results, Layard, Nickell, and Jackman suggest a variety of reforms to combat Europe's dual problems of high unemployment and long average duration of unemployment. With respect to the United Kingdom, they suggest reducing the potential duration of UI benefits, discarding policies that impose employment-adjustment costs on firms, and instituting subsidies to offset recruiting and training costs incurred by firms.

Layard, Jackman, and Nickell provide estimates of the impact of various labor market policies on unemployment and suggest reforms; however, they do not attempt to link their estimated employment effects to economic welfare. In contrast, Mortensen (1994) and Millard and Mortensen (1997) estimate the welfare effects of a variety of labor market policies including unemployment insurance. They use a general equilibrium search model so as to capture the cost of UI through its impact on the aggregate unemployment rate. In addition to the tax burden it creates, UI generates economic costs for two main reasons. First, as already discussed, more generous UI lowers the opportunity cost of unemployment and leads to lower search effort by the jobless. This increases the equilibrium rate of unemployment and reduces output. Second, because more generous UI makes the unemployed less likely to accept new jobs, the wage that firms must offer rises, making production less profitable. This decreases the total number of jobs available in the economy. This *job destruction* effect further lowers employment, production, and welfare. As discussed above, Baily's and Flemming's analyses do not model firm behavior, so this latter effect is absent.

For present purposes, the central results from Mortensen (1994) and Millard and Mortensen (1997) concern the UI programs in the United States and the United Kingdom. To estimate the impact of these programs, the authors calibrate their model using data on labor market flows in the United States during 1983–1992 and estimates of parameters that are obtained from the labor economics and macroeconomics literatures. Following Layard, Nickell, and Jackman, they recalibrate the model for the United Kingdom assuming that differences in the U.S.

and U.K. unemployment experiences can be attributed to differences in their labor market policies and union coverage rates.

In both papers, welfare is measured by aggregate income net of search, recruiting, and training costs. By this measure, Mortensen (1994) estimates that a 50 percent reduction in the U.S. replacement rate would reduce the equilibrium rate of unemployment by 1.48 percentage points and increase net output by slightly less than one percentage point. Mortensen also estimates that a 50 percent reduction in the potential duration of benefits would decrease the equilibrium rate of unemployment by 0.78 percentage points while increasing welfare by about 0.5 percentage points.

For the United Kingdom, Millard and Mortensen (1997) estimate that the welfare cost imposed by the current UI program is roughly 1.7 percent of net output—a large deadweight loss estimate. They also estimate that by limiting the benefit period to 2 quarters (as in the United States), the United Kingdom could increase welfare by more than one percentage point (and lower unemployment by over 2 percentage points). Moreover, Millard and Mortensen estimate that welfare in the United Kingdom would rise by as much as 3.5 percent if the employment-adjustment costs imposed by the government were also eliminated (as suggested by Layard, Nickell, and Jackman).

It is easy to infer from these results that the current UI programs in the United States and the U.K. impose significant welfare burdens on their economies. However, by using aggregate net income as their measure of welfare, the authors implicitly assume risk neutrality on the part of workers so that there is no need or desire for insurance of any kind. It follows that the positive aspect of UI—that it provides desired insurance against employment risk—gets no weight in the welfare calculation. The following two sections develop a model that captures the costs of UI (as do Millard and Mortensen) but that also assumes risk aversion on the part of workers so that insurance is valuable. The results of this exercise are then compared with those of Mortensen and Millard and Mortensen to illustrate the importance of risk aversion in determining the generosity of an optimal UI program.[3]

3. Model with Risk Aversion and Job Destruction

This section describes the model that is used in Section 4 to derive an optimal UI program. The model follows the tradition in this literature by using a search model of the labor market. It captures the benefits and costs of UI by focusing on the behavior of a typical unemployed worker who is searching for a job and desires employment insurance. This worker earns a wage of w each period while employed and collects UI benefits of x per period while unemployed provided that she has not exhausted her benefits. Benefits are provided by the government to jobless workers who have been unemployed for no more than T periods. Initially, then, all new job losers are assumed eligible for UI. In Section 4, the model is modified to account for the fact that the actual UI take-up rate is below 100 percent.

In the model, UI is funded by taxing all employed workers' earnings at a constant rate τ. This assumption, common in the optimal UI literature, is used to capture the notion that the incidence of a UI tax is likely to be borne by workers.

Unemployed workers are assumed to choose search effort (p) to maximize expected lifetime utility, and all workers are assumed to live forever. Each firm is assumed to hire at most one worker, and new firms enter the labor market until the expected profit from creating a vacancy is zero. Once a firm with a vacancy and an unemployed worker meet, they negotiate the wage. Following a well-established tradition in the search literature, the negotiated wage is assumed to split the surplus created by the job evenly (this will be made precise below). Total labor demand (F) and search effort together determine equilibrium steady-state unemployment (U).

The government's goal is to choose x and T to maximize aggregate expected lifetime utility. Increases in x and/or T provide unemployed workers with additional insurance but these increases also lower optimal search effort.[4] In addition, because a more generous UI program reduces the opportunity cost of unemployment, it increases the wage rate and makes it less profitable for a firm to create a vacancy. The reduction in search effort coupled with the destruction of job opportunities leads to an increase in unemployment. The optimal government policy must balance these costs and benefits.

This approach is similar to that of Mortensen (1994) and Millard and Mortensen (1997), except that workers are assumed to be risk averse. The model could also be viewed as an extension of Baily (1978) and Flemming (1978) in which (a) the potential duration of benefits is variable, (b) the UI take-up rate is allowed to be less than 100 percent, and (c) labor demand is modeled so that the job destruction effects of UI are accounted for.

The model is described in three steps. First, expected lifetime utility for all agents in the economy is determined and used to define welfare. Expected lifetime utility is also used to determine optimal search effort for unemployed workers. Second, total labor demand and search effort are combined to determine unemployment. Third, the model of firm behavior is introduced, and total labor demand and the wage are determined.

A few words about notation are in order. Throughout the analysis, variables such as search effort, expected lifetime utility, reemployment probabilities, and so on are defined that depend on the employment status of the worker. In each case, subscripts on the variables denote the employment status with, w representing employed workers, t denoting unemployed workers in their t^{th} period of search, and x denoting unemployed workers who have exhausted their benefits. For example, m denotes the reemployment probability, so m_t represents the reemployment probability of an unemployed worker in the tth period of search, and m_x represents the reemployment probability of an unemployed worker who has exhausted her benefits.

3.1 Expected Lifetime Utility, Search Effort, and Welfare

Let V_j denote expected lifetime utility for a worker in employment state j ($j = w$ if employed, t if unemployed for t periods, and x if unemployed and benefits have been exhausted). In addition, let $u(\ )$ represent the agents' common utility function. Per period utility takes the form $u(C) - c(p)$, with C denoting consumption, $c(p)$ denoting the cost of search, and p denoting search effort (if unemployed). The search cost function $c(p)$ is assumed to be convex with $c(0) = 0$. For now, assume that agents cannot save, so that in any given period consumption equals income. Section 5 describes how relaxing this assumption affects the results.

For employed workers, current income consists of two components—labor income, $w(1 - \tau)$, which is equal to the wage net of taxes, and nonlabor income, θ_w, which is equal to workers' share of the aggregate profits earned by the firms. Thus, current utility is given by $u[w(1 - \tau) + \theta_w]$. Clearly, employed agents incur no search costs. To determine expected lifetime utility, the worker's future prospects must also be considered. Let s denote the probability that in any given period the worker will lose her job. Then, with probability $(1 - s)$, the worker's expected future lifetime utility will continue to be V_w (since she remains employed). With probability s, the worker loses her job and her expected future lifetime utility falls to V_1. It follows that,

$$(1) \qquad V_w = u[w(1-\tau)+\theta_w] + [sV_1+(1-s)V_w]/(1+r).$$

Note that future utility is discounted at rate $(1 + r)$ with r denoting the interest rate.

Consider next the unemployed. For them, current income is equal to the sum of unemployment insurance (if benefits have not yet been exhausted) and profits. Let θ_u denote a typical unemployed worker's share of aggregate profits. Future income depends on future employment status. Let m denote reemployment probabilities, so that with probability m_t the worker finds a job and can expect to earn V_w in the future, while with probability $(1 - m_t)$ she remains unemployed and can expect to earn V_{t+1} in the future. Thus,

$$(2) \qquad V_t = u[x+\theta_u] - c(p_t) + [m_tV_w+(1-m_t)V_{t+1}] / (1+r) \qquad \text{for } t = 1,...,T.$$

$$(3) \qquad V_x = u[\theta_u] - c(p_x) + [m_xV_w+(1-m_x)V_x] / (1+r).$$

Welfare (W) can now be defined. Let U_t represent the number of workers who have been unemployed for t periods and define U_x analogously for UI-exhaustees. If

J is defined as the total number of jobs held in the steady-state equilibrium and aggregate expected lifetime utility across all agents, then

(4) $$W = JV_w + U_xV_x + \Sigma_tU_tV_t.$$

Search effort is chosen to maximize expected lifetime income, so that

(5) $$p_t = \arg \max V_t \qquad \text{for } t = 1,...,T.$$

(6) $$p_x = \arg \max V_x.$$

It will become clear in Section 3.2 that the reemployment probability (m) is an increasing function of search effort (p).

3.2 Determining Unemployment

This section shows how total labor demand (F) and search effort (p) can be combined to determine equilibrium unemployment. To do so, the reemployment probabilities and steady-state unemployment are first determined. Then the reemployment probabilities are shown to vary with search effort, labor demand, and other features of the labor market.

Let L denote total labor supply. Because every worker is either employed or unemployed,

(7) $$L = J + U.$$

In addition, given the definitions of U_t and U_x, total unemployment can be written as

(8) $$U = \Sigma_tU_t + U_x.$$

Consider next firms. For simplicity, each firm is assumed to provide only one job opportunity.[5] Thus, F denotes both the total number of firms and the total number of jobs available at any time. Each job is either filled or vacant, so if V denotes the number of vacancies in a steady-state equilibrium, it follows that

(9) $$F = J + V.$$

The dynamics of the labor market and the conditions that must hold for a steady-state equilibrium can now be described. These conditions guarantee that the unemployment rate and the composition of unemployment both remain constant over time. Recall that s is the economy's separation rate—that is, s denotes the probability that an employment relationship will dissolve in any given period. In addition, recall that reemployment probabilities are denoted by the m terms. Then, for any given worker, there are $T + 2$ possible employment states—U_1, U_2,...., U_T, U_x, and J. If employed (i.e., if in state J), the worker faces a probability s of losing her job and moving into state U_1. If unemployed for t periods (i.e., if in state U_t), the worker faces a probability of m_t of finding a job and moving into state J. With probability ($1 - m_t$) this worker remains unemployed and moves on to state U_{t+1}. Finally, UI-eligible exhaustees face a reemployment probability of m_x, in which case they move into state J. Otherwise, they remain in state U_x.

In a steady-state equilibrium the flows into and out of each state must be equal so that the unemployment rate and its composition do not change over time. Using the above notation, the flows into and out of state U_1 are equal if

(10) $$sJ = U_1.$$

The flows into and out of state U_t (for $t = 2,...,T$) are equal if

(11) $$(1-m_{t-1})U_{t-1} = U_t.$$

Finally, the flows into and out of state U_x are equal if

(12) $$(1-m_T)U_T = m_x U_x.$$

In each case, the flow into the state is given on the left-hand-side of the expression while the flow out of the state is given on the right-hand-side.

Equations (7)–(12) define the dynamics of the labor market given the reemployment probabilities and total labor demand. How does search effort translate into a reemployment probability for each unemployed worker? As described above, each unemployed worker chooses search effort (p) to maximize expected lifetime utility. Search effort is best thought of as the number of firms a worker chooses to contact in each period of job search. For workers who contact fewer than one firm on average, p_t could be thought of as the probability of contacting any firm. Once a worker contacts a firm, she files a job application if the firm has a vacancy. Because there are F firms, V of which have vacancies, the probability of contacting a firm with a vacancy is V/F. Once all applications have been filed, each firm with a vacancy fills it by choosing randomly from its pool of applicants. Thus, if N other workers apply to the firm, the probability of a given worker getting the job is $1/(N + 1)$. Because each other worker either does or does not apply, N is a random variable with a Poisson distribution with parameter λ equal to the average number of applications filed at each firm. It is straightforward to show that this implies that the probability of getting a job offer conditional on having applied to a firm with a vacancy is $(1/\lambda)[1 - e^{-\lambda}]$. The reemployment probability for any given worker is then the product of these three terms—the number of firms contacted, the probability that a given firm will have a vacancy, and the probability of getting the job conditional on having applied at a firm with a vacancy:

(13) $m_t = p_t(V/F)(1/\lambda)[1-e^{-\lambda}]$ for $t = 1,...,T$

(14) $m_x = p_x(V/F)(1/\lambda)[1-e^{-\lambda}]$

where

(15) $\lambda = \{\Sigma_t p_t U_t + p_x U_x\}/F.$

These equations define the reemployment probabilities of workers as a function of search effort and the length of time that they have been unemployed. Note that for any given worker, the search effort of other workers affects that worker's reemployment probability through λ.

Given the levels of search effort and expected lifetime utilities defined by (1)–(6), equations (7)–(15) can be solved for equilibrium unemployment (U), its composition (U_t for $t = 1,...,T$ and U_x), and the reemployment probabilities (m_t for $t = 1,...,T$ and m_x). If we stopped developing the model at this point, treating F and w as exogenous, the model would be almost identical to the one used by Flemming (1978). In fact, there would be only two substantive differences between the models—Flemming allows workers to save while employed and assumes that UI is offered indefinitely (the model here assumes that UI is offered for T periods). Below, the number of firms (F) and the wage (w) are made endogenous, and UI-ineligible workers are added to the model.

3.3 Firms

Firms are assumed to enter the market until the expected profits from doing so equal zero, making the number of firms endogenous. When a firm enters the market, it creates a vacancy and starts to accept applications from unemployed workers to fill it. Once the vacancy is filled, the firm produces and sells output as long as its vacancy remains filled. If the firm loses its worker, it must restart the process of filling its vacancy.

Let Π_V denote the expected lifetime profit for a firm that currently has a vacancy, and let Π_J represent the expected lifetime profit for a firm that has filled its vacancy. Thus, when a firm enters the market and creates a vacancy it can expect to earn Π_V in the future. Once it fills its vacancy, its expectations about future profits rise to Π_J. Firms enter until

(16) $\Pi_V = 0.$

To calculate Π_V and Π_J, the procedure that was used to determine expected lifetime utilities is again followed—the current and future prospects of typical firms are considered. Let q denote the probability of filling a vacancy, let K represent the cost of maintaining a vacancy, and let R denote the net revenue earned by a producing firm (net of K). Then, current profit for a firm with a vacancy is $-K$ while current profit for a producing firm is $R - w$. Now consider firms' future prospects. A firm that has an opening fills it with probability q, in which case its expected lifetime profits rise to Π_J. With the remaining probability the vacancy remains open and the firm continues to expect to earn Π_V. Accordingly,

$$(17) \qquad \Pi_V = -K + [q\Pi_J + (1-q)\Pi_V]/(1+r).$$

A firm that has already hired a worker keeps that worker with probability $(1-s)$ and continues to earn Π_J. With probability s, it loses its worker and sees its expected profits fall to Π_V. Hence,

$$(18) \qquad \Pi_J = R - w + [s\Pi_V + (1-s)\Pi_J]/(1+r).$$

Note that, as before, future profits are discounted at rate $(1 + r)$.

The probability of filling a vacancy, q, depends on the number of firms competing for the unemployed (V), the number of unemployed workers (U) and the search effort of workers. In any given period the number of unemployed workers who find new jobs is equal to $\Sigma_t m_t U_t + m_x U_x$ while the number of vacancies that are filled is equal to qV. These values must be equal, so that

$$(19) \qquad q = [\Sigma_t m_t U_t + m_x U_x]/V.$$

Note that the search effort of workers enters (19) through the reemployment probabilities.

Next, Π_V and Π_J are used to determine the profits that are distributed to workers in each period in the form of dividends (θ_w for the employed, θ_u for the unemployed). There are J jobs filled in equilibrium, with each one generating Π_J in expected lifetime profits, so aggregate expected lifetime profits are $J\Pi_J$. Thus, the aggregate per period profits equal $rJ\Pi_J / (1 + r)$. These profits must be distributed to workers each period. If these profits are distributed evenly to employed workers, with the unemployed receiving nothing, then $\theta_w = rJ\Pi_J / (1 + r)J = r\Pi_J / (1 + r)$, and $\theta_u = 0$. The assumption that the unemployed receive no profits is made for three reasons. First, relatively few unemployed workers have significant income from business assets, stocks, and bonds. Second, suppose that the government reduced the generosity of the UI program, and that aggregate profits increased as a result. If the unemployed were to receive a share of the increase, then the gain in nonlabor income could swamp the loss in UI and leave the unemployed better-off. Third, with this assumption, optimal UI will be less generous than in a model where the unemployed receive a share of firms' profits. As will be seen, even with this assumption, the model suggests that the existing UI program in the United States is probably not generous enough, so the assumption seems innocuous.

Finally, consider how the wage is determined. Following the general equilibrium search literature (see, for example, Diamond 1982 or Pissarides 1990), firms and workers are assumed to split the surplus created by the representative job evenly. When firms fill a vacancy, their expected profits rise from Π_V to Π_J. When an average worker becomes reemployed, his expected lifetime utility rises from V_u to V_w, where V_u denotes the average expected lifetime utility for an unemployed worker.[6] That is,

$$(20) \qquad\qquad V_u = [\Sigma_t U_t V_t + U_x V_x]/U.$$

It follows that the total surplus created by the average job *when measured in dollars* is $(\Pi_J - \Pi_V) + (V_w - V_u) / MU_I$ where MU_I represents the worker's marginal utility of income and allows transformation of the worker's gain, $V_w - V_u$ (which is measured in utility) into an appropriate dollar value. This surplus is split evenly between the firm and its employee if the wage satisfies

$$(21) \qquad\qquad \Pi_J - \Pi_V = (V_w - V_u)/MU_I.$$

In summary, the number of firms demanding labor (F) is determined by (16), and the equilibrium wage is determined by (21).

The government's problem is to choose x (the UI benefit level) and T (the potential duration of benefits) to maximize welfare (W, as given in equation 4) subject to the constraint that its budget balances. Because there are J employed workers, each earning a wage of w, total tax revenue is equal to $Jw\tau$. In equilibrium, $U - U_x$ unemployed workers receive benefits of x each period. Thus, the total cost of the program is $(U - U_x)x$. For the budget to balance it must be the case that

$$(22) \qquad\qquad (U - U_x)x = Jw\tau.$$

As noted above, an increase in x or T increases the level of insurance provided to unemployed workers, but both increase unemployment and require that τ increase in order to fund the expanded program.

This completes the description of the model. Its structure is similar to that of Mortensen (1994) and Millard and Mortensen (1997). The main difference is in the measurement of welfare—whereas the Mortensen and Millard-Mortensen models use aggregate income net of search, recruiting, and training costs as their measure of welfare, the model developed here uses aggregate expected lifetime utility. These two measures are identical if agents are risk neutral. However, if the utility function is concave, so that agents are risk averse, the measures differ. As argued above, it is important to assume risk aversion—otherwise unemployment insurance has no value to workers.

3.4 Properties of Equilibrium

Before turning to optimal policy, it is useful to describe the structure of equilibrium and some of its comparative dynamic properties. It is straightforward to show that in a steady-state equilibrium $V_w > V_1 > V_2 >...> V_T > V_x$. That is, expected lifetime income is highest for employed workers, lowest for unemployed workers who have exhausted their benefits, and decreasing in the number of weeks that a worker has been unemployed. Intuitively, workers in the early stages of a spell of unemployment have more weeks to find a job before they have to worry about exhausting their UI benefits. Because of this, workers who have recently become unemployed will not search as hard as those who have been unemployed for a longer period of time—that is, optimal search effort will be increasing in the number of weeks of unsuccessful search ($p_1 < p_2 <...< p_T < p_x$).

A decrease in either the UI benefit amount (x) or the potential duration of benefits (T) decreases the level of insurance offered unemployed workers and triggers an increase in search effort by all UI-eligible workers (and therefore lowers unemployment). Either change results in a decrease in V_t for all t, but decreases in x and T have opposite effects on the probability of exhausting benefits. A decrease in x makes it less likely that a worker will exhaust her UI benefits before finding a job (since she searches harder). But a decrease in T makes it more likely that benefits will be exhausted because the time horizon over which benefits are offered has been shortened (this is true even though search effort increases as T falls). Increases in x or T have the opposite effects.

Changes in the UI program also have implications for firm behavior and labor demand. Because increases in either x or T reduce the cost of being unemployed, they make workers less willing to search for and/or accept jobs. As a result, V_u increases and forces firms to increase the wage offered to new employees. The increased wage makes production less profitable and results in fewer firms and job opportunities—a job destruction effect that increases unemployment and lowers net output.

3.5 Calibration

Determining the optimal UI program requires (1) choosing values for the parameters of the model, (2) solving for the equilibrium generated by each pair of policy parameters (x and T), and (3) comparing the levels of welfare achieved in the different equilibria. Assuming that realistic parameter values are chosen, this exercise should yield ranges in which the optimal level of benefits and the optimal potential duration of benefits lie.

The parameters of the model are the separation rate (s), the interest rate (r), the size of the labor force (L), the search cost function ($c(p)$), the revenue earned by producing firms (R), the cost of maintaining a vacancy (K), and the utility function,

$u(C)$. Because we are interested in checking the sensitivity of the results with respect to the degree of risk aversion, we calibrate the model separately for a variety of different utility functions and compare the optimal programs that result.

The model is calibrated in two steps. First, the model developed in Sections 3.1 and 3.2 is treated as if it were self-contained—that is, the number of firms (F) and the wage (w) are treated as model parameters. To calibrate this portion of the model data collected to analyze the Illinois reemployment bonus experiment are used. Calibration of this abbreviated model is detailed elsewhere (Davidson and Woodbury 1993, 1997), so we provide only a short description here. Briefly, the abbreviated model is calibrated so that its predictions concerning the impact of a reemployment bonus offered to unemployed workers matches what was observed in the experiment for workers who were eligible for regular state benefits in Illinois (Davidson and Woodbury 1991). Treating F and w as fixed implies that the Illinois experiment had no wage or job creation/job destruction effects. These assumptions seem reasonable: The data indicate that there were no wage effects from the reemployment bonus (Woodbury and Speigelman 1987), and the bonus experiment was temporary, so it is not likely to have changed the number of firms seeking workers.

In the second step, the model is expanded (as in Section 3.3) so that F and w become endogenous. This adds two new parameters to the model—R (the revenue earned by the firm when producing) and K (the cost of maintaining a vacancy). These values are chosen so that the full model yields (a) a value for w that matches the data collected in Illinois, and (b) values for F that lie in the range predicted by the abbreviated model in the first stage of calibration.

When considering the abbreviated model (Sections 3.1 and 3.2), the parameters of interest are the separation rate (s), the interest rate (r), the wage (w), the number of firms (F), the size of the labor force (L), and the search cost function ($c(p)$). An estimate for s can be obtained from the existing literature on labor market dynamics. Ehrenberg (1980) and Murphy and Topel (1987) provide estimates of the number of jobs that break up in each period. Their work suggests that s lies in the range of 0.007 to 0.013 (with time is measured in 2-week intervals). The interest rate (r) is set to 0.008, which translates into an annual discount rate of approximately 20 percent. Because previous work (Davidson and Woodbury 1991, 1993) suggests that results from this model are not sensitive to changes in r over a fairly wide range, no other value of the interest rate is considered.[7]

The model is homogeneous of degree zero in F and L, so L can be set to 100 without loss of generality. If F is then varied, holding all other parameters fixed, the equilibrium unemployment and vacancy rates can be solved. Abraham's (1983) work suggests that the ratio of unemployment to vacancies (U/V) varies between 1.5 and 3 over the business cycle. Although the actual values of U and V depend on the other parameters, in order to obtain such values for U/V in this model with $L = 100$, F must lie in range of 95 to 97.5. Thus, in the second stage of the calibration, values of R and K must be chosen such that F lies in the range 95 to 97.5.

The remaining parameters in Sections 3.1 and 3.2 are the wage rate and the search cost function. These values are derived from the data and results of the Illinois reemployment bonus experiment. In the Illinois experiment a randomly selected group of new claimants for UI were offered a $500 bonus for accepting a new job within 11 weeks of filing their initial claim. The average duration of unemployment for these bonus-offered workers was approximately 0.7 weeks less than the average unemployment duration of the randomly selected control group (Davidson and Woodbury 1991). In previous work, we estimated the parameters of the search cost function that would be consistent with such behavioral results. That is, we assumed a specific functional form for $c(p)$ and then solved for the parameters that would make the model's predictions match the outcome observed in the Illinois experiment. The functional form used was $c(p) = cp^z$, where z denotes the elasticity of search costs with respect to search effort. The values for c and z that make the model's predictions match what occurred in Illinois depend upon the utility function that is assumed. For example, if the utility function is linear in consumption, then for the average biweekly wage rate observed in Illinois ($511), the values of c and z that are consistent with the Illinois experimental results are $c = 338$ and $z = 1.23$. On the other hand, if the utility function takes the form $u(C) = \ln(C)$, then the values of c and z that are consistent with the Illinois experimental results are $c = 2.05$ and $z = 1.38$.

Consider now the second stage of calibration. In order to make F and w endogenous, the equations in Section 3.3 are added to the model, adding two new parameters, R and K. In the Illinois data the average biweekly wage is $511, and from stage one of the calibration F must lie in the range 95 to 97.5. Next, x and T are set to their Illinois values—$242 for the average biweekly UI benefit (x), and 14 for the potential duration of benefits (T, because each period equals 2 weeks). The model is then solved to determine what values of R and K would lead the model to predict that $w = \$511$ and that F would fall in the range 95–97.5. The values of R and K depend on the assumed form of the utility function. If the utility function is linear in consumption, then when $R = 724$ and $K = 2,417$, the model predicts that $w = 511$ and $F = 96.25$. On the other hand, if $u(C) = \ln(c)$, then when $R = 1,469$ and $K = 10,863$, the model predicts that $w = \$511$ and $F = 96.25$.

When calibration is complete, the parameters are set at their calibrated levels and the model is solved for the welfare maximizing values of x and T. When the optimal values for x and T are obtained in one case, the parameters are varied over the ranges described above to test the sensitivity of the results with respect to each parameter. The results are largely insensitive to changes in all of the parameters except the degree of risk aversion. Accordingly, most of the results reported below are for a "reference case" in which $s = 0.010$ and in which R and K are chosen so that $F = 96.25$ and $U/V = 2$.

4. Results

This section begins by reviewing earlier results (Davidson and Woodbury 1997), in which the optimal UI program was solved in the abbreviated model outlined in Sections 3.1 and 3.2. These results are best thought of extensions of Baily's and Flemming's work to a setting in which (a) the potential duration of benefits can vary and be controlled by the government, and (b) not all unemployed workers are eligible for UI. Next, new results are presented on optimal UI when firm behavior is explicitly added to the model as in Section 3.3. This allows examination of how the initial results must be modified when the job destruction effects of more generous UI programs are taken into account. Finally, the model is extended again to allow for worker heterogeneity and to show how including workers with different labor market experiences in the model alters the results.

4.1 Optimal Potential Duration of Benefits without Job Destruction

A surprising result in the abbreviated model is that the optimal potential duration of benefits is infinite—that is, the government should offer benefits indefinitely to all unemployed UI-eligible workers. Although some details are omitted from the following reasoning,[8] the crux of the argument is as follows. Agents facing employment risk would prefer a program that allows them to smooth consumption as much as possible across spells of unemployment. Given a choice between two UI programs that provide the same level of total benefits, agents would choose the program that does the best job of smoothing consumption. With this in mind, consider the following two programs—the first program offers a benefit of x for T periods while the second program offers a benefit of x' for $T + 1$ periods where $x' < x$ and is chosen so that the two programs provide the same level of total unemployment benefits. Thus, the first program offers higher benefits per period but for fewer periods. The key to the argument is that the second program allows for greater consumption smoothing—in moving from the first program to the second program, benefits are lowered during the least adverse states of unemployment (i.e., the initial phase) and increased in one of the most adverse states (period $T + 1$ in which no benefits are offered in the first program) with total benefits provided remaining the same. By accepting slightly decreased benefits (and consumption) during the first T periods of unemployment, the unemployed can insure that benefits will not completely disappear for an additional period. Thus, all risk-averse unemployed workers prefer the second program.[9] Because this reasoning holds for all finite T, it follows that in an optimal UI program T must equal infinity.

This result has important implications for some of the work reviewed in Section 2. In particular, it suggests that conclusions drawn from models like Baily's and Flemming's need to be interpreted carefully. Both authors use models in which it is assumed that benefits are offered indefinitely; and in their models, it is indeed optimal to provide benefits indefinitely. Accordingly, the optimal replacement rates that they derive are correct—without savings, the optimal replacement rate is in the 60–70 percent range, and, with savings but imperfect capital markets, the optimal replacement rate is in the 40–50 percent range.[10] However, these replacement rates are optimal only if they are offered indefinitely. It follows that the conclusion that Baily and Flemming reach—that the 50 percent replacement rate in most states is probably too high—cannot be correct because the United States offers this rate for only 26 weeks. When the optimal replacement rate is solved in the abbreviated model with T set exogenously to 26 weeks, that rate is greater than 1. It follows that if one ignores the job destruction effect of UI, the current U.S. unemployment insurance program is not generous enough.

The finding that the optimal duration of benefits is infinite needs to be understood in context. That is, it is derived from a model in which the job destruction effects of UI are ignored. When the job destruction effects are taken into account, the result no longer holds (see below). For this reason, it is not likely that an optimal UI program would be characterized by an unlimited potential duration of benefits. However, the result does suggest that an optimal UI program is more likely to be characterized by low benefits and a long potential duration of benefits than by high benefits and a short potential duration of benefits. Programs with long potential benefit durations lead to smoother consumption paths and therefore reduce the risk associated with unemployment more than programs with short potential durations.

4.2 Optimal Replacement Rates with UI-Ineligibles in the Model

A second extension of the Baily and Flemming analyses in Davidson and Woodbury (1997) was to account for the fact that not all unemployed workers are eligible for UI. The importance of this extension is clear from Blank and Card (1991), who report that over 50 percent of unemployed U.S. workers are ineligible for UI and that of those who are eligible, only 75 percent claim benefits.[11] Storer and Van Audenrode (1995) estimate that 85–90 percent of UI eligibles in Canada actually claim benefits. Layard, Nickell, and Jackman (1991) report that up to 30 percent of unemployed U.K. workers are ineligible for UI.

These facts have important implications for the optimal replacement rate because more generous UI has positive spillover effects on UI-ineligibles. The reasoning is as follows. If the government institutes a more generous UI program, UI-eligibles respond by searching less hard for work. If UI-eligibles and UI-ineligibles compete for some of the same jobs, then the reduced search effort of UI-eligibles reduces the competition that UI-ineligibles face for jobs and increases their reemployment probabilities. The ineligibility of many workers for UI leads to positive spillover effects, and ignoring these effects leads to an underestimate of the optimal replacement rate.

To determine the optimal replacement rate when positive spillover effects exist, the abbreviated model of Sections 3.1 and 3.2 can be extended to allow for UI-ineligibility (Davidson and Woodbury 1997). Briefly, UI-ineligibles are modeled exactly as other workers except that they are not allowed to collect UI while unemployed. For example, equations analogous to (2) and (3) are used to define the expected lifetime utility for an unemployed UI-ineligible worker, and an equation analogous to (1) is used to define the expected lifetime utility for an employed UI-ineligible worker.

To be precise, let V_i represent the expected lifetime utility of an unemployed UI-ineligible worker, let V_{wi} denote the expected lifetime utility for an employed UI-ineligible worker, and use the subscript i on all other variables to denote UI-ineligibility. Then, the same logic used to derive (1)–(3) gives:

(23) $$V_{wi} = u[w(1-\tau)+\theta_w] + [sV_i+(1-s)V_{wi}]/(1+r)$$

(24) $$V_i = u[\theta_u] - c(p_i) + [m_iV_{wi}+(1-m_i)V_i]/(1+r).$$

Optimal search effort for UI-ineligibles is then the value of p_i that maximizes V_i:

(25) $$p_i = \arg \max V_i.$$

The remaining equations of the model can be modified in a similar fashion with only one new parameter added—the proportion of the unemployed who are ineligible for UI. This proportion can be set to 0.6 for the reference case (from Blank and Card 1991), and then varied from 0 (all unemployed workers eligible) to 0.6 to check the sensitivity of results.

Including UI-ineligibles in the model does increase the optimal replacement rate. Depending on the values of the other parameters, the spillover effects of UI on UI-ineligibles increase the optimal replacement rate by 6 to 10 percentage points. Thus, if agents cannot save and the job destruction effects of UI are ignored, an optimal UI program offers a replacement rate in the 65–75 percent range indefinitely. If, on the other hand, agents can save (but the job destruction effects of UI are still ignored), then an optimal UI program offers a replacement rate in the 45–55 percent range indefinitely.

This completes the description of our earlier results, all of which were derived assuming that utility is linear in consumption. If search costs had been assumed linear in effort as well, this would have been equivalent to assuming risk neutrality, and there would have been no demand for UI. However, because search costs were assumed convex in effort, each individual's optimization problem was concave in the choice variable and thus, each agent was risk averse.

To see how increasing the degree of risk aversion affects these results, the model can be recalibrated for two different utility functions, namely $u[C] = \ln(C)$ and $u[C] = \sqrt{C}$, and the optimal replacement rate derived again for each case. The log utility function is characterized by constant Arrow-Pratt relative risk aversion equal to one and is chosen because it is identical that used by Baily (1978). The square root utility function is characterized by constant Arrow-Pratt relative risk aversion equal to one-half and is used because its measure of risk aversion falls midway between the linear and log utility functions. Surprisingly, in the model without job destruction, the degree of risk aversion does not make much difference—optimal replacement rates fall, but only by a relatively small amount: about 6 percentage points when we go from the linear to the log utility function and about 2 percentage points when we go from the linear to the square root utility function.[12] The reason is that in recalibrating the model with the new utility functions, the values of the parameters change so that the model once again yields predictions that are consistent with the Illinois data.[13] For example, as the agents in the model are made more risk averse, the degree of convexity of the search cost function must also increase so that the model still yields correct predictions about a reemployment bonus. Because the model is recalibrated for each utility function so that the bonus impact is the same, it is not surprising that the models suggest similar optimal UI programs.[14]

In summary, our earlier work focused on extending the analyses of Baily and Flemming in two ways. They assumed that UI benefits would be offered indefinitely and that all agents are eligible for UI. Both of these assumptions led to a bias toward finding that less generous UI programs would be optimal. The next section further extends the model to allow for the job destruction effects of UI and forces further modifications to conclusions about an optimal UI program. This is done by endogenizing firm behavior.

4.3 Job Destruction and Risk Aversion

When firm behavior is endogenized, UI has several effects that have not been considered to this point. If a more generous UI program is offered, the average expected lifetime income for the unemployed (V_u) rises, and this triggers an increase in the equilibrium wage. The higher wage lowers profits for producing firms (Π_J) and lowers the expected lifetime profit to a firm creating a vacancy (Π_V). As a result, there are fewer firms (F) and fewer job opportunities. Regarding welfare, per period income for the employed could rise or fall (because the wage increases and nonlabor income from firms fall) while unemployment rises unambiguously due to the job destruction effect. Thus, the optimal UI program is likely to be *less* generous in a model with endogenous labor demand than in a model where firm behavior is ignored. The size of the job destruction effect determines just how much less generous.

In almost all cases reported below, the job destruction effect is large enough to overturn the result that it is optimal to offer UI benefits indefinitely. To see why, recall the earlier argument concerning the potential duration of benefits. For any UI program in which T is finite, there exists another UI program with longer potential duration of benefits and lower benefits that would cost the same to finance and would be strictly preferred by all agents. Thus, it would always be possible to increase T and raise welfare. This argument no longer holds when labor demand is endogenous because increasing T in this manner reduces the number of job opportunities and increases unemployment. This decrease in job opportunities must be weighed against the positive impact of smoothing consumption to determine whether the increase in T raises welfare. For almost all levels of risk aversion, the job destruction effect of increasing T eventually outweighs the consumption smoothing effect of increasing T so that benefits should eventually be cut off.

The optimal potential duration of benefits depends heavily on the degree of risk aversion. Consider three cases.

Case 1: Utility is linear in consumption. In this case, the degree of risk aversion is extremely low (recall that risk aversion enters through the convexity of the search cost function). This assumption and approach are very similar to that of Mortensen (1994) and Millard and Mortensen (1997), and the model yields predictions that are almost identical to those in Mortensen (1994)—the current UI program in the U.S. generates a deadweight loss of roughly 1.2 percent of welfare.[15]

With this low level of risk aversion, the optimal UI program is no program at all. That is, when the degree of risk aversion is low, the job destruction effect of UI is large enough to outweigh the positive impact of any insurance.[16] Clearly, this result stems from the fact that when utility is linear in consumption the demand for unemployment insurance is low.

Case 2: $U(C) = \ln(C)$. In this case the Arrow-Pratt measure of relative risk aversion is constant and equal to one. This is the utility function used by Baily (1978) and is probably the utility function that is most often used in the literature on decision making under uncertainty. With these preferences, the results are very different. First, in contrast to the results obtained with linear utility, the current U.S. unemployment insurance system (a 50 percent replacement rate for 26 weeks) *increases* welfare above the level that would be achieved without publicly provided UI. Moreover, the welfare gains are far from trivial—for the reference case, we estimate that welfare rises by 1.2 percent.

Second, without savings, this utility function yields an unappealing result—the optimal potential duration of benefits must be infinity. The reason is simple. Because an unemployed worker who exhausts benefits earns no income, that worker's instantaneous utility is $\ln(0) = -\infty$. Thus, if there is even the slightest probability of an unemployed agent exhausting her benefits, it follows that *all* agents' expected lifetime utility is $-\infty$. Any optimal UI program must therefore offer benefits indefinitely. This is clearly a knife-edge result—if UI exhaustees could count on even $1 of income from friends or relatives while unemployed, the result would vanish. Indeed, if one assumes that UI exhaustees do obtain a $1 transfer from family while unemployed, then the job destruction effect does overturn the result that benefits should be offered indefinitely (even with this high level of risk aversion). Nevertheless, the optimal value of T remains quite large—90 weeks in the reference case and from 74 to 104 weeks in the other cases (see Table 8.1)—so that benefits should be offered for as long as two full years. Thus, the job destruction effect is much less important when agents are reasonably risk averse.

Third, when agents cannot self-insure by saving, the optimal replacement rate is about 64 percent. With savings, this rate is likely to fall below 50 percent (see Section 5 below). The conclusion is that with reasonable assumptions about risk aversion, the optimal UI program offers benefits somewhat below 50 percent for almost two years. The model predicts that such a UI program would raise welfare above the level achieved with the current U.S. program by 5.5 percent—a striking potential welfare gain.

Case 3: $U(C) = \sqrt{C}$. This utility function has a constant Arrow-Pratt measure of relative risk aversion equal to one-half, so that it falls midway between the other two utility functions. With this utility function the current UI program in the United States is about right—the optimal program involves offering a replacement rate of 61 percent for 26 weeks in the reference case, with programs of similar duration and

Table 8.1. Optimal UI Programs for Log Utility.

	Potential Duration	Replacement Rate
Reference Case* $s = 0.010, F = 96.25$	90 weeks	64%
Few Firms $s = 0.010, F = 95$	84 weeks	64%
Many Firms $s = 0.010, F = 97.5$	94 weeks	64%
Low Turnover $s = 0.007, F = 96.25$	74 weeks	68%
High Turnover $s = 0.013, F = 96.25$	104 weeks	61%

*In each case F (total demand for labor) is endogenous with parameters R (firm revenue) and K (the cost of maintaining a vacancy) chosen so that F matches the values listed. s denotes the bi-weekly separation rate.

replacement rates in all other cases (see Table 8.2). This optimal program increases welfare above the levels that would be achieved without a UI program by about 2 percent.

The differences among the three sets of results indicate that the assumptions made about risk aversion are crucial. Thus, it is important to determine which utility function best represents workers' degree of risk aversion. Two contradictory strands of literature address this issue. First, there is the empirical literature on consumption behavior that attempts to estimate directly agents' degree of risk aversion (see, for example, Zeldes 1989), which suggests that the best point estimate of the Arrow-Pratt measure of relative risk aversion is 2. The other literature, which is theoretical, attempts to infer risk aversion from observed behavior. For example, one can observe how agents adjust their investment portfolios as their wealth changes and build models of investment under uncertainty to explain such behavior. Most work in this area finds that the theories of choice under uncertainty are consistent with observed behavior only if the Arrow-Pratt measure of relative risk aversion is less than one (see, for example, Hadar and Seo 1993).

That these two literatures contradict one another is troubling and leaves us (and economists generally) in an uncomfortable position. The work reported above suggests that if the Arrow-Pratt measure of relative risk aversion is close to (or above) one, then the current UI program in the United States is not nearly generous enough. However, if the Arrow-Pratt measure of relative risk aversion is close to one-half, then the current system is about right. If one finds the empirical literature on consumption convincing, then the former outcome is more likely than the latter. It follows that in the most general model, with what appears to be the best supported assumption about risk aversion, the optimal UI program offers benefits that are close

Table 8.2. Optimal UI Programs for Square Root Utility.

	Potential Duration	Replacement Rate
Reference Case* $s = 0.010, F = 96.25$	26 weeks	61%
Few Firms $s = 0.010, F = 95$	24 weeks	61%
Many Firms $s = 0.010, F = 97.5$	28 weeks	61%
Low Turnover $s = 0.007, F = 96.25$	20 weeks	66%
High Turnover $s = 0.013, F = 96.25$	32 weeks	56%

*In each case F (total demand for labor) is endogenous with parameters R (firm revenue) and K (the cost of maintaining a vacancy) chosen so that F matches the values listed. s denotes the bi-weekly separation rate.

to the levels currently offered by most states in the U.S. but offers those benefits for a longer period of time—between 1.5 and 2 years. In other words, the current U.S. program offers too little unemployment insurance.

4.4 Discussion

The finding that the optimal UI program is characterized by fairly a low replacement rate and a long potential duration of benefits conflicts with most of the previous literature.[17] However, we now argue that this result should have been expected because it is consistent with a large abstract literature on optimal insurance contracts in the presence of moral hazard.

Three issues have been addressed in the abstract literature on optimal insurance contracts that have implications for the design of an optimal UI program. The first concerns the design of an optimal insurance contract when the insured agent's behavior can affect the probability of a loss occurring (i.e., moral hazard is present). To investigate this issue, it is assumed that the agent's behavior cannot be observed by the insurance provider so that the contract must be structured in a manner that makes putting forth effort optimal for the agent. The problem then is how to provide adequate insurance without reducing the agent's incentive to avoid the loss. Shavell (1979) is a well-known article in this area.[18]

The second issue concerns the optimal sharing of risk between a risk neutral insurance provider and a risk averse agent when the total level of insurance coverage is fixed (i.e., in terms of expected indemnification). Raviv (1979) provides the classic treatment of this issue (see also Arrow 1974).

The final issue concerns the design of insurance contracts in the presence of adverse selection—the situation in which agents differ in a way that is unobservable to the insurers and affects the probability that they will suffer a loss. The main problem in this case is to devise insurance contracts that will lead agents to self-select into groups and therefore reveal their personal characteristics. The classic article on this topic is Rothschild and Stiglitz (1976).

These strands of the literature are remarkable because, although they ask different questions, in at least the simplest models they all deduce the same answer— optimal insurance contracts take the form of a "deductible policy" in which coverage is not provided for losses below a certain level.[19] The reasoning is as follows. When agents face uncertainty in income they would like to smooth income as much as possible by purchasing insurance. In the absence of moral hazard, the optimal insurance contract in a competitive insurance market provides full coverage so that income is the same in all circumstances. However, when moral hazard is present, the market breaks down when full insurance is provided because, in that case, no agent would have any incentive to take care to avoid large losses. With no one taking care, large losses would occur and insurance providers would go broke compensating the insured. Thus, given that full insurance will not be provided, what type of insurance is best? To answer this, note that agents are most concerned about avoiding catastrophes—that is, extremely large losses. It follows that the outcomes that they most want to insure against are the most adverse outcomes, and any optimal insurance contract will have to provide coverage in such cases. The insurance contract must also provide incentives to avoid losses, and this is provided by not covering small losses—there is a deductible that the insured agent must cover any time a loss occurs. In summary, a deductible contract forces agents to cover all small losses and provides coverage against large losses. It is optimal because it provides coverage in the cases that agents are most concerned about and includes incentives for agents to make efforts to avoid losses.

What are the implications of this literature for UI? Workers suffer large losses when they suffer long spells of unemployment. An optimal UI program, then, should compensate those who have a particularly difficult time finding reemployment. This is why a long potential duration of benefits is optimal. A deductible has been ruled out in the model we use by requiring the replacement rate to remain constant over the spell of unemployment until benefits are exhausted.[20] Therefore, the only way to force agents to search for employment is to keep the replacement rate relatively low. This explains why the model yields optimal replacement rates at or below the current rates offered in the United States.

The results from the optimal insurance literature also imply that the current UI program in the United States is reverse of what it should be. By offering benefits to most workers for 26 of the first 27 weeks of unemployment, the UI system covers the majority of short spells of unemployment—that is, the small losses. By cutting off benefits after 26 weeks of payments, the government provides inadequate coverage in catastrophic cases—ones in which agents suffer large losses due to long spells of unemployment.

A UI program with low benefits offered for a long period of time would have the additional benefit of reducing the subsidization of temporary layoffs by firms. It is well-known that because the payroll tax that funds UI is incompletely experience rated in the United States (and not experience rated at all in other countries), firms have an incentive to exploit the system by temporarily laying off workers and then recalling them when their benefits are exhausted. Existing estimates suggest that 25 to 50 percent of all layoffs in the United States can be explained by incomplete experience rating of the payroll tax (Card and Levine 1994; Topel 1994). If laid-off workers received lower benefits during the early weeks of unemployment, they would have an incentive to seek new jobs rather than wait for recall. And if workers were unwilling to wait for recall, then firms would be less likely to lay them off.

Previous results have suggested that such a program might be more efficient than current UI programs. For example, O'Leary (1998) used a consumer theoretic approach to examine UI benefit adequacy and found that the current U.S. system overcompensates short spells of unemployment and undercompensates long spells. This conclusion is consistent with the type of policy shift suggested above. Using a different framework, Wang and Williamson (1996) argue for a UI program similar to the one suggested here. In particular, they suggest a UI program that offers benefits for more than 5 quarters.[21]

5. Extensions

Up to this point, all workers have been assumed identical and unable to self-insure by saving. This section extends the model to see how the results would be altered by relaxing these assumptions.

5.1 Savings

Allowing workers to save while employed should reduce the generosity of the optimal UI program because workers will be able to supplement UI benefits by dissaving during the early stages of a jobless spell. For workers who suffer long spells of unemployment, however, savings will eventually be depleted, leaving them with only their UI benefits to finance consumption.

Extending the model to allow for savings is nontrivial. Doing so rigorously would require choosing between assuming constant absolute risk aversion on the part of workers (so that consumption and savings in each period are independent of assets, as in Acemoglu and Shimer 1998) and modeling the consumption/ savings decision faced by each worker in each stage of employment and unemployment. In the latter case, optimal consumption would depend on a worker's complete labor market history and would require tracking each worker's employment history and the economy-wide distribution of assets. Such a wholesale extension is beyond the scope of this paper.[22]

Instead, Gruber's (1997) empirical findings on the consumption smoothing benefits of UI (from the Panel Study of Income Dynamics) can be used to extend the model marginally and still gain insight into how savings would alter the optimal UI program. Gruber's sample consists of individuals who were employed at the time of an annual interview in year $t-1$ and then unemployed at the time of the interview in year t. He compared the yearly consumption levels by these individuals and concluded that with a UI replacement rate of 50 percent, consumption in year t would be 94 percent of consumption in year $t-1$. In addition, he estimated that a replacement rate of roughly 80 percent would fully smooth consumption across the unemployment spell. Gruber's conclusion is that UI does allow workers to smooth consumption. His findings also suggest that personal savings alone are not sufficient to smooth consumption.

Gruber's findings can be used to gauge how the model's results would be altered if agents saved while employed. Doing so requires some simplifying assumptions. First, assume that a worker who was employed at time t-1 was employed for the full year, whereas a worker who was unemployed at time t suffered one spell of unemployment during the year and that the spell was of average duration (one quarter). Second, assume that while employed, all agents save a constant fraction of their income (denoted by σ) and that these savings are then used to finance consumption by unemployed workers not receiving UI (UI-exhaustees and UI-ineligibles) and to supplement benefits for those who are collecting UI. Assume also that the amount of savings transferred to those receiving benefits is independent of the number of weeks the worker has been unemployed and that the amount transferred to UI-exhaustees and UI-ineligibles is the same. To make this precise, let C_w denote consumption by an employed worker, let C_u represent consumption by an unemployed worker who is collecting UI-benefits, and let C_x denote consumption by UI-exhaustees ad UI-ineligibles. Then $C_w = [w(1 - \tau) + \theta_w](1 - \sigma)$. Furthermore, for C_w and C_u to be consistent with Gruber's findings, it must be that when the replacement rate is 50 percent (as in Gruber's sample), then

$$0.25C_u + 0.75C_w = 0.94C_w$$

because a worker who is unemployed at time t is assumed to have been unemployed for one-quarter and employed for three quarters. This implies that if the replacement rate is 50 percent, then $C_u = 0.76C_w$—that is, an unemployed worker collecting UI benefits consumes 76 percent as much as an employed worker. Most of this consumption is covered by UI benefits while the remainder is paid for by savings.

Deriving the optimal UI program requires knowing how consumption varies with the replacement rate. Such a formula can be derived by making use of Gruber's estimate that a replacement rate of roughly 80 percent would allow unemployed workers to fully smooth consumption across the jobless spell. This implies that $C_u = C_w$ when the replacement rate is 0.80. Combining these two results gives us the following relationship between C_u, C_w, and RR:

(26) $C_u = (.36 + .8RR)C_w.$

For UI-ineligibles and UI-exhaustees, one more estimate from Gruber can be used. He estimates that with a replacement rate of zero, consumption in year t would be approximately 78 percent of what it had been in year $t - 1$. For UI-ineligibles who are unemployed at time t, C_x and C_w should therefore satisfy $0.25C_x + 0.75C_w = 0.78C_w$. It follows that $C_x = 0.12C_w$—that is, while unemployed, consumption by UI-ineligibles and UI-exhaustees falls to 12 percent of consumption while employed. This consumption is fully financed by savings. While this rate of consumption may seem low, it is similar to the rate used by Wang and Williamson (1996) and Fredriksson and Holmlund (1998), who set consumption by UI-exhaustees equal to 17 percent of consumption by employed workers.

To complete the extended model, all savings must be accounted for. Because there are J employed workers who each save $[w(1 - \tau) + \theta_w]\sigma$, total savings are $J[w(1 - \tau) + \theta_w]\sigma$. These savings are used to finance consumption by the unemployed. UI-eligibles who have not exhausted their benefits receive $C_u - x$, while UI-ineligibles and UI-exhaustees receive C_x. Thus, for total savings to equal total payments it must be that

$$(27) \qquad J[w(1 - \tau) + \theta_w]\sigma = (U - U_x - U_i)(C_u - x) + (U_x + U_i)C_x.$$

Adding (26), (27), and the equation $C_x = 0.12C_w$ to the model puts us in a position to see how savings affect the results. To do so, then model is recalibrated for the square root and log utility functions to get estimates of the parameters that make the model's predictions consistent with the Illinois reemployment bonus experiment. The model is then solved for the optimal UI program in the reference case for each of the two utility functions.

As expected, in each case the optimal UI program is less generous than it would be in the absence of savings. Self-insurance lowers the optimal replacement rate by a significant amount and reduces the optimal potential duration of benefits as well. When the degree of relative risk aversion is one-half (the square root utility function), the optimal UI program is characterized by a replacement rate of 28 percent offered for 24 weeks. Compared with the optimal program without savings ($RR = 61\%$, $T = 26$), the main impact of self-insurance is to reduce the optimal replacement rate. When the degree of relative risk aversion is equal to one (the log utility function), the optimal UI program in the reference case is characterized by a replacement rate of 46 percent and a potential duration of benefits of 44 weeks. Thus, with log utility the ability to self-insure causes both the replacement rate and the potential duration of benefits fall significantly. Nonetheless, in both cases the main result with respect to potential duration remains—with a square root utility function the current system (with potential benefit duration of 26 weeks) is about right, whereas with the log utility function the current system does not offer benefits for a long enough period of time. Both models suggest that current benefit rates are too high, although the model that is closest to existing empirical estimates of risk aversion (the log model) yields a replacement rate quite close to current rates.

Although the approach to savings taken here is ad hoc and relatively simplistic, it generates optimal replacement rates that are quite similar to those found by Wang and Williamson (1996) and Valdivia (1994), who handle savings in a more rigorous way.

5.2 Worker Heterogeneity

All existing work on optimal UI assumes that all agents are alike. Empirically, however, workers are subject to a wide variety of labor market experiences. Some workers are never unemployed, others find jobs quickly, and some face long spells of unemployment when they lose a job. In addition, some workers regularly take advantage of the UI system while others never consider claiming benefits. This implies that workers have different preferences for UI based on their labor market histories and expectations. Moreover, the number of workers that attempt to exploit the system may depend upon the generosity of the program.

In order to take worker heterogeneity into account, the model is extended to allow for three different classes of workers. The first represents the bulk of the labor force and is described by the model developed above. These workers face employment risk, losing their jobs with probability s in each period, and actively search for a new job once unemployed.

The second class consists of workers who are never unemployed. We refer to this group as "professionals," for lack of a better term, and use φ to denote the proportion of the labor force that falls into this class. Also, L_p denotes the number of such workers, and V_p denotes their expected lifetime utility. Because these workers are never unemployed, they earn w in each period of life, so that $V_p = u(w)(1+r)/r$. The total contribution of these workers to social welfare is therefore L_pV_p, and adding professionals to the model is accomplished by adding this term to W as defined in equation (4).

The third class of workers consists of agents who try to take advantage of the system. We refer to such workers as "opportunists." These agents work only to become eligible for UI and live off of the dole as much as possible. L_o denotes the number of opportunists, and V_o represents their expected lifetime utility. Thus, their contribution to social welfare (W) is L_oV_o.

Presumably, the number of opportunists in the labor force will depend on the generosity of the system—a more generous UI program should result in more opportunists. To measure the generosity of the system, consider the following variable G:

$$G = \{u(x)/u(w)\}\{1 - (1/1+r)^T\},$$

which measures the ratio of utility received from collecting UI benefits to utility from working for wage w during one spell of unemployment that lasts T periods (the potential duration of benefits). If $x = 0$ or $T = 0$, so that no UI is offered, $G = 0$. On the other hand, as the replacement rate approaches 1 and T approaches infinity, G approaches 1. Increases in G represent increases in the generosity of the UI program. We assume that the proportion of the labor force that are opportunists, denoted by α, is linearly related to G: $\alpha = \eta G$.

To complete the extended model, the determination of η and V_o need to be described. Consider V_o first. Because these agents work as little as possible, they contribute less to social welfare than the average unemployed agent (who is seeking a job). Thus, because V_u is the average expected lifetime utility for unemployed workers, we set $V_o = \Omega V_u$ with $\Omega < 1$. Ω can then be varied to see how the optimal UI program is affected. Note that Ω measures the relative contribution of opportunists to social welfare.

For η (the extent to which opportunists increase with increases in UI generosity), the model is solved assuming that the current U.S. program is in effect (a 50 percent replacement rate offered for 26 weeks); then η is varied so that α ranges from 0 to 0.05. This implies considering values of η such that between 0 percent and 5 percent of the labor force exploits the system.

Results for the square-root utility function are summarized in Tables 8.3 and 8.4 and results for the log utility function are reported in Tables 8.5 and 8.6. These tables report the optimal UI program for various values of α, Ω, and φ with all other parameters set at the reference case values. In each cell, the optimal UI program is reported by first listing the optimal replacement rate and then listing the optimal potential duration of benefits. Tables 8.3 and 8.5 show how the optimal UI program varies with α and Ω when there are no professionals in the model (i.e., $\varphi = 0$). For example, using the square-root utility function and $\alpha = 0$ (so that there are no opportunists in the model), the optimal program offers a 61 percent replacement rate for 26 weeks. As the number of opportunists increases, the generosity of the optimal program declines regardless of the value of Ω. This is hardly surprising—with more opportunists in the economy the government needs to make the program less generous in order to discourage exploitation of the system.

Tables 8.3 and 8.5 also indicate that the generosity of the optimal program is decreasing in Ω (the parameter that measures the amount that opportunists contribute to social welfare). As Ω decreases, opportunists contribute less to social welfare and it becomes more important for the government to discourage exploitation. Tables 8.3 and 8.5 clearly indicate the importance of the actual values of α and Ω. If α is low or if Ω is close to one, then the optimal program is quite close to the optimal program in the model that ignores exploitation. But for large values of α and low values of Ω (e.g., $\alpha = 0.05$ and $\Omega = 0.7$), the optimal program is considerably less generous.

Table 8.3. Optimal UI Programs with Opportunists but No Professionals Using Square-root Utility (replacement rate, potential duration in weeks).

Ω	$\alpha = 0$	0.01	0.02	0.05
0.9	(61%, 26)	(59%, 24)	(56%, 22)	(48%, 16)
0.8	(61%, 26)	(60%, 22)	(55%, 20)	(42%, 14)
0.7	(61%, 26)	(58%, 22)	(54%, 18)	(36%, 12)

α is the proportion of the labor force comprised of opportunists; Ω is the relative contribution of opportunists to social welfare.

Table 8.4. Optimal UI Programs with Professionals and Opportunists Using Square-root Utility (replacement rate, potential duration in weeks).

φ	α = 0	0.01	0.02	0.05
0	(61%, 26)	(60%, 22)	(55%, 20)	(42%, 14)
0.1	(64%, 28)	(60%, 26)	(57%, 22)	(45%, 14)
0.2	(66%, 32)	(63%, 28)	(61%, 24)	(47%, 16)
0.3	(68%, 36)	(67%, 32)	(64%, 28)	(51%, 18)

α is the proportion of the labor force comprised of opportunists; φ is the proportion of the labor force comprised of professionals; Ω is the relative contribution of opportunists to social welfare; $\Omega = 0.8$ in all cells.

Table 8.5. Optimal UI Programs with Opportunists but No Professionals Using Log Utility (replacement rate, potential duration in weeks).

Ω	α = 0	0.01	0.02	0.05
0.9	(64%, 90)	(62%, 86)	(60%, 82)	(53%, 76)
0.8	(64%, 90)	(62%, 84)	(59%, 78)	(47%, 70)
0.7	(64%, 90)	(61%, 82)	(56%, 74)	(40%, 66)

α is the proportion of the labor force comprised of opportunists; Ω is the relative contribution of opportunists to social welfare.

Table 8.6. Optimal UI Programs with Professionals and Opportunists Using Log Utility (replacement rate, potential duration in weeks).

φ	α = 0	0.01	0.02	0.05
0	(64%, 90)	(62%, 84)	(58%, 74)	(48%, 60)
0.1	(66%, 94)	(65%, 88)	(61%, 77)	(51%, 62)
0.2	(68%, 100)	(67%, 92)	(64%, 80)	(55%, 66)
0.3	(70%, 102)	(68%, 96)	(66%, 84)	(58%, 70)

α is the proportion of the labor force comprised of opportunists; φ is the proportion of the labor force comprised of professionals; Ω is the relative contribution of opportunists to social welfare; $\Omega = 0.8$ in all cells.

Tables 8.4 and 8.6 report the optimal program when both opportunists and professionals are included in the model. These results are derived assuming that $\Omega = 0.8$ (as in the middle row of Tables 8.3 and 8.5). Tables 8.4 and 8.6 indicate that as the proportion of professionals rises the optimal program becomes more generous. The reasoning is as follows. With professionals in the model, the tax burden of UI is shared by a group of workers who never use the system, which allows for a more generous system. As in Tables 8.3 and 8.5, knowing the correct value of φ is important. For example, using the square-root utility function and setting $\alpha = 0$, the optimal UI program when 10 percent of the work force is made up of professionals offers a replacement rate of 64 percent for 28 weeks. In contrast, when 30 percent of the work force are professionals, the optimal program offers a replacement rate slightly higher (68 percent) but for a much longer time (36 weeks).

To summarize, the main result holds up to extensions that allow for saving by workers and worker heterogeneity. Although the approaches taken to modeling savings and worker heterogeneity are relatively simple, we believe that they point toward answers that could be expected if more comprehensive approaches were taken. Regarding savings, the approach taken is consistent with the limited empirical work on this topic, however simple it may be. Regarding worker heterogeneity, although two new groups are added to the model, transitions between the groups have not been modeled (although the number of opportunists does depend on the generosity of the program in the model). To some extent, efforts in these directions may be limited until more is known about the composition of the labor force (that is, the proportions of workers that can be considered "opportunists," "professionals," and so on) and the extent to which workers may move among various labor force groups. There is clearly a need for additional work on optimal UI when workers are heterogeneous and can save.

6. Conclusion

This paper has developed a general equilibrium search model of the labor market in order to determine the optimal UI program when the government sets the optimal potential duration of benefits and when the replacement rate must remain constant until UI benefits are exhausted. The model developed has several features that have not been included in earlier work on optimal UI. First, it is an equilibrium model that allows one to estimate the costs of different UI programs through the impact on search effort, job creation, and unemployment. Second, the model incorporates the assumption that workers are risk averse. As a result, the various UI programs examined provide insurance against the risk of unemployment and have measurable welfare benefits. Third, the model allows the potential duration of benefits to vary, includes workers who are ineligible for UI, takes account of firm behavior so that the job destruction effects of UI can be measured, and allows for worker heterogeneity and private savings. These features make the model developed here relatively comprehensive.

The main finding is that current statutory UI replacement rates offered in the United States are about right (or slightly too high), but that UI benefits are offered for too short a period of time. In the latter sense, the U.S. system is not generous enough. The finding depends heavily on the assumed degree of worker risk aversion and on the assumption that all unemployed workers are alike. If workers differ significantly in their labor market experiences, the division of the labor force into "professionals" and "opportunists" becomes important as well. The result appears to be much less sensitive to assumptions about whether workers can save. Unfortunately, little if any evidence exists on the degree of worker risk aversion or the division of the labor force into different groups. Empirical work aimed at clarifying these parameters would have high value.

Notes

1. There is a cap on benefits which reduces the replacement rate below 50 percent for most high-wage workers.

2. Articles that consider the optimal path of benefits over the unemployment spell include Shavell and Weiss (1979) and Hopenhayn and Nicolini (1997). These papers address the following question: given that the government is going to spend a fixed amount of money on unemployment compensation, how should the benefits be paid out to the unemployed (i.e., how should the benefits vary over the spell of unemployment)? The optimal size of the program is an open question in these papers.

3. Valdivia (1995) extends the Mortensen (1994) analysis to allow for risk aversion and finds optimal replacement rates of approximately 30 percent for the United States. However, this rate is derived assuming that benefits are offered indefinitely (as in the Baily/Flemming analyses). Fredriksson and Holmlund (1998) allow for risk aversion in a model in which the potential duration of benefits is finite and stochastic and the benefit rate is allowed to change once over the spell of unemployment. Their main goal is to argue that a two-tier system in which the benefit rate drops at some point in time dominates a program with a uniform replacement rate. With a uniform benefit structure, they find optimal replacement rates between 27 and 42 percent, depending on the degree of risk aversion.

4. A more generous UI program may also induce entry into the work force. We return to this issue in Section 4.4 when we extend the model to allow for worker heterogeneity.

5. This assumption is commonly used in general equilibrium search models (see, for example, Diamond 1982 or Pissarides 1990). Alternatively, one could assume that each firm recruits for and fills each of its many vacancies separately.

6. Strict application of the Nash bargaining solution would require a different threat point for unemployed workers who have been unemployed a different length of time. For example, the threat point for an unemployed worker in her t^{th} period of search would be V_{t+1} while the threat point for an unemployed worker who has exhausted her benefits would be V_x. This would result in the firm paying different wages to workers with different unemployment histories and would imply that the firm would prefer to hire a long-term unemployed worker rather than someone who had been unemployed for a relatively short time (since the firm could offer a lower wage to the worker who has been unemployed for a long time). The result would be a more complicated analysis without additional insight into the design of an optimal UI program. For simplicity, then, we assume that the threat point is the same for all unemployed workers and that this threat point is the average utility of all unemployed agents. This allows us to capture the notion that the average wage will rise when the utility of the unemployment increases.

7. For details on the sensitivity of the results with respect to the interest rate, see footnotes 13 and 14 of Davidson and Woodbury (1997).

8. See Davidson and Woodbury (1997) for details.

9. In the terminology of decision making under uncertainty, the unemployed prefer the second program to the first program because it makes unemployment "less risky" in the Rothschild-Stiglitz sense.

10. The abbreviated model yields almost identical predictions concerning optimal replacement rates, as shown in Table 5 of Davidson and Woodbury (1997).

11. McCall (1995) reports that only 60 percent of UI eligibles claimed their benefits between 1984 and 1990.

12. Although the optimal replacement rate falls slightly when risk aversion is increased, the true level of insurance provided by these benefits is higher than the level provided under linear utility. The level of insurance can be measured by comparing *utility* while receiving UI benefits with *utility* while employed. With a linear utility function this ratio is identical to the replacement rate. But with concave utility, this ratio and the replacement rate are quite different. For example, with log utility a replacement rate of 0.60 (implying a bi-weekly benefit of $305 for a worker with pre-layoff bi-weekly wages of $511) gives a utility ratio of 0.91. Thus, optimal insurance is increasing in the degree of risk aversion.

13. When Baily and Flemming changed the degree of risk aversion in their models, they held all other parameters fixed.

14. When the model is recalibrated for the square root utility function in the reference case (s = 0.010), the following values are obtained for the key parameters—c = 11.2, = 1.284, R = 881, K = 4.196.

15. Recall that the abbreviated model of Sections 3.1 and 3.2 yielded results quite similar to those found in Baily (1978) and Flemming (1978). Thus, the model seems able to reproduce existing results in the literature once the assumptions are altered to match the models used by previous authors. This is true even though the previous models were calibrated in different ways using data from a wide variety of different sources.

16. This result holds for all of the parameter values considered.

17. For an important exception, see Wang and Williamson (1996).

18. The parallel between garden-variety insurance, such as fire insurance or automobile insurance, and UI is incomplete because moral hazard arises in a different way in each. With fire insurance, moral hazard occurs through lack of care in preventing a single event that results in a single insurance payment. With UI, it could be argued that moral hazard occurs mainly after a precipitating event—involuntary job loss—followed by lack of effort to gain reemployment. The lack of effort to gain reemployment results in a stream of insurance payments.

19. In the case of adverse selection it is necessary to offer a menu of deductible policies so that agents with different characteristics choose different policies. However, each of the offered policies includes a non-zero deductible.

20. This requirement also rules out a deductible in the form of a waiting period, which is a common feature of UI in the United States.

21. The government has much more power in Williamson and Wang's model than in ours. In Williamson and Wang, the replacement rate is allowed to vary over the spell of unemployment, the government is allowed to control consumption, and the government can offer reemployment bonuses to workers. Nevertheless, they find that it is optimal to offer positive benefits for over one year.

22. For example, with constant absolute risk aversion, expected utility maximization implies that a worker will always invest the same absolute amount in risky assets regardless of her wealth. That is, the assumption leads to the counter-factual result that all wealth increases are invested in riskless assets.

References

Abraham, Katherine G. "Structural/Frictional vs. Deficient Demand Unemployment: Some New Evidence." *American Economic Review* 73 (September 1983): 708–724.

Acemoglu, Daron and Robert Shimer. "Efficient Unemployment Insurance." National Bureau of Economic Research Working Paper No. 6686, 1998.

Arrow, Kenneth. "Optimal Insurance and Generalized Deductibles." *Scandanavian Actuarial Journal* 1: 1–42.

Baily, Martin N. "Some Aspects of Optimal Unemployment Insurance." *Journal of Public Economics* 10 (1978): 379–402.

Blank, Rebecca M. and David E. Card. "Recent Trends in Insured and Uninsured Unemployment: Is there an Explanation?" *Quarterly Journal of Economics* 106 (November 1991): 1157–1189.

Card, David and Phillip B. Levine. "Unemployment Insurance Taxes and the Cyclical and Seasonal Properties of Unemployment." *Journal of Public Economics* 53 (January 1994):1–29.

Davidson, Carl and Stephen A. Woodbury. "Effects of a Reemployment Bonus under Differing Benefit Entitlements, or, Why the Illinois Experiment Worked." Manuscript, Department of Economics, Michigan State University, and W.E. Upjohn Institute for Employment Research, March 1991.

_____. "The Displacement Effect of Reemployment Bonus Programs." *Journal of Labor Economics* 11 (October 1993): 575–605.

_____. "Optimal Unemployment Insurance." *Journal of Public Economics* 64 (1997): 359–387.

Diamond, Peter. "Wage Determination and Efficiency in Search Equilibrium." *Review of Economic Studies* 49 (April 1982): 217–228.

Ehrenberg, Ronald G. "The Demographic Structure of Unemployment Rates and Labor Market Transition Probabilities." *Research in Labor Economics* 3 (1980): 214–291.

Flemming, J. S. "Aspects of Optimal Unemployment Insurance." *Journal of Public Economics* 10 (1978): 403–425.

Fredriksson, Peter and Bertil Holmlund. "Optimal Unemployment Insurance in Search Equilibrium." Department of Economics, Uppsala University Working Paper, 1998:2.

Gruber, Jonathan S. "The Consumption Smoothing Benefits of Unemployment Insurance." *American Economic Review* 87(1): 192–205.

Hadar, Josef and Tae Kun Seo. "Sensible Risk Aversion." Southern Methodist University Working Paper, September 1993.

Hamermesh, Daniel S. *Jobless Pay and the Economy.* Baltimore, MD: Johns Hopkins University Press, 1977.

Hopenhayn, H. A. and J. P. Nicolini. "Optimal Unemployment Insurance." *Journal of Political Economy* 105 (1997): 412–428.

Layard, Richard, Stephen Nickell and Richard Jackman. *Unemployment: Macroeconomic Performance and the Labor Market.* Oxford University Press, 1991.

Ljungqvist, Lars and Thomas Sargent. "The European Unemployment Dilemma." *Journal of Political Economy* 106 (1998): 514–550.

McCall, Brian. "The Impact of Unemployment Insurance Benefit Levels on Recipiency." *Journal of Business and Economics Statistics* 13 (April 1995): 189–198.

Millard, Stephen and Dale Mortensen. "The Unemployment and Welfare Effects of Labor Market Policy: A Comparison of the USA. and UK." In *Unemployment Policy: Government Options for the Labor Market,* edited by Dennis J. Snower and Guillermo de la Dehesa. Cambridge: Cambridge University Press, 1997. Pp. 545–572.

Mortensen, Dale. "Reducing the Supply-Side Disincentives to Job Creation." In *Reducing Unemployment: Current issues and Policy Options.* Federal Reserve Bank of Kansas City, 1994.

Murphy, Kevin M. and Robert H. Topel. "The Evolution of Unemployment in the United States: 1968-1985." In *NBER Macroeconomics Annual 1987*, edited by Stanley Fischer. Cambridge, MA: MIT Press, 11–58.

OECD (Organization for Economic Cooperation and Development). *Employment Outlook*. Paris, France: OECD, 1995.

O'Leary, Christopher J. "The Adequacy of Unemployment Insurance Benefits." In *Reform of the Unemployment Insurance System*, edited by Laurie J. Bassi and Stephen A. Woodbury. Stamford, CT: JAI Press, 1998. Pp. 63–110.

Pissarides, Christopher. *Equilibrium Unemployment Theory*. Basil Blackwell, 1990.

Raviv, Arthur. "The Design of an Optimal Insurance Policy." *American Economic Review* 69 (1979): 84–96.

Rothschild, Michael and Joseph Stiglitz. "Equilibrium in Competitive Insurance Markets: An Essay on the Economics of Imperfect Information." *Quarterly Journal of Economics* 90 (1976): 629–649.

Shavell, Steven. "On Moral Hazard and Insurance." *Quarterly Journal of Economics* 93 (November 1979): 541–562.

Shavell, Steven and Laurence Weiss. "The Optimal Provision of Unemployment Insurance Benefits over Time." *Journal of Political Economy* 87 (December 1979): 1347–1362.

Storer, Paul and Marc Van Audenrode. "Unemployment Insurance Take-up Rates in Canada: Facts, Determinants, and Implications." *Canadian Journal of Economics* 28 (November 1995): 822–835.

Topel, Robert. "Financing Unemployment Insurance: History, Incentives, and Reform." In *Unemployment Insurance: The Second Half-Century*, edited by W. Lee Hanson and James F. Byers. Madison, WI: University of Wisconsin Press: 108–135.

Valdivia, Victor. "Evaluating the Welfare Benefits of Unemployment Insurance." Northwestern University Working Paper, 1994.

Wang, Cheng and Stephen Williamson. "Unemployment Insurance with Moral Hazard in a Dynamic Economy." *Carnegie-Rochester Conference Series on Public Policy* 44 (June 1996): 1–41.

Zeldes, Stephen. "Consumption and Liquidity Constraints: An Empirical Investigation." *Journal of Political Economy* 97 (April 1989): 305–347.

9

Macroeconomic Policy and the Theory of Job Search

Bruce C. Fallick
Board of Governors of the Federal Reserve System

William L. Wascher
Board of Governors of the Federal Reserve System

Abstract

Search theory has provided a foundation for the way many policymakers think about the macroeconomics of the labor market—including a general belief in the existence of a "natural" rate of unemployment, a recognition of the role that frictional unemployment plays in determining the natural rate, and a reliance on some form of the Phillips curve model of the inflation process. We outline the major contributions of the theory, but also argue that theoretical developments have far outpaced their practical relevance to economic policy. We conclude that researchers should direct their efforts towards developing stronger empirical connections between theory and the practical workings of the macroeconomy, testing models more rigorously, examining in more detail the role of the demand side of the market, and analyzing the movements of nominal quantities.

1. Introduction

Search theory has provided a foundation for much of the way policymakers now think about the macroeconomics of the labor market. The concept of a natural rate of unemployment and the associated representations of the Phillips curve, one cornerstone of applied macroeconomics, rest on this foundation. However, while search models of the labor market have come a long way in theoretical development since the inception of this body of research in the 1960s (as can be seen in the other chapters of this volume), their relevance to economic policy has not developed in a parallel fashion. Indeed, an uncomfortably large proportion of what the theoretical search literature has contributed to "practical" macroeconomics can already be found in the early collection of papers in Phelps (1970). In our view, the discrepancy between advances in modeling and in policy relevance can be traced to two factors. First, the existing literature has made only limited progress in developing the strong empirical connections necessary to guide policymakers from the theoretical models of job search to the practical workings of the macroeconomy. Second, researchers have paid relatively little attention to nominal quantities and to the demand side of the market in general. In this chapter, we outline the important contributions and limitations of the existing research on search unemployment from the point of view of those concerned with implementing macroeconomic stabilization policy.

2. Contributions of Search Models to Macroeconomic Policy

2.1 The Existing Paradigm

We begin by summarizing our impressions of how a typical policymaker might think about unemployment in a macroeconomic context. Given the breadth of international experience with both labor market institutions and economic performance and given the variety of viewpoints within each country, our attempt at generalization will undoubtedly give short shrift to a number of alternative views. However, to provide at least some flavor of what might be considered the mainstream framework used by policymakers as a reference point, we turn to two documents that are considered by many to be representative of the views of policymakers in more developed nations: The 1994 *OECD Jobs Study* and the 1997 *Economic Report of the President*.

   The OECD (Organization for Economic Cooperation and Development) is an international agency that is supported by the more developed countries of the world. Although the OECD has its own staff, its activities are often guided by and undertaken in close cooperation with official representatives (ministers) from the member countries.[1] In 1992, the OECD ministers issued a mandate to the OECD staff to examine the theoretical and empirical evidence on the causes of high and persistent unemployment in the OECD economies and to issue a set of policy options designed to address the unemployment problem. The 1994 *OECD Jobs Study* is the culmination of this effort.

The study is wide ranging, and much of the research pertains as much to the microeconomics of search models discussed in previous chapters of this book as to the discussion here. However, the macroeconomic framework in which possible sources of unemployment are examined is clearly stated at the outset, and potential macroeconomic policies aimed at reducing unemployment are examined as well. As an example, consider the following paragraph taken from Chapter 2 of the *Jobs Study*:

> Economic analysis generally distinguishes between the actual unemployment rate prevailing at any time, and the "natural" (or "structural") unemployment rate. The latter, which is a longer-term equilibrium concept, is determined by the underlying structural factors affecting the supply of and demand for labor. These factors include the demographic composition of the labor force, and the various regulations and institutions that influence the operation of the labor market, including employment protection legislation and the unemployment compensation system. Unfavorable shifts in these basic determinants of the natural unemployment rate will be reflected in higher actual unemployment if various systems of labor market imbalances, such as an ever-accelerating inflation rate, are to be avoided.

There are three things to note about this passage. First, and perhaps most importantly, a distinction is made between cyclical and structural unemployment, and there is a clear reference to a "natural" rate of unemployment. Second, there is a presumption that the natural rate varies over time with changes in structural factors and institutional arrangements. Third, there is a presumed linkage between cyclical unemployment and inflation, and indeed one method advocated by the OECD for deriving an estimate of structural unemployment is to make use of the relationship between the unemployment rate and changes in the rate of wage inflation. Elsewhere, in the context of hysteresis, the OECD document also expresses the view that the level of equilibrium unemployment at any given time may not be unique and that prudent macroeconomic policies might be able to reduce the equilibrium rate.

A framework similar to the OECD's is presented in the 1997 *Economic Report of the President*, a document written by the Council of Economic Advisers (CEA) that traditionally sets forth the U.S. Administration's economic plan for the coming year. In particular, Chapter 2 of the 1997 *Economic Report* contains an extensive discussion of the links between the actual unemployment rate, the natural rate of unemployment, and changes in inflation. As in the OECD study, the 1997 *Economic Report* advocates estimating the natural rate by way of the relationship between unemployment and inflation (although price changes rather than wage changes are used here) and presumes that the natural rate of unemployment may change over time. Factors potentially affecting the natural rate are designated as "supply shocks" in the *Economic Report*, but include many of the same elements as discussed in the

OECD study (e.g., demographics and labor market institutions).[2] Similarly, the *Economic Report* suggests that macroeconomic policies might be able to influence the equilibrium unemployment rate, although its authors state that there is little evidence for this in the United States.[3]

Thus, the typical policymaker (if there is one) might be viewed as accepting the notion that some unemployment will exist in equilibrium, that structural policies are the most efficient means of reducing unemployment in the long run, and that macroeconomic policies are most appropriate for addressing cyclical fluctuations in unemployment. Indeed, the "natural rate" concept highlighted in both the OECD and CEA reports has clearly dominated policy discussions over the past twenty years, with government agencies, private forecasters, and academics producing estimates of the natural rate (or more precisely, the Nonaccelerating Inflation Rate of Unemployment) nearly continuously. For our discussion of the role of search theory, such a focus is especially convenient, given the theory's importance in the original formulation of the concept.

In terms of a macroeconometric model of inflation, Blanchard and Katz (1997) succinctly summarize this "natural rate" concept using the following equation:

(1) $\Delta p_t = \alpha + \Delta p_{t-1} - \beta u_t + \varepsilon_t$

where p refers to the (log) price level and u is the unemployment rate.[4] In this framework, the natural rate is taken to be the unemployment rate consistent with no change in the inflation rate. Modelers will undoubtedly view this equation as overly simplistic, but it does capture the essence of much of the policy debate surrounding cyclical and structural unemployment—namely that macroeconomic policies designed to reduce the unemployment rate may have undesirable implications for inflation. Given this framework, it seems clear that, if they are to be taken seriously by policymakers, proponents of various theories of unemployment—including search models—must clearly spell out their implications for links between unemployment and inflation.

2.2 Theoretical Contributions of Search Models to the Framework

As we indicated at the outset, the theoretical research on search unemployment has played a prominent role in helping to shape the way policymakers think about the macroeconomics of the labor market. In particular, search theory contributed formal representations of a number of ideas that had surfaced repeatedly in economic thought, but that had not entered the mainstream, in part because economists had not yet provided the theoretical microeconomic underpinnings to support them. Chief among these contributions, perhaps, was the development of a formal basis for the idea that there will be some amount of unemployment even at "full employment." That is, given the current structure of the labor market, the economy would not tend toward a zero rate of unemployment even in the absence of adverse shocks. Moreover, the theory argues that the structure determines, at any moment, the positive "natural" rate of unemployment to which the economy would tend and below which no amount of aggregate demand could keep the economy indefinitely without undesirable consequences (if at all).

In its simplest forms, search theory provides a formal description and rational justification (in terms of the individual actors) of "frictional" unemployment: job separation or labor force entry often leads to a temporary period of unemployment during which the individual is searching for a job. However, the theory is actually much richer, in that it also provides a single framework into which the concepts of frictional, structural, and cyclical unemployment can be easily fit. In doing so, it risks blurring the lines between these three types of unemployment, in the sense that all unemployment can be thought of as search unemployment. But at the same time, the ability to model all three types of unemployment in a common framework invites the economist to make the definitions more explicit and to make the intuitive distinctions between these potential sources of unemployment operational.

For example, frictional unemployment may be defined as the unemployment resulting from the (rational) search behavior of workers doing their best to find a good job in an environment of incomplete information and transactions costs, under "normal" conditions. Structural unemployment is unemployed search in excess of frictional unemployment that arises because a person faces an "abnormally" low rate of arrival of acceptable offers, for individual-specific reasons, perhaps involving a mismatch of location or skills between jobs and the worker. Finally, cyclical unemployment may be thought of as unemployment in excess of frictional and structural that arises because people in general face an abnormally low rate of arrival of offers (per searcher). Under this categorization, which labor market institutions, policies, beliefs and technologies are considered to constitute "normal" conditions distinguish between frictional and structural unemployment, and the generality of the circumstances that cause conditions to deviate from normal distinguishes between structural and cyclical unemployment. Other reasonable taxonomies are possible, of course, but they, too, can typically be conveniently expressed in a search framework.

From a practical standpoint, the ability of the theory to distinguish among various types of unemployment suggests that search models should be useful in identifying factors that influence the natural rate of unemployment. And, indeed, there are numerous such factors noted in the literature: the demographic composition of the labor force, the rate of entry into the labor force, the propensity of workers to quit without another job in hand (and thus become unemployed), and the rate at which firms discharge workers (the amount of turnover or "churning" in the labor market), as well as the "technology" of job search (including such elements as the growth in temporary help firms or the Internet),[5] policies that affect the flow of information (such as advance notice of layoffs), and the degree of heterogeneity across workers and across jobs. In addition, some researchers have emphasized the role of mismatches between the locations and skill-requirements of jobs and the locations and skills of workers, policies (such as taxes or unemployment insurance) that affect the relative disposable incomes from employment and unemployment, and productivity growth. Also, as a general principle, the framework emphasizes that any policy that would have a lasting effect on the natural rate must influence the rates of flow into or out of unemployment; a one-time change in the level of unemployment will soon be undone by the equilibrating effects of the enormous, continual flows between labor market states.

According to search theory, changes in these factors will lead to changes in the natural rate. In addition, the natural rate may evolve over time, and particularly over the business cycle, due to the dynamics of the search process itself. Search takes time, and changes in rates of flow caused by changes in the search environment take time to fully manifest themselves in stock measures like the unemployment rate. So, for example, when the business cycle turns up, the search process may cause the unemployment rate to remain, for a time, higher than would eventually be consistent with the higher underlying level of labor demand. This extra frictional unemployment will fade away, since the exits of these "extra" people from unemployment are no longer being matched by new transitions from employment into unemployment. This lag between labor demand and the unemployment rate need not be symmetric, however. When labor demand falls early in a downturn, there is no search-related lag in dismissing or laying-off employees or in declining to hire, although anticipation of the search time and costs involved in future hiring may dampen a firm's enthusiasm for reducing the size of its workforce in response to a perceived temporary demand shock.

Finally, if one "undesirable consequence" of attempting to reduce the unemployment rate below its natural rate is an ever-increasing rate of inflation, then the natural rate of unemployment corresponds to the NAIRU. Indeed, one important early application of search theory to macroeconomics was to provide a formal theoretical basis for the Phillips curve relationship between unemployment and inflation. Depending critically on how expectations are formed and other aspects of the search process, search theory makes predictions about the shape of the Phillips curve and about the restrictions that might, therefore, be placed upon an empirical Phillips curve equation. In addition, these early applications helped to generate an active interest by economists in empirically assessing the causes and properties of equilibrium unemployment, the topic of the next section.

2.3 Empirical Investigations of Microeconomic Factors with Macroeconomic Implications

Empirical analyses of individuals' transitions between unemployment and employment, within, or at least inspired by, the search framework, have provided evidence on the importance of a number of the factors that theory suggests may influence the natural rate of unemployment. The various contributions are too numerous for us to cover completely in this paper, but we have included a few examples of areas of study using microdata that have provided policymakers with useful evidence on the causes of structural/frictional unemployment and on potential specification issues in modeling the relationship between unemployment and inflation.

Perhaps the most striking characteristic of the microeconomic data, although rarely itself a focus of study, is the enormous heterogeneity across individuals. Heterogeneity is a feature of many theoretical search models and, in particular, can lead to cyclical movements in the natural rate in such models. Empirically, heterogeneity is manifested in the negative duration dependence in the transition rate from unemployment to employment that is typically found before heterogeneity (both observed and unobserved) is taken into account, as those workers with the highest transition rates leave the pool of the unemployed disproportionately early. Moreover, there is ample evidence of substantial differences in exit rates from unemployment by education, gender, race, the cause of separation from employment, and the characteristics of the previous job. Heterogeneity across jobs (beyond differences in wage rates) is evident also: the nonwage attributes of jobs may influence exit rates (Devine and Kiefer, 1991, p. 308), and the experiences of displaced workers (e.g., Farber, 1993) suggest that the transition to a full-time job may differ from the transition to a part-time job. Evidence on true duration dependence in the rate of exit from unemployment, which would also have implications for the cyclical behavior of the natural rate, is, unfortunately, less clear.

A topic that has received more explicit attention is the influence of the amount and duration of unemployment insurance benefits on exit rates from unemployment. As expected by theory, exit rates are inversely related to the generosity of the UI program. Likewise, measures that reward a worker for finding a job quickly, such as in several recent reemployment bonus experiments, should increase exit rates from unemployment (Meyer, 1996).[6] In general, such studies suggest that a more generous UI system could be expected to raise the natural rate of unemployment.

Another policy that has received considerable attention is advance notice of job loss. Whether provided voluntarily or mandated by law, advance notice would seem a straightforward way to improve the "technology" of search by allowing workers to begin searching before becoming unemployed. The evidence produced thus far suggests that advance notice has only a modest effect on average unemployment durations and thus that such provisions are not of much use in reducing search unemployment (Fallick, 1996). However, our impression is that the available data pertaining to this issue are not yet of sufficient quality to provide firm conclusions and that more research will be needed before the true impact of advance notice can be accurately determined.

Empirical work has also demonstrated that local economic conditions—local unemployment rates in particular—are an important determinant of transition rates out of unemployment (Devine and Kiefer, 1991; Fallick, 1996). Depending upon the form of this relationship, it may raise questions about the adequacy of aggregate measures of labor market conditions, like the national unemployment rate, for policy purposes. In particular, even if different localities have identical natural unemployment rates, the inflationary pressures associated with a given unemployment rate might differ depending on the distribution of unemployment across geographic areas. For example, as was noted in some of the early research on Phillips curves (e.g., Archibald, 1969; Thomas and Stoney, 1971), the typical nonlinear relationship posited between unemployment and inflation, $\Delta p = f(1/U)$, would lead to positive relationship between the geographic dispersion of the unemployment rate and inflation.

Another specification issue on which the microeconomic evidence has proven fruitful is the direction of the relationship between unemployment and wage changes. Various theoretical search models of the Phillips curve relationship have produced differing points of view on this question, emphasizing either the influence of the unemployment rate (as an indicator of offer-arrival rates) on wage inflation (e.g., Phelps, 1968, 1970) or the influence of unexpected wage inflation on acceptance probabilities and thereby on the unemployment rate (e.g., Mortensen, 1970). Attempts to estimate structural models of search, as well as the limited evidence on employer behavior, suggests that variation in transition rates into employment primarily reflects variation in offer arrival rates rather than in acceptance probabilities (Devine and Kiefer, 1991). This evidence favors the former groups of models, providing some justification for the standard practice of treating the unemployment rate as the independent variable in Phillips curve equations.

3. Limitations of the Current Research Agenda: Why Has the Search Literature of the 1980s and 1990s Had So Little Influence on Policy?

In the previous section we described several ways in which search theory has contributed to the specification of reduced-form models of the Phillips curve that are an important tool used by policymakers. However, the basic form of these equations can be derived from the search theory of twenty-five years ago. Models of search and matching in the labor market have developed a good deal since then, but few of these developments appear to have had much influence on the way policymakers think about macroeconomics or on the equations estimated in mainstream macroeconomic models. Nor are policymakers today likely to employ a structural search model to analyze the economic situation. Search models of the business cycle, in particular, do not appear to have made much headway in the policy arena. In this section we give our view of the main reasons for this lack of connection between the theoretical research program and practical applications of search unemployment models: a lack of attention paid to aggregate demand and to nominal prices, a lack of consensus about important theoretical details, and problems with the empirical implementation of the models.

3.1 Emphasis of Analysis

From a theoretical standpoint, much recent research has concentrated on embedding models of the business cycle into a search framework. These have tended to be of the "real" business cycle variety, which typically includes no role for demand management. Such models can be useful to makers of monetary policy if one thinks of them as models of fluctuations in the natural rate of unemployment in the face of supply shocks rather than as comprehensive models of the business cycle. However, despite the focus of the early literature on explaining the Phillips curve, the more recent literature has had little interest in nominal quantities and therefore is of limited use in identifying inflationary pressures or in describing the behavior of inflation.

An additional issue is the existence of multiple equilibria in many models. While multiple equilibria may be a desirable feature in a model, especially in view of persistent international differences in labor market outcomes in seemingly similar countries, research has not focused on the issues of most importance to policymakers: what determines which equilibrium obtains and how an economy can be moved from one equilibrium to another. Diamond and Fudenberg (1989) show that expectations provide one mechanism in a search framework through which policymakers might be able to influence an economy's steady state equilibrium path. But other avenues seem possible as well, and even for expectations, practical models of their influence on equilibrium outcomes in the context of search unemployment have not been adequately developed.[7]

3.2 The Sensitivity of Theoretical Results to Assumptions

All search models proceed from the basic notion that information in the job market is incomplete and that search (i.e., gathering information) is time-consuming or otherwise costly. However, as described elsewhere in this volume, search models differ on such fundamentals as whether search is modeled as an active or a passive pursuit, and whether wage offers are one-sided or subject to bargaining. Do firms and workers formulate search strategies, possibly including decisions about where and how much to search and about which job offers should be accepted, or do exogenous matching functions determine the extent of search unemployment?

Models differ along other dimensions, too. One important example is the structure of transitions out of employment. Is employed search permitted? Is it as costly or efficient as unemployed search? Do exogenous dismissals occur? What determines the probability of dismissal? Are there costs to being dismissed (e.g., transitions costs or loss of human capital)?

The problem is that such differences in structural assumptions often have a substantial influence on the predictions from theoretical models of job search. Take as an example the widely-alleged decrease in job security in the United States. How might, say, an exogenous increase in the rate at which firms dismiss workers— holding constant the long-run aggregate level of employment—influence the natural rate of unemployment and pressures on wage rates? An increase in the dismissal rate increases the rate of flow of workers into unemployment. At the same time it increases the vacancy rate. Even if there is no change in the long-run level of employment, the time-consuming nature of job search means that frictional unemployment will increase. Whether this is the end of the story depends upon the particulars of the model. For example, if search intensity is endogenous, then an increase in the rate of dismissal, by decreasing the expected future value of taking any particular job, decreases the optimal intensity of search, which exacerbates the increase in frictional unemployment.

What happens to wage rates? In a basic search model with endogenous acceptance decisions, an increase in the dismissal rate *lowers* the reservation wage.[8] If a worker's wage rate affects the probability of dismissal that worker faces, workers may further decrease their reservation wages in response to the systemic increase in dismissal rates. However, if there are costs to losing one's job beyond the income foregone while searching again (costs to the transition, or perhaps earnings losses that can be anticipated from having to draw again from a wage-offer distribution that has deteriorated over time), then an increase in the dismissal rate may *raise* the reservation wage. In a matching/bargaining sort of model, the question is whether the higher dismissal rate shifts bargaining power toward firms or toward prospective workers, which, in turn, depends on how the bargaining process is modeled, if it is modeled at all. On the employers' side, any given unemployment rate now represents a higher vacancy rate, which may induce firms to raise their wage offers in order to induce greater search intensity (if search intensity is modeled as endogenous) or greater acceptance probabilities on the part of unemployed workers. And as any change in the equilibrium level of wage rates plays out over time, it could show up in the data as a change in wage inflation, with whatever implications the model provides for inflationary expectations.

Thus, while the wide range of search models evident in the literature generally concur that an increase in the dismissal rate would raise the natural rate of unemployment (by raising frictional unemployment), the theory provides murkier guidance on how large this effect might be or on how wage rates are likely to be affected. Moreover, the implications of the variations in the assumed structure of the labor market have received little attention in general equilibrium or business cycle models of search. As a result, we do not know which structural features are critical and which might be dispensed within the interest of settling upon an operationally useful model. Such ambiguities obviously limit the usefulness of search theory to macroeconomic modeling in particular and, more generally, to policy discussions.

3.3 Empirical Strategies

To the extent that researchers have engaged in empirical research aimed at explaining macroeconomic fluctuations, the emphasis has been on the use of calibration techniques rather than the traditional statistical methods that have dominated the empirical research on macroeconomics for the past 30 years, or even the newer simulation methods developed by Fair (1992), Taylor (1993), and others. Such an emphasis is understandable, and perhaps even necessary, given the complexity of many of the models under consideration. But the use of calibration techniques comes at the cost of a lack of the strong empirical roots needed to convince policy practitioners to take the results of these models seriously. To quote Hansen and Heckman (1996, p. 90):

> Such models are often elegant, and the discussions produced from using them are frequently stimulating and provocative, but their empirical foundations are not secure. What credibility should we attach to numbers produced from their "computational experiments," and why should we use their "calibrated models" as a basis for serious quantitative policy evaluation?

Although this comment was directed at the research program advocated by real business cycle researchers, we fear that the empirical approach currently used to "test" the macroeconomic implications of search unemployment has too often ventured down the same path.

To be more specific, Hansen and Heckman make two important criticisms of calibration methods in the context of real business cycle models that we think also reduce the relevance of the empirical representations of search models to macroeconomic policy discussions. First, there appears to be a lack of rigor when it comes to choosing the parameters of the models, with the parameters taken either from available microeconometric studies or from simple time-series averages of the data. For example, in simulating their matching model, Mortensen and Pissarides (1994) use a combination of parameters taken from sample averages (e.g., gross employment flows, U.S. interest rates, and the scale parameter of the matching function), parameters based on other econometric studies (e.g., the search elasticity of the matching function), and arbitrarily set parameters (e.g., bargaining power). Similarly, in incorporating search into real business cycle models, both Andolfatto (1996) and Merz (1995) use parameter values based on sample means and evidence from econometric studies of cross-sectional data, following the empirical strategy suggested by Kydland and Prescott (1982).

One problem with this approach is that there is often a wide range of estimates of the parameters of interest in the existing literature. Yet, there is typically little discussion of why one parameter value is chosen over another, and virtually no recognition of the uncertainty surrounding the parameter estimates chosen to calibrate the model. Moreover, the data from which the parameters were taken (whether they be sample means or more sophisticated econometric estimates) may not correspond well with the basic assumptions of the model being calibrated. For example, Mortensen and Pissarides use a value for the search elasticity of the job matching function taken from *separate* studies of Great Britain and the United States, which (at least for the U.S.) used gross *worker* flows from the Current Population Surveys.[9] They then simulated their model and compared the results to the gross *job* flows in *U.S. manufacturing* reported by Davis and Haltiwanger (1990). However, except for drawing the arrival rate from a uniform distribution over a given interval, there is no discussion of the sensitivity of the simulation results to potential errors in the parameters used to calibrate the model or of the issue of applying a model of the aggregate economy to data for a specific industrial sector.

We recognize, of course, that a lack of adequate data sometimes presents practical difficulties in calibrating models, just as the need for proxies makes empirical estimation less precise. For example, if there existed good estimates of job flows, Mortensen and Pissarides presumably would have used them, as would Blanchard and Diamond. But we also think that conceptual problems in linking data to model parameters can often diminish the usefulness of calibrated model simulations. Indeed, in some cases, there may not exist any empirical counterpart, measured or not, to the theoretical construct of a specific component of a model. This should not be taken as a criticism of the models themselves; using idealized or fictional components is one way in which a researcher achieves the simplified, idealized representation of the world that is a model. But it is another thing again to take an estimate from the data that resembles in some respects the idealized component, but that is also the product of myriad other influences, and use it as *the* value of that component.

Second, even aside from downplaying the difficulty and uncertainty inherent in obtaining the parameter values used in their simulations, researchers traditionally have provided little guidance as to how the performance of calibrated models should be judged. Typically, the model simulations are compared to the first (and sometimes the second) moment of the data, with the claim that the model fits the facts "reasonably well" or explains x percent of the observed time-series fluctuations in some data series. For example, Merz (1995) includes a detailed and informative discussion comparing her calibrated model simulations with moments and correlations in various U.S. time series, but there is little hard evidence presented on the overall performance of the model other than a general statement that "[t]he model performs well in generating the relative cyclical behavior of the variables that are related to the labor market..." (p. 280). Watson (1993) suggests one approach to judging the performance of calibrated models, by examining the amount of stochastic error needed to exactly match the second moments of the data. We are unaware of any explicit applications of this method to search models. However, Watson's tests of standard real business cycle models using this method suggest that the researchers simulating those calibrated models were probably overstating the capability of their models to mimic the underlying time-series processes generating the data.

Moreover, as Fair (1991) points out, the narrow focus among researchers using calibration methods on the ability of their simulated models to predict particular moments of the data provides only a very limited test of these models. He suggests instead that researchers compute root mean squared errors of the observation-by-observation predictions of their models and compare this RMSE with the errors generated by some other model. To quote Fair, "Having the computed path mimic the actual path for a few selected moments is a far cry from beating even a first-order autoregressive equation (let alone a structural model) in terms of fitting the observations well according to the RMSE criterion" (p. 141).

To these criticisms, we would add another comment, which we view as particularly relevant for the recent search unemployment literature: Perhaps because theoretical search models have become increasingly linked to the real business cycle literature, there seems to be a tendency for researchers using calibration methods to attempt to devise stochastic equilibrium models that completely "explain" unemployment fluctuations. For example, Cole and Rogerson (1996) show that the Mortensen-Pissarides model can account for business cycle fluctuations in unemployment "reasonably well" only if the average duration of unemployment is much longer than that suggested by the data and argue that this failing suggests that the model should be extended to incorporate "heterogeneity in search intensity across workers at a point in time as well as allowing for quits and temporary separations."

In our view, this tendency to judge search models on how well they mimic aggregate fluctuations is asking too much of these models and has, in fact, contributed to the skepticism with which their results have been viewed by the mainstream paradigm. It certainly is not necessary for search models to explain all movements in employment and unemployment for the theory to be relevant to policy discussions. It seems more appropriate to take a pragmatic approach, and to view search dynamics as a piece of the unemployment puzzle rather than as a complete description of the labor market.

In this light, we do not wish to suggest that researchers should turn their attention to estimating all of the parameters of a search model, so as to maximize the fit of its predictions. Estimation of the highly nonlinear and stylized system of equations characterizing the newer models of search unemployment would undoubtedly present problems of identification and overfitting, and one would be justifiably reluctant to trust the out-of-sample predictions from such estimated models. Rather, we would argue that a more useful approach for policy purposes would be to use the new implications from advances in search models at either the theoretical or microeconometric level to improve the specification of the time-series representations of the unemployment-inflation process now employed in the natural rate framework, which, after all, has its own roots in search theory. While the simpler reduced-form relationships that are now used by the CEA, the OECD, and others are subject to the criticism that they often are only linear descriptions of potentially nonlinear economic processes, importing new insights from theory might reduce the potential for such reduced-form models to fail when the underlying process is not linear.

4. Promising Directions in the Empirical Research on Search Unemployment

While there have been few, if any, comprehensive empirical macroeconomic studies of search models that have had an influence on how policymakers think about unemployment fluctuations, there have been several lines of research that have attempted to incorporate some of the implications from search models of unemployment into the mainstream paradigm. We now turn to a few examples of important contributions that have influenced the policy debate or where we think recent developments are particularly promising.

Our first example is quite old by now, but we believe still worth mentioning. As we noted in section II, early versions of search models not only postulated the existence of a natural rate of unemployment, but also predicted that it would change over time in response to structural or institutional changes in the labor market. Responding to this prediction, there was a fairly large body of literature in the 1970s and 1980s that attempted to identify and estimate the importance of potential determinants of the natural rate. Efforts to account for movements in frictional unemployment associated with demographic changes in the work force may have been the most influential among this literature, and indeed this is now the primary adjustment made to the natural rate in the wage-price sectors of mainstream large-scale econometric models.[10] But other factors were considered as well, including the effects of changes in union wage premiums on "wait" unemployment (e.g., Summers, 1986), the gap between differences in aspiration wages and real wages associated with changes in productivity growth rates (e.g., Braun, 1984; Bruno and Sachs, 1985), and the energy shocks of the 1970s (e.g., Nordhaus, 1980). The extent to which these authors linked their analysis directly to theory varied considerably, but there are at least some references in this literature to the basic tenets of the early search models developed by Phelps and others.

An area where the empirical analyses have been more explicitly linked to the macroeconomic predictions of search models is in the debate over the importance of sectoral reallocations in generating relatively high-frequency movements in unemployment. David Lilien (1982) argued that much of what were referred to as "cyclical" fluctuations in the unemployment rate in the 1970s were actually associated with the reallocation of labor following sectoral demand shocks rather than with disturbances in aggregate demand. Lilien did not explicitly refer to the search models existing at the time (rather he asserts that the Lucas-Prescott (1974) spatial model is most relevant to his work). However, models of the search process clearly indicate that frictional unemployment associated with labor market search will be influenced by the pace of sectoral reallocation in the labor market. A lively debate ensued, in which Abraham and Katz (1986) used the Conference Board's Help-wanted index as a proxy for the vacancy rate and presented evidence more favorable to the notion commonly accepted by policymakers that aggregate demand shocks are the primary reason for changes in the unemployment rate.

Although the evidence ultimately convinced mainstream economists that cyclical shocks rather than sectoral shifts were the dominant factor influencing short-term unemployment fluctuations, the discussion helped to rejuvenate two lines of empirical research with roots in search theory that, although not yet part of the usual dialogue in discussions about macroeconomic policy options, have crept onto the scene. The first was a renewed emphasis on the importance of analyzing gross job flows to determine the sources of unemployment fluctuations (Abowd and Zellner, 1985; Poterba and Summers, 1986; Leonard, 1987; and Blanchard and Diamond, 1990b). Particularly notable is the recent research by Davis, Haltiwanger, and Schuh (1996), who document extensively the magnitudes and patterns of job reallocation flows in U.S. manufacturing and bemoan the fact that, despite the theoretical advances in search models, "most analyses of business cycles and aggregate fluctuations ignore or downplay the role of allocative shocks and reallocation frictions."

Arguably, the main contribution of this research to date has simply been to make economists and policymakers more aware of the substantial reallocation that is ongoing in the labor market. That is, although cyclical unemployment may dominate the movements in the aggregate unemployment rate, the potential for significant movements in frictional and structural unemployment associated with changes in the reallocation process cannot be dismissed on the grounds that the resulting flows in and out of unemployment are small. However, these analyses have also yielded important additional insights that are less widely cited in general discussions of macroeconomic policy. For example, the evidence presented by Davis, Haltiwanger, and Schuh suggests that the amount of job reallocation varies over the business cycle, with the pace apparently higher in recessions than in expansions; they also find that an increase in job destruction is the main characteristic of a recession.[11] Consistent with this latter finding, Blanchard and Diamond (1990b) report that changes in the flow of workers out of employment dominate movements in the unemployment rate, while flows into employment are relatively stable over the business cycle. The implication of both of these studies is that short-term fluctuations in unemployment are largely determined by changes in the pace at which matches are terminated rather than by variation in the rate at which new matches are formed.

The second strain of empirical research motivated by the sectoral shifts debate involved extending the single-minded focus on the Phillips curve type relationships of equation (1) to a more general focus on both unemployment and vacancies by incorporating the Beveridge curve into the analysis of unemployment and inflation.

As we noted earlier, search models of the Phelps (1970) vintage recognized a relationship between unemployment and vacancies. However, the potential importance of job vacancies as an economic indicator received scant attention in the policy discussions of subsequent decades, despite intermittent attempts to revive interest in their role as an indicator of labor market slack (e.g., Abraham, 1987) and as a method for distinguishing cyclical and structural unemployment (Abraham and Katz, 1986).[12] Indeed, even the OECD Jobs Study mentions vacancies only briefly, although there is clearly an indication in the document that OECD economists have investigated how to incorporate the Beveridge curve into their analyses of unemployment and inflation (chapter 2, p. 67).

Toward the end of the 1980s, there was a resurgence of interest in empirical representations of the Beveridge curve, led by a series of papers by Blanchard and Diamond (1989, 1990a). In particular, they laid out more clearly the macroeconomic evidence on the importance of the Beveridge curve as it pertains to search unemployment, illustrated how this framework could be used to translate movements in vacancies, unemployment, and labor supply into a decomposition of changes in unemployment into its structural and cyclical components, and made some attempt to incorporate these insights into an empirical model of wage determination. Similar to Abraham and Katz's findings, Blanchard and Diamond report that "short- and medium-term fluctuations in unemployment have been due mainly to aggregate activity shocks, ... rather than to changes in the degree of reallocation intensity..." (1989, p. 50). They subsequently attempted to integrate this analysis into a model of aggregate wage determination, by including separately each piece of the decomposition of unemployment fluctuations resulting from their Beveridge curve analysis. As they report (1990a, pp. 196–97), their evidence is mixed. As predicted by their model, the cyclical component of unemployment has a significant negative effect on wage inflation. Contrary to their predictions, however, the reallocation component has an even stronger negative impact (rather than no effect) on wage changes. They suggest that these results might reflect problems in incorporating productivity growth into the model, a hypothesis bolstered by the fact that their results using a reduced-form price model are more in line with their expectations.

Did the empirical research on the macroeconomic implications of job search have a noticeable influence on policy discussions? Given the extensive attention paid to potential movements in the natural rate in the *OECD Jobs Study* and the *Economic Report of the President*, it seems clear that the early research on the determinants of the natural rate effectively flowed through to the policy arena. We would argue that the later research has contributed to a lesser extent, and in a way that is not so readily apparent. Our view of the body of research on gross flows and the Beveridge curve is that, although it correctly pointed out the potential importance of sectoral reallocation as a determinant of unemployment, it also confirmed the intuition of mainstream macroeconomists that cyclical movements in the unemployment rate were largely demand driven; in this respect, one might say that an important contribution of this research program was to prevent policymakers from heading down a wrong path.

Thus far, however, this research has not led to significant improvements in the specification of short-term forecasting models of unemployment or inflation, nor in identifying the longer-term determinants of structural unemployment (or the matching function).

In this sense, it must be recognized that the usefulness to policymakers of even the greatest theoretical insights is limited by the availability of data that is both sufficiently timely and of sufficiently high quality to serve as a practical guide to decision-making. Unfortunately, in the case of search models, the necessary data are often belated, of questionable quality, or are unavailable at all, problems which have undoubtedly inhibited the employment of such models for policy purposes. For example, the U.S. gross job flows data analyzed by Davis, Haltiwanger, and Schuh are only available with a lag of several years and currently only cover a minority of the jobs in the economy (e.g., manufacturing jobs). And, while gross flows from the CPS can be constructed in a relatively timely manner, past research indicates that these data are subject to severe conceptual and measurement problems. Similarly, the best measure of vacancies in the United States is the Conference Board's Help-Wanted Advertising Index. However, using this series requires the researcher to make numerous ad-hoc adjustments to correct for inconsistencies in this series over time (Abraham, 1987; Braun and Otoo, 1994). In the United States, at least, better data on vacancy rates and gross flows would allow policy makers to incorporate these aspects of search models into a richer set of empirical tools.

5. Conclusions

There should be no doubt that theoretical models of search unemployment have had an important role in the development of the macroeconomic tools used by policymakers over the past 25 years. The contributions by Phelps and others in the late 1960s and early 1970s provided a sound theoretical basis for many of the empirical correlations that had been uncovered over the previous decade and argued persuasively that there were limitations on how much macroeconomic policies could do to reduce aggregate unemployment. To be sure, research on other potential explanations of equilibrium unemployment (e.g., efficiency wages; sticky prices) have contributed importantly to our understanding of unemployment fluctuations. But, after more than two decades of investigation, it seems evident that the natural rate theory is still the mainstream paradigm used by policymakers today.

Despite the successes of the early research on search unemployment, more recent developments have been largely ignored in policy discussions. Indeed, we are skeptical that existing search models—as they stand—will ever be of much direct use to policymakers as tools for policy analysis. The lack of attention paid to search models (and our skepticism regarding their future) reflects shortcomings in both the existing literature and in how policymakers use the results of economic analysis in setting policy. In terms of the latter, we would venture to guess that one reason the natural rate model became so much a part of macroeconomic policy discussions was the ability of its proponents to synthesize the model into a "rule of thumb" that could be easily understood. Given policymakers' reliance (whether appropriate or not) on relationships that can be summarized in simple equations, it seems doubtful that the stochastic general equilibrium models of search unemployment will make their way into policy discussions unless their results can be summarized in a form more easily accessible by noneconomists.

Even more problematic, in our view, has been a tendency for researchers in this area to focus on simulations of complicated models using assumptions about deep structural parameters rather than on estimation of more tractable reduced-form versions of search models (e.g., Mortensen and Pissarides, 1994; Merz, 1995; and Andolfatto, 1996). In addition to the conceptual and econometric difficulties inherent in attempting to link structural model parameters to their empirical counterparts, the fact that the theoretical models of search unemployment are difficult to work through immediately throws up a barrier to those who might be interested in the policy implications of these models. That the "real world" tests of the models with data lack a strong empirical foundation then provides a reason to dismiss the models out of hand.

Despite our criticisms, we are also optimistic that the many insights produced by more recent models of search unemployment will increasingly find their way into the practical (as opposed to academic) discussions of appropriate macroeconomic policies. Important progress already has been made in this direction, and we have highlighted some of the research that we think is most relevant. However, there is still much to be done, and making the leap from theory to policy will require, in our view, a greater emphasis by researchers on the appropriate statistical tests of the implications of the theory and on how these implications can be integrated into the real-time empirical models used by forecasters and policymakers.

Notes

We thank Carl Davidson and Stephen Woodbury for helpful comments. The views in this paper do not necessarily reflect those of the Board of Governors of the Federal Reserve System or its staff.

1. In the United States, representatives include members of the Council of Economic Advisers, the Department of the Treasury, and the Board of Governors of the Federal Reserve System.

2. In addition to the factors listed, the 1997 *Economic Report* also suggests a role for productivity to influence the natural rate in the medium term, through potential differences in real wage aspirations and labor productivity. According to this analysis, however, any influence of productivity disappears in the long run as real wage aspirations adjust to the underlying trend rate of productivity growth.

3. Stiglitz (1997), who was CEA chairman at the time, makes many of the same arguments.

4. This equation is readily recognized as the expectations-augmented Phillips curve developed in the late 1960s and early 1970s. See, for example, Perry (1970).

5. An interesting side-note is the implication that to the extent that employed search is a substitute for unemployed search, anything that lowers the cost of the former relative to the latter should lower the natural rate of unemployment.

6. There is little evidence for the mitigating possibility that the higher reservation wage induced by UI results in higher-quality matches (Decker, O'Leary, and Woodbury, 2001). It is also possible that the UI program increases the exit rate into unemployment by reducing the incentive for workers and firms to avoid layoffs and discharges (Deere, 1991; Topel, 1983).

7. The role of expectations was clearly recognized in the early search literature as well. Indeed, representations of the expectations-augmented Phillips curve in the 1970s provided a mechanism for expectations to influence the equilibrium rate of inflation, although not the natural rate of unemployment.

8. Intuitively, it is less worthwhile to wait for a better offer if the expected duration of that better job is shorter.

9. In particular, the parameter value is described as "midway between the estimate obtained by Blanchard and Diamond (1989) using U.S. data and that of Pissarides (1986) from U.K. data." Blanchard and Diamond's estimates, in turn, are based on a combination of the CPS gross flows data and the Conference Board's Help-Wanted Advertising index. But even the CPS data are incomplete because they exclude worker flows directly from one job to another. Blanchard and Diamond adjusted for this shortcoming using estimates derived by Akerlof, Rose, and Yellen (1988) from a 1961 special survey of job changers. Needless to say, the estimates of the resulting matching function are not likely to be without error.

10. See, for example, Hall (1970), Perry (1970), and Wachter (1976), among others.

11. However, this question is not settled. See Boeri (1996) and Foote (1997).

12. In part, this may be due to the lack of explicit data on job vacancies in the United States. In Europe, where vacancy data are more readily available, there has been greater attention paid to using such data in macroeconomic models.

References

Abowd, John M., and Arnold Zellner. "Estimating Gross Labor Force Flows." *Journal of Business and Economics Statistics* 3 (1985): 254–283.

Abraham, Katharine G. "Help-Wanted Advertising, Job Vacancies, and Unemployment." *Brookings Papers on Economic Activity* (1987): 207–248.

Abraham, Katharine G., and Lawrence F. Katz. "Cyclical Unemployment: Sectoral Shifts or Aggregate Disturbances?" *Journal of Political Economy* 94 (1986): 507–522.

Akerlof, George, Andrew Rose, and Janet Yellen. "Job Switching and Job Satisfaction in the U.S. Labor Market." *Brookings Papers on Economic Activity* (1988): 495–592.

Andolfatto, David. "Business Cycles and Labor Market Search." *American Economic Review* 86 (1996): 112–132.

Archibald, G. C. "The Phillips Curve and the Distribution of Unemployment." *American Economic Review* 59 (1969): 124–134.

Blanchard, Olivier Jean and Peter Diamond. "The Aggregate Matching Function." In *Growth/Productivity/Unemployment*, edited by Peter Diamond. Cambridge, Massachusetts: MIT Press, 1990a. Pp. 159–201.

_____. "The Cyclical Behavior of Gross Flows of Workers in the U.S." *Brookings Papers on Economic Activity* (1990b): 85–155.

_____. "The Beveridge Curve." *Brookings Papers on Economic Activity* (1989): 1–60.

Blanchard, Olivier and Lawrence F. Katz. "What We Know and Do Not Know About the Natural Rate of Unemployment." *Journal of Economic Perspectives* (1997): 51–72.

Boeri, Tito. "Is Job Turnover Countercyclical?" *Journal of Labor Economics* 14 (1996): 603–25.

Braun, Steven N. "Productivity and the NIIRU (and Other Phillips Curve Issues)." Economic Activity Working Paper No. 34. Washington, DC: Board of Governors of the Federal Reserve System, 1984.

Braun, Steven N. and Maria W. Otoo. "The Help Wanted Index Among Alternative Indicators of Labor Market Slack." Unpublished manuscript, Board of Governors of the Federal Reserve System, 1994.

Bruno, Michael and Jeffrey D. Sachs. *Economics of Worldwide Stagflation*. Cambridge, Massachusetts: Harvard University Press, 1985.

Cole, Harold L. and Richard Rogerson. "Can the Mortenson-Pissarides Matching Model Match the Business Cycle Facts?" Research Department Staff Report 224. Minneapolis, Minnesota: Federal Reserve Bank of Minneapolis, 1996.

Council of Economic Advisers. *Economic Report of the President*. Washington, DC: U.S. Government Printing Office, 1997.

Davis, Steven J. and John C. Haltiwanger. "Gross Job Creation and Destruction: Microeconomic Evidence and Macroeconomic Implications." *NBER Macroeconomics Annual* 5 (1990): 123–168.

Davis, Steven J., John C. Haltiwanger, and Scott Schuh. *Job Creation and Destruction*. Cambridge, Massachusetts: MIT Press, 1996.

Decker, Paul T., Christopher J. O'Leary, and Stephen A. Woodbury. "Impacts on Employment and Earnings." In *Reemployment Bonuses in the Unemployment Insurance System*, edited by Philip K. Robins and Robert G. Spiegelman. Kalamazoo, Michigan: W. E. Upjohn Institute, 2001. Pp. 151–174.

Deere, Donald R. "Unemployment Insurance and Employment." *Journal of Labor Economics* 9 (1991): 307–24.

Devine, Theresa J. and Nicholas M. Kiefer. *Empirical Labor Economics: The Search Approach*. New York: Oxford University Press, 1991.

Diamond, Peter and Drew Fudenberg. "Rational Expectations Business Cycles in Search Equilibrium." *Journal of Political Economy* 97 (1989): 607–619.

Fair, Ray C. "The Cowles Commission Approach, Real Business Cycle Theories, and New-Keynesian Economics." In *The Business Cycle: Theories and Evidence*, edited by Michael T. Belongia and Michelle R. Garfinkel. Norwell, Massachusetts: Kluwer Academic Publishers, 1991. Pp. 133–147.

_____. *Testing Macroeconomic Models*. Cambridge, Massachusetts: Harvard University Press, 1992.

Fallick, Bruce C. "A Review of the Recent Empirical Literature on Displaced Workers." *Industrial and Labor Relations Review* 50 (1996): 5–17.

Farber, Henry S. "The Incidence and Costs of Job Loss: 1982–91." *Brookings Papers on Economic Activity: Microeconomics* (1993): 73–132.

Foote, Chris. "Trend Employment Growth and the Bunching of Job Creation and Destruction." Unpublished manuscript, Harvard University, 1997.

Hall, Robert E. "Why Is the Unemployment Rate So High at Full Employment?" *Brookings Papers on Economic Activity* (1970): 339–96.

Hansen, Lars Peter and James J. Heckman. "The Empirical Foundations of Calibration." *Journal of Economic Perspectives* 10 (1996): 87–104.

Kydland, Finn E. and Edward C. Prescott. "Time to Build and Aggregate Fluctuations." *Econometrica* 50 (1982): 1345–70.

Leonard, Jonathan S. "In the Wrong Place at the Wrong Time: The Extent of Frictional and Structural Unemployment." In *Unemployment and the Structure of Labor Markets*, edited by Kevin Lang and Jonathan Leonard. New York: Basil Blackwell, 1987. Pp. 141–63.

Lilien, David M. "Sectoral Shifts and Cyclical Unemployment." *Journal of Political Economy* 90 (1982): 777–93.

Lucas, Robert E. and Edward C. Prescott. "Equilibrium Search and Unemployment." *Journal of Economic Theory* 7 (1974): 188–209.

Monika Merz. "Search in the Labor Market and the Real Business Cycle." *Journal of Monetary Economics* 36 (1995): 269–300.

Meyer, Bruce. "What Have We Learned from the Illinois Reemployment Bonus Experiment?" *Journal of Labor Economics* 14 (1996): 26–51.

Mortensen, Dale T. "A Theory of Wage and Employment Dynamics." In *Microeconomic Foundations of Employment and Inflation Theory*, edited by Edmund S. Phelps. New York: W. W. Norton, 1970. Pp. 167–211.

Mortensen, Dale T. and Christopher A. Pissarides. "Job Creation and Job Destruction in the Theory of Unemployment." *Review of Economic Studies* 61 (1994): 397–415.

Nordhaus, William. "Oil and Economic Performance in Industrial Countries." *Brookings Papers on Economic Activity* (1980): 341–88.

Organization for Economic Cooperation and Development. *The OECD Jobs Study*. Paris: OECD, 1994.

Perry, George L. "Changing Labor Markets and Inflation." *Brookings Papers on Economic Activity*, (1970): 411–441.

Phelps, Edmund S. "Money Wage Dynamics and Labor Market Equilibrium." In *Microeconomic Foundations of Employment and Inflation Theory*, edited by Edmund S. Phelps. New York: W. W. Norton, 1970. Pp. 124–166.

_____. "Money-Wage Dynamics and Labor Market Equilibrium." *Journal of Political Economy* 76 (1968): 679–711.

Pissarides, Christopher. "Unemployment and Vacancies in Britain." *Economic Policy* 3 (1986): 499–560.

Poterba, James M. and Lawrence H. Summers. "Reporting Errors and Labor Market Dynamics." *Econometrica* 54 (1986): 1319–38.

Stiglitz, Joseph. "Reflections on the Natural Rate Hypothesis." *Journal of Economic Perspectives* 11 (1997): 3–10.

Summers, Lawrence H. "Why Is the Unemployment Rate So Very High Near Full Employment?" *Brookings Papers on Economic Activity* (1986): 339–96.

Taylor, John B. *Macroeconomic Policy in a World Economy*. New York: W. W. Norton, 1993.

Thomas, R. L. and P. J. M. Stoney. "Unemployment Dispersion as a Determinant of Wage Inflation in the U.K.: 1925–1966." *The Manchester School* 39 (1971): 83–116.

Topel, Robert H. "On Layoffs and Unemployment Insurance." *American Economic Review* 73 (1983): 541–59.

Wachter, Michael L. "The Changing Cyclical Responsiveness of Wage Inflation." *Brookings Papers on Economic Activity* (1976): 115–167.

Watson, Mark W. "Measures of Fit for Calibrated Models." *Journal of Political Economy* 101 (1993): 1011–1041.

Index

Lightning Source UK Ltd.
Milton Keynes UK
UKOW07n1706131114

241504UK00002B/202/P